THE BOOK OF SURVIVAL TO THRIVAL

CREATED BY

MULTI #1 INTERNATIONAL BESTSELLING AUTHOR & AWARD WINNING SPEAKER

ERIK SWANSON

THE BOOK OF

SURVIVAL TO THRIVAL

COURAGE

ERIK SWANSON

50 AMAZING STORIES OF TRIUMPH

ALSO FEATURING CELEBRITIES

THERESA "TGO" GOSS, SEAN KANAN & JOHNNY WIMBREY

Quantity sales special discounts are available for corporations, associations, and other organizations with quantity purchases. For more information, please contact the publisher at the address above.

Orders from U.S. trade bookstores and wholesalers are available. Manufactured and printed in the United States of America and distributed globally by **Integrity Publishing International**.

Paperback ISBN: 978-1-964330-28-0

Hardback ISBN: 978-1-964330-29-7

www.IntegrityPub.com

Global Speakers Mastermind & Habitude Warrior Masterminds

Join us and become a member of our tribe! Our Global Speakers Mastermind is a virtual group of amazing thinkers and leaders who meet twice a month. Sessions are designed to be 'to the point' and focused while sharing fantastic techniques to grow your mindset as well as your pocketbooks. We also include famous guest speaker spots for our private Masterclasses. We also designate certain sessions for our members to mastermind with each other & and counsel on the topics discussed in our previous Masterclasses. It's time for you to join a tribe who truly cares about *YOU* and your future and start surrounding yourself with the famous leaders and mentors of our time. It is time for you to up-level your life, businesses, and relationships.

For more information to check out our Masterminds:
Team@HabitudeWarrior.com
www.DecideToBeAwesome.com

BECOME AN INTERNATIONAL
#1 BESTSELLING AUTHOR & SPEAKER

Habitude Warrior International has been highlighting award-winning Speakers and #1 Bestselling Authors for over 25 years. They know what it takes to become #1 in your field and how to get the best exposure around the world. If you have ever considered giving yourself the GIFT of becoming a well-known Speaker and a fantastically well known #1 Best-Selling Author, then you should email their team right away to find out more information in how you can become involved. They have the best of the best when it comes to resources in achieving the bestselling status in your particular field. Start surrounding yourself with the N.Y. Times Bestsellers of our time and start seeing your dreams become reality!

For more information to become a #1 Bestselling Author
& Speaker on our Habitude Warrior Conferences
Please text the word AUTHORS to 619-304-6268
And also go to:
www.DecideToBeAwesome.com

CONTENTS

INTRODUCTION

THE BOOK OF SURVIVAL TO THRIVAL

. . . .

A TRANSFORMATIONAL SERIES ON
RISING ABOVE & THRIVING

The Book of Survival to Thrival is a transformative book series designed to help you achieve personal breakthroughs and empower the human spirit through real stories of grit, growth, and grace.

Each of us may experience trials in life. Some come suddenly and shake our world, while others may quietly wear some of us down over time. But there is a defining choice in every challenge: we can merely survive—or we can rise and thrive.

This series was created by Erik Swanson and was born from that choice to thrive. Through the voices of courageous contributing co-authors in each volume, *The Book of Survival to Thrival* invites you into the most personal moments of pain, truth, resilience, and victory. These are not just stories—they are blueprints for transformation. You'll learn how people just like you made the decision to grow instead of break, to forgive instead of stay bitter, and to persevere instead of give up.

With each volume, we explore a core human quality required to go from surviving life... to thriving in it.

VOLUME 1 ~ COURAGE

Courage is the first step in the journey from survival to thrival. It's a steady resolve to rise, even when fear, pain, or uncertainty threatens to hold us down.

In this powerful first volume, **courage** sets the tone for everything that follows. The authors in this book didn't wait for fear to disappear. They stepped into their battles while still trembling. They moved forward while still doubting. They showed us that real courage isn't reserved for heroes—**it's a choice that everyday people make in extraordinary moments.**

This collection of stories invites you into the deeply personal turning points of people who dared to face what tried to break them. These stories are not just inspiration—they are activation. You'll discover how courage looks different for everyone:

• For some, it was choosing forgiveness over resentment.

• For others, it was starting over with nothing but faith.

• For many, it was showing up for others when they could barely show up for themselves.

You'll also uncover patterns: that courage is a habit, built one small brave step at a time. It grows stronger through adversity. Let this volume be your reminder: You don't have to be fearless to be brave. You don't have to have it all together to take the next step. You just have to **decide**—to try, to rise, to keep going.

VOLUME 2 ~ FORGIVENESS

Forgiveness is highly misunderstood, yet the most transformative force in the human experience. Many believe it's about excusing wrongdoing, forgetting betrayal, or minimizing the damage done. But in reality, **forgiveness is not about the past—it's about your future**. It's about releasing yourself from the chains of bitterness, resentment, guilt, or shame that keep you stuck in survival mode.

In this second volume, our authors pull back the curtain on what it really means to forgive—and how that decision can radically change your life. Through real-life stories of heartbreak, betrayal, self-blame, and deep emotional wounds, you'll witness the rawness of the human spirit and the courage it takes to move forward. These stories are deeply personal accounts of people who had every reason to stay angry, to hold on, to let their pain define them. And yet, they chose healing, growth, and **freedom**.

Our authors reveal that **forgiveness is not a one-time event** but a process—a practice—a path to reclaiming peace and restoring personal power. **Forgiveness is one of the boldest acts of strength you will ever make.** It is the turning point where survival ends and thriving begins. It's how you stop carrying what was never meant to define you and start living in alignment with who you're becoming.

You don't need permission to forgive. You don't need the apology. You just need the willingness to take one step toward healing. Allow our authors to help guide you in the blissfulness of forgiveness.

VOLUME 3 ~ PERSEVERANCE

Getting started is brave. Finishing is bold. But the space in between—the messy, painful, uncertain middle—that's where **perseverance** lives. And that's where most people give up.

In this third volume, we explore what it truly takes to **keep going**. This volume is a tribute to the quiet, relentless spirit that refuses to quit.

Our co-authors know what it's like to feel stuck, exhausted, or even defeated. But they also know what it's like to keep showing up, one small step at a time, until breakthroughs happen.

Perseverance is not just for athletes or entrepreneurs or the "strong-willed." It's a human skill we all need to develop to thrive in today's world. And it's more available than you think.

This volume isn't about pushing through blindly. It's about pressing forward **with clarity, compassion, and conviction**— even when no one sees you trying. It's about staying true to your values when shortcuts are tempting. It's about embracing the process, not just the outcome.

Let these stories renew your strength. Let them remind you that you are not alone, and that even in the silence of your struggle, something powerful is being built inside you.

You don't have to have it all figured out. You just have to keep going. Because perseverance is how thrival becomes your reality.

A NOTE FROM OUR SERIES CREATOR
ERIK SWANSON

This series is more than a collection of stories. It's a movement.

I created *The Book of Survival to Thrival* to share with the world that our hardest moments can become our greatest turning points. Whether you're in the middle of a storm or reflecting on past pains, these stories will meet you where you are and walk with you to where you want to be. Shoutout to Eric D. Jackson for the conversations that sparked the creation of the stories you are about to embark on.

Let these stories lift you. Let them heal you. Let them remind you that thriving is your birthright—and the journey starts with one courageous step.

"NDSO!"

No Drama, Serve Others!
With strength, grace, and perseverance,
~ Erik Swanson, Integrity Publishing International

ERIK SWANSON

ACTIVATE YOUR INNER WARRIOR!

. . . .

"It takes courage to grow up and become who you really are!"
~ **E.E. Cummings**

Let's get something straight right out of the gate: **you were not born just to survive.** You were born to THRIVE. To conquer, to shine, to elevate everyone around you by rising into your highest self. But sometimes—let's be real—life doesn't hand us the easy path. Sometimes we're crawling, clawing, doing everything we can just to *make it through the day.* That's survival mode.

And if that's where you are right now, guess what?

That's okay.

Because survival is your starting line. It's your classroom. It's where your COURAGE is forged. And that, my friend, is how you begin the journey toward thriving.

THE HABITUDE WARRIOR SURVIVAL ZONE: YOUR GREATEST TRAINING GROUND

So, what does it mean to be in survival mode?

21

It means you're reacting instead of creating. You're waking up already tired. You're on edge. You're saying things like:

- "I just need to get through this week."
- "Once this problem is fixed, then I'll be okay."
- "I can't catch a break!"

Does this sound familiar? Yeah, we've all been there. Even your favorite speakers and mentors—myself included—have found ourselves knee-deep in challenges we didn't see coming.

But here's what I know: Survival isn't the enemy. It's the invitation.

See, survival mode is life's way of whispering, "Hey, are you ready to grow?" It doesn't always feel like a whisper. Sometimes it feels like a gut punch. But within every challenge is a CHOICE: Stay where you are… or build your wings and rise.

Here's the deal—**thrivers aren't born, they're built.** They're built in the fire. They're built in the unknown. They're built in those three a.m. moments when your mind is racing and your heart is pounding, but you make the decision to keep going anyway.

That's survival transformed. That's the first spark of COURAGE.

COURAGE: YOUR SUPERPOWER IN DISGUISE

Let me ask you something: What if courage isn't the absence of fear, but the *reclamation* of your power?

Courage is the bridge between survival and thriving. It's the voice inside you that says, "I don't know what tomorrow looks like, but I'm showing up anyway." It's the decision to have the hard conversation. To start the business. To leave the relationship that's holding you back. To walk into the unknown with your head held high, even if your knees are shaking.

Listen, I'm not talking about the movie-style courage where you're scaling mountains or running into battle with a sword in your hand. (Though hey, if that's your thing—more power to you!)

I'm talking about the *real stuff*. The raw stuff. The courage to be vulnerable. To admit you need help. To try again after failing. To choose faith over fear when nothing makes sense.

COURAGE IS ACTION IN MOTION IN SPITE OF FEAR!

It doesn't require a perfect plan. It requires a commitment to yourself. It's you saying, "I'm worth the effort. I'm worth the comeback. I'm worth the life I envision."

Would you like to hear an awesome truth bomb? **You've already survived 100% of your worst days.** That's not luck—that's strength. That's resilience. That's inner fire that hasn't gone out—it's just waiting for you to fan the flame.

THE THRIVING MINDSET: SHIFTING YOUR FREQUENCY

Now let's talk about the GOOD stuff. The thriving. The joy. The magic of living on purpose and with intention.

Thriving doesn't mean your life is perfect. Thriving means you're *aligned*. You're in tune. You're not just reacting anymore—you're designing your reality.

When you thrive, your frequency changes, and you become what I call a "Habitude Warrior!" You walk into a room, and people feel your energy before you say a word. You become magnetic—not because of what you have, but because of who you *are*, and more importantly, who *they* are and how you make them feel! That's the gift of doing the inner work. That's the reward of choosing courage over comfort.

So, how do you shift from surviving to thriving?

Let me give you five powerful steps in what I call the **Habitude Warrior Pathway**:

1. OWN WHERE YOU ARE

Stop pretending. Drop the mask. The first step to thriving is *radical honesty*. Look at your life and ask, "Where am I just surviving?" Is it your career? Your health? Your mindset? Your relationships? Or all of the above?

Get real, because truth is the foundation of transformation.

2. ACTIVATE YOUR HABITUDE WARRIOR INNER CIRCLE

No one thrives alone. You may want to read that again! You need mentors. You need allies. You need people in your corner who challenge you, cheer for you, and hold you accountable to your greatness. There's a saying that you are the compilation of the five people you surround yourself with. Do you need new friends?

If you're the smartest person in the room, find a new room!

3. UPGRADE YOUR HABITUDES

Your habits and your attitude—your *habitudes*—are either lifting you or limiting you. Ask yourself:

- What do I do *daily* that feeds my mind?
- What do I do *daily* that raises my frequency?
- What do I need to *release* that's been dragging me down?

Thriving is a byproduct of aligned habitudes.

4. SPEAK LIFE

Your words are frequency carriers. Speak possibility. Speak gratitude. Speak in advance. Speak positively. Speak promptly. Speak victory—even when the evidence hasn't shown up yet. Say things like:

- "I'm proud of how far I've come."
- "I attract the right people and opportunities."
- "I am no longer available for anything that diminishes my light."
- "I am ready for greatness, and greatness is ready for me."
- "I attract abundance and attract amazing success."

Words matter. Frequency matters. Speak with intention and change your life.

5. CELEBRATE THE JOURNEY

This one's BIG. Don't wait until the mountaintop to celebrate. Celebrate the climb. Celebrate the grit. Celebrate the fact that you *didn't quit* when you could have. Celebrate the people who support you in your journey. And, even celebrate those who doubted you and show them by your amazing and awesome success.

That's thriving—living in gratitude while chasing growth.

STORIES OF SURVIVAL TO THRIVING SUCCESS

Let me take a moment and share some quick stories from people I've met through Habitude Warrior Conferences and beyond—people just like YOU.

Jenny—The Courageous Entrepreneur

Jenny lost her job in 2020 and went into survival mode fast—financial fear, panic, self-doubt. But instead of crumbling, she asked the big question: "What do I *want* to create?"

She took a leap and started a business helping others build their resumes and confidence. Now, she's thriving with a six-figure income and a purpose-driven platform.

What changed? Not her resources—her *resourcefulness*. Her *courage!*

Marcus—The Wellness Warrior

Marcus was one hundred pounds overweight, depressed, and stuck in a loop of negative self-talk. He started with one walk. Then two. Then a gym membership. Then a coach. Then a transformation.

Today, he's a motivational speaker helping teens build self-esteem. His survival story became his superpower. He is a true Habitude Warrior!

Maria Elena—The Frequency Shifter

Maria Elena was surrounded by toxic relationships and a job that drained her soul. One day, she declared: "I deserve more!"

She invested in herself. She joined our Habitude Warrior Mastermind, which she could attend virtually through our Zoom platform. She learned to set boundaries. She shifted her frequency, and her friends changed. Her opportunities changed. Her entire *life* changed.

These aren't fairy tales—these are real people who chose courage and rewrote their stories.

YOUR TURN: CLAIMING YOUR THRIVING LIFE

So, here's where I turn the spotlight on YOU. Where are you just surviving? Where are you being called to step up with courage? What would thriving actually *look* like for you?

Let me challenge you right now, future Habitude Warrior, to write it down. Vision it out. Make it real. Don't worry if it feels far away. Everything great starts with a decision.

And if that voice of doubt starts whispering, "Who do you think you are to want that?" answer back louder and louder and louder: "I'm someone who has *survived* more than I thought I could... and I'm *not stopping now!*"

You don't need to be perfect. You just need to be *willing*. Willing to grow. Willing to rise. Willing to choose the path of the THRIVER instead of the victim.

IT'S TIME FOR YOU TO RISE UP!

Survival is not your destination—it's your *launchpad*.

Courage is not optional—it's your *gateway*.

Thriving is not just for "them"—it's your *birthright*.

I believe in you. I see you. And more importantly, it's time that *you* **believe in yourself!**

You've got this! Now get out there... and THRIVE like the world depends on it. Because guess what? Someone out there *needs your light*. Let's go! It's time for you to become a fearless, courageous, thriving Habitude Warrior!

ERIK SWANSON

As an Award-Winning International Keynote Speaker and Multi-Time #1 International Bestselling Author, Erik Swanson is in great demand around the world! He speaks to an average of more than one million people per year. Mr. Swanson has the honor of having been invited to speak to many schools around the world, including the prestigious Harvard University. He is also a recurring faculty member of CEO Space International and an alumnus keynote speaker at Vistage Executive Coaching.

Mr. Swanson is also the recipient of the 2024 International Book Impact Award and the United States Presidential Lifetime Achievement Award presented by the White House in 2024 for his ongoing community service and philanthropy work. Erik's speeches can be found on Amazon Prime TV, as well as on TED Talks, where he has contributed his speeches titled, "A Dose of Awesome" and "NDSO ~ No Drama, Serve Others."

Erik got his start in the self-development world by mentoring directly under Brian Tracy. Quickly climbing to become the top trainer around the world from a group of over 250 handpicked coaches, Erik started to surround himself with the best of the best and very quickly started to be invited to speak on stages alongside such greats as Jim Rohn, Bob Proctor, Les Brown, Sharon Lechter, Jack Canfield, Lisa Nichols, and Joe Dispenza—just to name a few.

Erik has created and developed the super-popular Habitude Warrior Conferences and Speaker Hearts Mastermind & Retreats, which have a two-year waiting list and feature thirty-three top-named speakers from around the world. They are "TED Talk" style events which have quickly climbed to the top ten events not to miss in the United States! He is the creator, founder, and CEO of the Habitude Warrior Mastermind, Global Speakers Mastermind, and Cafe Mastermind. He is also the creator and publisher of many book series, such as *The 13 Steps To Riches* book series, as well as *The Principles of David & Goliath* book series. His motto is clear: "NDSO!" No Drama – Serve Others!

www.SpeakerErikSwanson.com

SEAN KANAN

THE FIVE MIGHTY MASTS

Living well is indeed the best revenge. Sounds easy enough, right? Silence the haters, doubters, and naysayers by leading an extraordinary and enviable life. Simply put, don't just survive—thrive. But what does thriving really mean, and more importantly, how do you transform this witty saying into a tangible and meaningful life experience?

Surviving, while obviously important, represents the bare minimum of the human experience. The metaphorical ocean separating those who survive from those who thrive runs deep and vast, yet remains simple to traverse.

As with most worthy challenges, the solution is simple but rarely easy. Frequently, the journey offers a greater reward than the destination. Moments of challenge and struggle serve as a fiery crucible, forging the steel of our character and refining authenticity.

Overcoming life's challenges requires a positive mindset and strategic action, which together function as the ship carrying you across these often choppy waters, delivering you to the warm, sandy beaches of achievement. Stop waiting for your ship to come in and build it yourself.

Your ship requires five mighty masts to propel you toward a thriving life. The first four are authenticity, self-awareness, personal success, and meaningful happiness. However, there is a caveat: there's no free lunch. The materials needed for their construction come at a price. Only by paying it can you erect the final mast, which we will discuss shortly.

Rest assured, the map to thrive does not hide deep within some arcane puzzle or lie camouflaged amidst a carefully guarded secret known only to a select few; the course to navigate this map remains available to all. Joseph Campbell illuminated the path when he wrote, "The cave you fear to enter holds the treasure you seek." Zen masters pose the following riddle to their students: "How did the ship enter the bottle?" The answer? It was already there. Everything you need to build your ship and traverse the journey already exists within you. Locating the raw materials is your responsibility. Here are the strategies I used to build the masts on my ship.

1. AUTHENTICITY

Authenticity—living a life of truth, in sync with the universe and your intended existence within it—requires freedom. It necessitates liberating yourself from the prison of your mind and breaking free from the chains of reactive emotionality. This begins with personal responsibility and accountability, acknowledging that you are not a victim. Your life is your responsibility.

If you feel confined by the challenges you face and the reality in which you live, understand that your past choices have brought you to this point. Your choices from this moment forward will determine your future, whether you merely survive or thrive. It's up to you to find the key that unlocks the cell where you currently reside and to shatter the shackles of victimhood that restrain you.

These chains aren't forged from iron but rather the stories we tell ourselves. Take a good, hard look at the excuses and rationalizations you employ as coping mechanisms to explain away challenges and disappointments when life feels difficult and seems unfair. Newsflash: LIFE ISN'T FAIR! Get used to it.

Too often, humans struggle to see the big picture or anticipate what lies ahead. Our aversion to the unknown causes anxiety. The desire to eliminate that anxiety leads us to categorize people, places, and experiences in simple, binary terms: good or bad, positive or negative, beneficial or detrimental. Very few things are monolithically all one thing or all another. Most things, whether experiences or people, contain shades of gray. The rush to assign a label shapes the stories we tell ourselves, influencing our future decisions. Often, what feels catastrophic in the moment proves to be a blessing with the passage of time.

Decades ago, I experienced a painful divorce, which led me to attach the disempowering story that I was unlovable. This was not only inaccurate but also a rationalization I created to avoid taking responsibility for my own behavior. That story caused a great deal of self-inflicted suffering. After much introspection and upon achieving some self-awareness, I realized that my painful divorce was one of the best things that ever happened to me; it opened the door for me to meet my incredible wife.

The flip side is just as true. We've all heard tales of lottery winners who, after a few years, find themselves broke and miserable, viewing what was once perceived as a windfall as one of the worst things to happen to them. The key is to understand that our stories shape how we perceive our experiences, and recognizing their fluidity can save us a lot of emotional turmoil.

Humans have an uncanny ability to create wildly inaccurate narratives about the events and circumstances that define their lives. These narratives are not reflections of reality; rather, they are often distortions shaped by the unique perspectives of each storyteller, frequently diverging from the truth. Individuals tend to adopt an idiocentric viewpoint, positioning themselves as the main characters in their stories, often casting themselves as victims instead of heroes. This inclination not only distorts their understanding of reality but also magnifies the harmful and constricting effects of such narratives.

What stories do you tell yourself?

- "I'm too old to change."
- "I'll lose weight after the holidays."
- "If you're successful, you must have stepped on someone to get there."

Negative stories are rooted in a mindset of victimhood. You are not a victim. You are not here to settle for mediocrity; you are destined to radiate with such brilliance that the world is drawn to you just to bask in your light. This transformation is within your reach if you take action. Challenge and reframe those disempowering narratives and remove the obstacles that keep you stuck. Transform yourself and you will transform the world.

The following anecdote illustrates how two individuals can experience identical events and then attach very different stories, resulting in vastly different lives.

A journalist writing an article about Skid Row in Los Angeles interviewed a homeless man, a hopeless alcoholic. She inquired how he came to arrive at this place in his life. He responded, "My father drank a pint of whiskey every night, beat my mother, beat me and my twin brother, and couldn't keep a job. How else would I have grown up?" The journalist was so intrigued, she sought out the man's twin brother.

Upon arriving at the address, she thought to herself, "This can't be right." The house was a large and expensive home. She knocked on the massive front door, and soon a fit and vibrant older man opened it, smiling warmly. The journalist noted a slight resemblance to his twin brother on Skid Row. He graciously invited her in, introducing his loving family, and recounted that he had practiced medicine in the community for decades.

The journalist asked him how he arrived at this place in his life. He responded, "My father drank a pint of whiskey every night, beat my mother, beat me and my twin brother, and couldn't keep a job. How else would I have grown up? I've never touched alcohol." Two identical experiences, two very different stories. One led to despair and the other to abundance.

Stories are rarely completely accurate representations of events. It's essential to move beyond victimhood and propel yourself to overcome, succeed, and thrive.

Many years ago, I faced a life-altering decision. Fate positioned me at the intersection of two roads, one leading to defeat and the other to triumph. The story I adopted changed the trajectory of my life.

Christmas Eve, 1988. While most people celebrated with family and friends, I found myself in a Las Vegas emergency room, bleeding to death. I was just twenty-two years old. For days, I had dismissed a nagging pain in my upper left thigh as fatigue from relentless martial arts training for my role as the new villain, Mike Barnes, in The Karate Kid III. In reality, that pain marked the slow dripping of blood from my femoral artery, a consequence of a stunt I performed. My blood pressure plummeted, causing me to collapse.

Paramedics rushed me to the hospital as the pain intensified. Struggling to remain conscious, I was handed a consent form by a nurse, informing me that surgeons needed to operate immediately and that they couldn't guarantee my survival. I was no longer fighting for a film role; I was fighting for my life. As the anesthesia took hold in the operating room, I felt myself slipping away.

I survived and woke to a painful twelve-inch wound on my abdomen, held together by steel staples. Shortly after, the director called with an ultimatum: return to set within two weeks or face termination. A bitter thought crept in: "Welcome to Hollywood, kid."

That moment demanded that I make a choice. How would I write the next chapter in the story of my young life? Would I sink into victimhood, decrying the seemingly cruel twist of fate, or would I assume the role of the hero fighting to overcome the daunting odds? I decided that this setback would not define me, but would instead reveal a part of my character that was yet unknown, even to myself.

I hadn't realized how weak I had become; surgery had taken its toll, dropping me from 180lbs of muscle to a severely underweight 155lbs. Each agonizing step and grueling workout was driven by a single thought: Fight. It was up to me to save myself, as no one else could.

Despite the odds, I pushed through the painful recovery, determined to reclaim my title as "Karate's Bad Boy." I ultimately returned to the set, performed all my own martial arts stunts, and completed the film. I chose the road less traveled, a life-defining decision between two narratives: victim or victor. That decision has made all the difference.

2. SELF-AWARENESS

Understanding the world and the people around us begins with self-awareness. It begins with accepting the fact that the reality we live in is a construct based on our perceptions and influences, rather than what truly is. Reaching this moment of self-awareness is simultaneously enlightening and potentially frightening. Remember Neo in *The Matrix*? Here, we all face a choice: continue to live in the relative bliss of self-delusion or embark on the journey of personal deconstruction leading to self-awareness. Do you take the blue pill or the red pill?

Most of us struggle with self-awareness, but it's not entirely our fault. It is, however, our responsibility to face this challenge and work to overcome it. From the moment we are born, parents and society pressure us to become a success, become a winner, to become someone.

But what if this prescribed path is flawed, leading us astray? What if true success and meaningful happiness lie not in becoming, but in unbecoming—rediscovering, healing, and reconnecting with our authentic selves? Achieving this requires shedding the emotional armor we've developed over the years as a defense against toxic shame, withering criticism, and harsh judgments from the outside world.

True self-awareness demands detaching ourselves from a mindset formed from years of negative external influences. Easier said than done. Politically divisive media, 24-hour news cycles, and the relentless noise of social media surreptitiously try to seduce us into becoming someone other than our true selves. Internally, we also grapple with the incessant mental chatter amplifying doubt and fear. Reflect on your true identity—can you remember who you were before external pressures dictated who you should become?

Much of who we are today has been shaped by old wounds of the heart and painful memories of the mind, creating trauma that lingers within us. These emotional scars reside in what we refer to as "the inner child." Healing this aspect of ourselves is essential for dismantling the distorted image we hold of our past and for recognizing our true selves in the present. When we neglect this inner healing, we remain tethered to our past experiences.

Many of us carry a vivid image of our inner child, which can evoke feelings of anger directed both at that child and at our current selves for failing to protect them. This anger stems from the helplessness our inner child experienced in the face of past traumas, whether it involved confronting bullies or witnessing abuse within the family.

Frustration over our inability to resolve these painful issues often leads us to mistakenly blame the vulnerable child who embodies our suffering. This unresolved anger can evolve into rage towards our adult selves, accompanied by guilt and a sense of inadequacy for not having safeguarded our inner child when they needed us most. Ultimately, our inner child was defenseless, longing for the support that we were unable to provide at that time.

So, what's the solution? We must learn to embrace the parts of ourselves that feel unlovable. Try this exercise. Find an image that represents your inner child and connect with the emotions it evokes.

Speak to your inner child with compassion: "You are a part of me that I cherish and need, but you do not define who I am today." Repeat this affirmation daily until it truly resonates with you. Seek forgiveness for the moments you may have used your inner child as an excuse for victimhood. Forgive yourself, recognizing that you did the best you could, both as a child and now as an adult. Remember, healing takes time and patience, and you are already on the right path.

3. TRUE SUCCESS

Part of thriving comes from feeling successful. That success, however, must be *your* personal definition of success, not the one foisted upon us by society, whose primary metrics focus upon material acquisition and financial assets. Your life must be more than the sum of your possessions. You are not your home, your car, or your job—no matter how much you think your work defines you. Character is what defines us.

Success is not the unrealistic physical images plastered across the glossy covers of fashion and fitness magazines. It's not the constant bombardment of television commercials telling us what we must have, and it's definitely not what you see on social media, where influencers parade their luxury cars and extravagant lifestyles. Having worked in Hollywood for over thirty years, I can tell you that many of those so-called "extraordinary" lives are carefully curated by publicists, Photoshop, and filters, not by meaningfully happy individuals.

Our society places tremendous importance on results. Results are indeed important. However, one of life's great ironies is this: If you want results, ignore them. Instead, focus on the process necessary to achieve those results. Concentrate on your habits and actions.

Whether you realize it or not, you probably already do this in certain areas of your life. Take driving as an example. I bet we all follow the same basic steps. We don't grip the steering wheel with constant anxiety, worrying about whether we'll make it. We expect to arrive at our destination. Why? Because we have created a bulletproof process for driving. Build a bulletproof process for any goal, apply it consistently, and adjust as needed. Focusing on results means thinking about the future, which is unknown. This creates anxiety, diverting energy and effort from the present.

Part of success requires accepting failure as an essential part of the process. Once you view failure as a teacher, you will always succeed. Sounds oxymoronic, but it's true. Failure helps you learn what works and what doesn't, which in turn refines your bullet-proof process. You will either win or you will learn. Try attaching that story when you don't immediately achieve the desired result.

4. MEANINGFUL HAPPINESS

The art of strategic surrender is critical to achieving meaningful happiness. To whom do we wave the proverbial white flag? Not to whom but to what. The incessant need to control. Control is one of life's greatest illusions. What we attempt to control often ends up controlling us. A clear reminder of this is our planet's dependence on our sun, a dying star that will one day go supernova, ultimately collapsing into a black hole and consuming our Earth. Still believe you are in control?

The only aspect of life we control is our emotional response to the constant stream of external stimuli we encounter. How we react to situations is a choice. Therefore, choose wisely, as your decisions can initiate a domino effect, shaping the narrative you attach to events. Before trying to control others, focus on gaining mastery over yourself—this may be a challenging but rewarding journey.

The universe behaves with an inherent fluidity. Resisting its natural ebb and flow leads to feelings of being out of sync. You might have experienced days where you feel like a baby salmon swimming upstream—that sense of struggle indicates you're misaligned with the world or your true self. Trying to impose control over external factors is like forcing a round peg into a square hole, resulting in frustration and anger rather than meaningful happiness.

Living in the present represents an essential component of meaningful happiness and, subsequently, thriving. This means accepting the fact that sometimes your circumstances are suboptimal. Meaningful happiness doesn't mean life won't be uncomfortable or even painful. It means accepting circumstances as they are. Acceptance doesn't mean you don't adapt and work to resolve challenges. It does mean meeting life on life's terms, maintaining a sense of gratitude for what you have, and living in abundance, not scarcity. Exude this vibration, and the universe will match it.

5. SERVICE

Assuming you have erected the preceding four masts on your ship, you are ready to construct the final and most essential mast that will power your ship, transporting you to a life that thrives. This mast is constructed through acts of service. The unselfish desire to bring value to everyone you encounter.

Tune into the voice within your heart that speaks to your authentic self. Here you will learn the secret to life, discovering your unique gift with which you were born. Pay attention to the voice of the universe that guides you toward balance, peace, and harmony. Here you will learn the meaning of life: Sharing that gift with others and transforming the world. The fastest way to achieve what you want —a life in which you thrive—comes from helping others achieve the same.

Someday, in the not-too-distant future, I expect to stand upon the deck of my ship, gaze across the bow, and view millions of other ships all sailing toward a shared destination, a world in which we all thrive.

SEAN KANAN

Sean Kanan won the 2021 Daytime Emmy for Outstanding Limited Series as the Executive Producer/Creator of Studio City, exclusively on Amazon Prime. He previously received four nominations for Studio City in the categories of Outstanding Lead Actor and Outstanding Writing Team. He also won the Indie Series Award for Outstanding Lead Actor for his heartbreaking and humorous portrayal of Sam Stephens, aka Dr. Pierce Hartley.

On the big screen, Sean began this year starring in back-to-back films with Bruce Willis. Both *Survive the Game* and *The Fortress* were produced by Emmett/Furla and filmed in the mountains and jungles of Puerto Rico. Lionsgate Entertainment will distribute.
Next up is a lead role in the suspense thriller, *Killer Ambition,* for Lifetime. He recently rejoined the cast of *The Bold and the Beautiful* on CBS, reprising his role of bad boy Deacon Sharpe.

Proving himself a "triple threat," Sean has recently launched his third and most personal book, *Way of the COBRA*. Drawing upon intimate personal stories, *Way of the COBRA* details the strategies and philosophy that Sean uses to achieve success in his life.

" 'Transform yourself and you can transform the world.' Way of the Cobra is a compelling book by Sean Kanan that is both intriguing and motivational, offering food for thought. It is a great source of inspiration for anyone, and it is highly recommended for all."
~ Markos Papadatos, Digital Journal

Sean's first book, *The Modern Gentleman: Cooking and Entertaining with Sean Kanan,* received rave reviews. His second book, *Success Factor X,* became an Amazon New Release Bestseller in one week and was recently named one of the twenty most inspirational books of the last two decades by Book Authority.

Sean's acting career exploded with his breakout performance as iconic villain, Mike Barnes, in *The Karate Kid III,* beating out over two thousand hopefuls in an open call. He won an award for his role in daytime television, playing the black sheep, AJ Quartermaine, on *General Hospital.* His critically acclaimed portrayal of Deacon Sharpe on *The Young and the Restless* and *The Bold and the Beautiful,* television's most syndicated show in history, has been seen in dozens of countries.

Recently, the popularity of Netflix's hit show *Cobra Kai* has sparked international speculation of whether or not Kanan will reprise his role as Mike Barnes. Having appeared in over 1,000 episodes of network television and more than twenty feature films, Sean is recognized worldwide.

Whether lobbying on Capitol Hill, raising awareness about bullying, or taking his stand-up comedy act to Bosnia to entertain the troops with the USO, Sean remains active in numerous charitable organizations, including the American Cancer Society, various animal advocacy groups, and serving as the international youth ambassador for Boo2Bullying.

Sean and his wife, Emmy-winning producer and writer, Michele Kanan, live in Palm Springs, where he has a star on the Walk of Fame. He spends his free time practicing martial arts, cooking, traveling, and studying multiple foreign languages, including Italian and Mandarin.

www.WayOfTheCobra.com

DR. THERESA "TGO" GOSS
THE TRUTH ABOUT COURAGE

I grew up on the Southside of Chicago—and if you know, you know. That means survival wasn't optional, and playing small wasn't even on the table. It means you grow up fast, learn the streets like scripture, and figure out early that softness can cost you more than you can afford. But even with all that noise outside, my foundation was shaped by something deeper—something rooted in generations of survival, pride, and pain that refused to be forgotten.

My parents were warriors long before I ever showed up. They were born into a world where Black folks didn't get to dream—they were expected to endure. My mother and father were sharecroppers until their teenage years in Arkansas and Mississippi during the 1920s and '30s, working land they'd never own, living under systems designed to keep them stuck. And when they adopted me in the 1960s, they brought that entire legacy into our house: the strength, the survival, the silence—and the fire.

I remember that my mother hated cotton. Not just the crop, but the memory. She wouldn't even allow it in the house. She'd make me pull the cotton out of the medicine bottles before putting them away. That's how deep it went. That's how close the pain still was. And yet, she never made it a spectacle. She didn't sit me down for some dramatic monologue about racism or poverty. She just lived her truth and expected me to rise because of it.

45

I remember sitting at our kitchen table, her voice low but steady, telling me stories of Arkansas—about fields that felt endless, stores she wasn't allowed to enter, and days she swore she'd never go back to. And when she looked me in the eye, without even raising her voice, the message was clear: "You are going to do something different. You are going to BE something different."

So, I did.

But it wasn't easy.

We didn't have a lot of money. But we had faith—and I had a mind that couldn't sit still. I've been building since I was ten years old. That's when I launched my first business doing odd jobs in the neighborhood. I wasn't just hustling for pocket change —I was hiring my friends to work with me, tracking what we earned, and reinvesting like a baby CEO. By twelve, I was making more money than my parents—not because I was lucky, but because I saw opportunity where others saw limits. I used to joke that I was running the neighborhood like a mini CEO—only half-kidding. My Aunt would just shake her head and say, "Lord, she's got more ideas than time."

That drive never left me. In high school, while other kids were worried about prom or popularity, I was falling in love with computers. I started learning how to code—teaching myself logic, structure, and how to solve problems line by line. I didn't realize it then, but I was training for the digital legacy I'd one day build.

After high school, I joined the United States Navy. I didn't enlist because it was trendy—I joined because I needed direction, discipline, and a way to prove to myself that I could stand under pressure. The Navy gave me structure, but more than that, it gave me a sense of accountability I hadn't experienced before. I learned how to lead without needing a title, how to follow when it counted, and how to stay focused even when everything around me was chaos. That foundation became a part of my DNA.

When I left the Navy, I didn't waste a minute. I took all that training—mental, emotional, and spiritual—and poured it into entrepreneurship, building platforms that would allow others to be seen, heard, and empowered.

When other people were dreaming about fame, I was trying to figure out how to own the cameras, the lights, and the network. I didn't want to be on the stage. I wanted to build the whole damn thing—and then teach others how to do the same. And I did. But not without sacrifice.

Let me give it to you straight: being a woman in media, in tech, in leadership—especially over forty—comes with a kind of pressure that'll eat you alive if you're not grounded. I've walked into rooms where people assumed I was the assistant. I've had clients tell me they couldn't "picture someone like me" running a full-scale production. I've had people ask if my husband was the brains behind the business. I don't have a husband.

What I do have is receipts, and the paper trail is deep.

I've produced hundreds of TV episodes. I've built media platforms and tech-driven brands from scratch. I earned a Ph.D. while building businesses that uplift other people's legacies. And I've mentored women who were scared to speak, scared to shine, scared to charge their worth—and watched them bloom into icons. That's not ego. That's impact.

But here's what they don't see:

They don't see the nights I cried in my car because the payroll didn't match the bank account. They don't see the days I worked sixteen hours only to come home to silence. They don't see the fear I swallowed when everything depended on *me* and I didn't know if I had another ounce of strength left.

And they definitely didn't see 1995…

47

That was the year I hit rock bottom. I had planned it all out—how I was going to drive up one of the mountains and just… not come back. I didn't want to wake up anymore. I didn't want to fight anymore. And yet somehow, instead of ending my life, I ended up parked outside a public library. I don't even remember how I got there. But I was sitting there crying like my soul had finally broken open.

Something told me to go inside.

I walked up to the front desk and told the librarian, "I need something to motivate me." Her eyes softened, and she said, "I can see that. Now, I don't know much about this motivation stuff, but there's a whole section with tapes along that wall." Tapes. Cassette tapes.

I walked over and saw names like Zig Ziglar, Rita Davenport, and Les Brown staring back at me. I picked up a Zig Ziglar audio series and popped it into a cassette player. I pressed play, and the first thing I heard was: "I have brought for you a brand-new pair of glasses! These are not rose-colored glasses, but they will help you see life more clearly."

That was it. I was hooked.

I sat in that library until closing, listening like my life depended on it—because it did. The librarian saw me sitting there, lost in the tape, and asked if I wanted to check the tapes out. I didn't even have a library card. So, she rented them for me under *her* name. She didn't flinch—she just did it. A complete stranger who saw I needed help and gave me a lifeline.

I sat in my car and listened until I ran out of gas. I wasn't sure where I was going, but I knew one thing: I wasn't going off that mountain.

Those voices—Zig, Rita, Les—became my companions. My lifelines. I listened so much that I memorized every word. To this day, I still say they saved my life. I haven't met Les Brown yet, but I've had the honor of interviewing Zig Ziglar's son and calling Rita Davenport not just a mentor, but a dear friend. In fact, I had the privilege of honoring her as the 2023 NOW Honors Woman of the Year.

That's how life works when you keep going. When you hold on. When you decide, even in the darkest moment, that maybe—just maybe—there's still something left for you. That was courage. Not loud, not flashy. Just a broken woman, in a borrowed chair, listening to strangers talk about hope.

That moment gave me everything I needed to rebuild.

So, if you take nothing else from this chapter, take this:

You're allowed to change the game. You're allowed to want more. You're allowed to demand space, not ask for it.

It's not just about the big speeches or the shiny moments. Courage is layered. It's textured. It's messy. Sometimes, it looks like speaking up in a room full of people who don't want to hear you. Sometimes, it looks like walking away from what's comfortable to chase what's calling you. Sometimes, it's sitting still in your storm because moving too fast would break everything.

And I've done all of it.

I've lost people who didn't understand the mission. I've walked away from money that didn't align. I've stood my ground when it cost me opportunities. Because here's the truth—I didn't come this far to be controlled. I didn't build this from the ground up just to play nice and play small.

I came to disrupt. I came to rebuild. I came to remind people—especially the ones who look like me, who come from where I come from—that courage isn't just for the chosen few. It lives inside all of us. But you've got to choose it. You've got to fight for it. And sometimes, you've got to fight like hell to remember it.

There was a time I forgot who I was.

There was a season where I got lost trying to help everybody else rise. I gave too much. I said yes too often. I dimmed just a little so others could shine. But dimming doesn't serve anybody. Shrinking doesn't create legacy. So, I had to come back home to myself.

That's courage, too.

Courage is returning to your own voice after everyone else has had their say. It's rewriting your own story when life hands you a script you didn't ask for. And it's realizing that survival may have raised you—but thrival is your birthright.

Don't wait to feel fearless. That's a lie. Move anyway. Speak anyway. Build anyway. I did.

And I'm still doing it.

Let's get real. This part isn't for applause.

It's for the ones in the grind. The ones holding it all together with duct tape and deadlines. The ones who smiled through hell and still showed up like it was Sunday. This is for you if you've ever looked around and thought, "Damn, is this it?" If you've ever built something just to watch it fall apart. If you've ever been the strong one for so long that nobody checks if you're okay anymore. I see you. I've been you.

So, here's what I'll say—not as Dr. TGo, not as the media strategist, not as the one with the show, the mic, or the degrees, but just as a woman who's been broke, broken, doubted, underestimated, and still standing:

You don't need motivation. You need honesty. You need someone to remind you that being tired doesn't mean you're weak. That starting over doesn't mean you failed. That wanting more doesn't make you ungrateful.

Stop apologizing for your ambition. Stop asking for permission to dream. Stop trying to make yourself easier for other people to digest.

Be full. Be fierce. Be undeniable.

And when they try to box you in with their rules, their labels, their limitations—you lean in and say:

"Don't confuse my shine with luck. This glow came from the ashes—and I set the fire myself."

You don't owe anyone an explanation for why you're still here. You owe yourself a reminder that you've always had it in you.

So, go.

Say the thing. Write the book. Launch the business. Start the show. Ask for the room. Walk away from what drains you. Walk toward what sets you on fire.

You're the one. You've always been the one.

I didn't forget. And now you won't, either.

Walk like you've already survived the fire—because you have. Speak like you remember who you are—because you do. Build like the world has been waiting on you—because it has.

This is your time. No more shrinking. No more silence. No more playing small to make others comfortable.

You didn't come this far to play by their rules. You came to break the mold. You came to leave a mark.

Now, go do it.

And the next time you look in the mirror, I want you to see more than survival. I want you to see power. Process. Possibility. Not what life has taken—but what you've taken back.

Say it out loud if you have to: *"I've earned this voice. I've earned this space. And I'm just getting started."*

Oh, and if you're still waiting for a sign, let this be it: *Your Fear Is Not Bigger Than Your Fire.*

~ TGo

Special thanks to the voices who helped save me—Zig Ziglar, Rita Davenport, and Les Brown. This chapter includes a direct quote from Zig Ziglar's work, used with gratitude and respect.

DR. THERESA "TGO" GOSS

Theresa "TGo" Goss is more than a media strategist or producer —she is a powerhouse of innovation and a passionate advocate for community service and women's empowerment. Known for her visionary spirit and indomitable will, TGo's story is a remarkable journey of breaking barriers and creating impactful change.

From a young age, TGo demonstrated extraordinary entrepreneurial talents, outshining adults in business initiatives and laying the groundwork for her future successes. After a distinguished stint in the United States Navy, she ventured into the technology sector, where she flourished as a computer programmer and creative director, pioneering projects that bridged technology with artistic vision.

In 2004, TGo broke new ground with the launch of "BIM" (Black Insight Magazine), the first all-digital interactive magazine for African Americans, reaching 1.8 million subscribers and reshaping digital media engagement. Her ventures into television have further solidified her legacy, with her work earning her accolades such as the ATHENA International TV & Producer Award and induction into the Nevada Women's Hall of Fame for Entertainment & Media.

Beyond her professional achievements, TGo is deeply committed to community service and advocacy. She has served as the administrative director and volunteer coordinator for the League of Women Voters Illinois (Citizens Information Services) and the Chicago Area Runners' Association, dedicating her skills to enhancing civic engagement and community health initiatives. As a devoted caregiver and cancer patient advocate over the years, TGo has touched many lives with her compassion and support.

Her commitment to women's empowerment is evident in her role as the founder of NOW (Network of Outstanding Women) and the Power of PINK Summit. These platforms have become catalysts for women to excel, collaborate, and transform societal norms. TGo is also a steadfast supporter and volunteer for multiple nonprofits in Nevada, including the Women's Chamber of Commerce, Corner4Success Charitable Foundation, and the Roger's Foundation's CORE program.

TGo's life and career are not just a narrative of success but a profound influence that inspires and empowers. As she continues to pioneer groundbreaking projects and champion causes close to her heart, Theresa "TGo" Goss remains a beacon of creativity and a relentless advocate for positive change in every community she touches.

www.HeyTGo.com

JOHNNY WIMBREY

ESTABLISHING ACCOUNTABILITY IN THE AGE OF DISTRACTIONS

We live in a world of instant gratification. Scroll, swipe, like, repeat. It's never been easier to get distracted and never been harder to stay focused. In a culture where comparison is currency and attention spans are shorter than ever, how do you anchor yourself to your goals long enough to see them through?

Let me take you back to a moment when I had nothing but a dream, a beat-up pair of shoes, and a burning desire to become a first-generation millionaire. That dream was fragile. It had value, but only if I protected it, nurtured it, and, most importantly, held myself accountable.

THE POWER OF PRESENCE, NOT JUST INTENTION

You can have the clearest vision board, the boldest affirmations, and even the best mentor in your corner, but none of that matters without consistent action. And consistent action requires consistent accountability.

Accountability isn't about punishment. It's about progress. It's about positioning someone in your life to lovingly call you out when your actions don't match your ambition. In the early 2000s, I found that someone.

His name was Christopher Lloyd.

We met during a church leadership program in 2002. I was twenty-seven, broke, and hungry. My first daughter had just turned one, and my wife was pregnant with our second. I had every excuse to quit, but I kept showing up—week after week, leadership class after leadership class. I served until I had holes in my shoes—literally.

In those moments of grit, I was surrounded by people with real purpose. Christopher stood out. He wasn't just polite; he was *present*. When he asked, "How are you?" it wasn't small talk. It was soul talk. And that made all the difference.

SILENT OBSERVERS MAKE THE BEST MENTORS

Back then, part of our service involved acting as security detail, hotel greeters, and drivers for global leaders who came through the program. The one rule was simple: Don't speak unless spoken to. So, I didn't speak. I watched. I absorbed. I treated every encounter like a private masterclass.

Christopher and I went through this process together. We weren't just attending training—we were being *transformed*. We were witnessing world-class leadership while quietly mastering the art of presence, humility, and service.

Years later, when I set out to write my first book, *From the Hood to Doing Good*, I found myself in a creative stall. I had the message. I had the story. But the pages weren't getting written.

FROM FINE TO FINISHED

Every time Christopher saw me, he'd ask, "How's the book coming along?"

"Fine," I'd say.

"Fine" was a lie. Nothing was happening. No drafts, no chapters, just ideas and excuses. But I kept saying "fine" to avoid the truth —that I wasn't doing the work.

Until one day, something snapped. I looked Christopher in the eye and said, "Don't ask me how it's going anymore. From now on, ask me what page I'm on."

That moment changed everything. I knew I couldn't see him week after week and keep saying, "Page one."

ARTIFICIAL INTELLIGENCE VS. ACTUAL ACCOUNTABILITY

Fast-forward to today. We have AI tools that can write a book in minutes and productivity apps that schedule our lives down to the second. But here's the truth: No piece of technology will replace real human accountability.

There's a difference between automation and alignment. You can automate your reminders, but you need someone who *reminds you of your greatness* when you forget.

Christopher did that for me. Without fanfare. Without judgment. Just presence.

I finished the book within thirty days of that new accountability rule. Every time Christopher asked what page I was on, I gave him a new number. I wasn't just writing a book—I was rewriting my identity—from a "starter" to a "finisher," from a dreamer to a doer.

PROTECT YOUR PEARLS

There's an ancient proverb that says, "Do not cast your pearls among swine." Why? Because pigs can't comprehend value. They'll eat a million dollars in cash just as fast as they'd eat trash.

Your dreams are pearls.

Be cautious of who you allow to speak over them. Not everyone deserves access to your goals, especially when those goals are still in incubation. One careless voice can sow seeds of doubt. One insecure friend can hijack your momentum.

Accountability is sacred. Choose wisely.

YOUR INNER CIRCLE IS YOUR FUTURE

In 2025, we live in a world obsessed with visibility. Everyone wants to go viral, but very few want to go vertical. They want fame without foundation.

Here's a truth most won't tell you: Your private disciplines create your public victories.

You don't rise in public until you conquer in private. That means surrounding yourself with people who will check your blind spots, correct your course, and call out your inconsistencies.

Not critics. Not fans. Builders.

ACCOUNTABILITY WITHOUT PERMISSION

The best accountability doesn't wait for an invitation. It steps in— sometimes boldly, sometimes quietly, but always intentionally.

Christopher didn't need to become my coach or call himself my mentor. His consistent presence and genuine care made him the perfect accountability partner. I trusted him because I *felt* his investment in my future.

And I didn't give him permission to hold me accountable. I *assigned* him that role through my expectation. There's a difference.

Accountability is your responsibility. Not theirs.

FROM SURVIVAL TO THRIVAL

Courage isn't loud. It doesn't always show up on a stage. Sometimes, it whispers: *Keep going. Don't quit. Turn the page.*

In that season of my life, courage looked like writing through the fear of failure. It looked like telling someone to hold me accountable, even when it made me uncomfortable. It looked like saying, "Ask me what page I'm on," instead of hiding behind a lie.

Courage was showing up with holes in my shoes and fire in my heart.

MODERN LESSONS FOR A DISTRACTED WORLD

We need more Christophers in today's world. Not followers, but *finishers*—people who show up, ask the real questions, and care enough to remember your goals.

And we need to become that person for someone else.

Start here:

- Pick one goal.
- Choose one person you trust.
- Make them your page counter.
- Give them permission to ask uncomfortable questions.
- Then do the work.

Accountability is the bridge between survival and thrival. It's not enough to dream. You have to decide. And after you decide, you have to *deliver*.

In a world obsessed with filters, likes, and curated success, courage is raw, messy, and unfiltered. But it's real.

That's the kind of courage that turns authors into bestsellers. That's the kind of courage that turns ideas into income. That's the kind of courage that builds a legacy.

As you rise into the next chapter of your life, remember this:

Your goals don't need more inspiration. They need accountability.

And not just from others, but from you.

Be the one who finishes what you start. That's what courage looks like in 2025. That's what thrival feels like.

And that's the legacy you're writing—one courageous page at a time.

DR. JOHNNY WIMBREY, PH.D

Dr. Johnny Wimbrey is an international motivational speaker, bestselling author, and award-winning orator whose voice has inspired audiences across six continents. With a signature style rooted in transparency, resilience, and transformation, Johnny has delivered electrifying keynote addresses for Fortune 500 companies, global conferences, and leadership summits, sharing his message of overcoming adversity and building a life of purpose without compromise.

Rising from a troubled youth to global prominence, Johnny's journey has been featured in multiple national and international media outlets. His bestselling books—including *From the Hood to Doing Good* and *Building a Millionaire Mindset*—have impacted readers worldwide, providing a blueprint for turning struggle into strength and pain into purpose. His story of redemption and elevation is not only inspiring but also a powerful testament to personal accountability and unshakable faith.

As a media-trained speaker and certified mindset strategist, Johnny has shared stages with world-renowned figures in personal development, captivating audiences with bold storytelling, actionable wisdom, and a larger-than-life presence that commands the room. His presentations are consistently ranked among the most memorable at high-level events, and his voice is often requested for major platforms seeking authenticity with impact.

Johnny holds an Honorary Doctorate of Divinity from Trinity International Seminary, conferred after delivering a powerful commencement keynote. He is also the recipient of the Key to the City of Fort Worth, awarded by the mayor's office in recognition of his service, transformation, and influence—symbolically reclaiming the same city where he once faced incarceration.

Whether on stage, in print, or on camera, Johnny Wimbrey speaks with conviction, clarity, and courage—guiding audiences to shift their mindset, own their greatness, and never settle for anything less than their full potential.

www.Wimbrey.com

JON KOVACH JR.

COURAGE IN THE SHADOW OF FEAR

Courage isn't the absence of fear—it's doing the right thing even when fear is present.

I've always been an underdog.

From when I was a little boy to now in the professional world, life has never handed me an easy ticket. I wasn't the tallest, I wasn't the strongest—and although I was close, I was never quite the fastest. But what I lacked in handouts, I made up for in grit, work ethic, and a relentless commitment to show up and be my best.

I've been incredibly blessed in many areas of life. My family is amazing. I was raised by two loving parents—my father, an honest and hardworking man, and my mother, a woman of unconditional love for her family and everyone she encountered. They both led with proper leadership and paved a blueprint path for us: to serve, love, and live honorably.

Growing up in a strict Christian household wasn't always easy. It made us different. We stood out from our friends, neighbors, and classmates. Our church beliefs often kept us from participating in things other kids took for granted—sports games played on

Sundays or extracurriculars that required travel or expenses we couldn't afford.

There were four of us kids. All of us were incredibly talented. But there weren't enough resources to pour into just one of us to reach the top, so we stayed local. We kept things simple. And we learned to thrive within our means.

IT TAKES COURAGE TO BE DIFFERENT

It's hard when society praises uniqueness, but in reality, those differences often create distance. I remember the countless Sunday hangouts I had to miss, the parties I knew I couldn't go to, or the curfews that made me feel like the odd one out.

Yet, somehow, I'm grateful. I learned early on what it meant to say "no" to things that didn't align with our values—and to show up the next day with my head held high, even when everyone else was talking about things I wasn't part of.

Courage is often quiet.

It's the invisible sacrifice you make when no one's watching.

As I've written in some of my other books, backpacking in the wilderness has been one of the greatest teachers of humility and courage. Being out in nature quickly reminds you of who's really in charge. And for me, that has always been the one and almighty Creator.

Those quiet moments in the wild taught me that humility and courage often go hand in hand. Without humility, I don't think courage would exist.

LOCKER ROOM ARROGANCE

One story that always comes to mind when I think about courage is from my junior year of high school. I was honored to lead the fastest 4x800m relay team in Colorado. At one track meet, a reporter approached me to get a quote for an article. But they caught me at the wrong time—my adrenaline was sky-high after just finishing our race.

When asked, "What would you say about your competition today, Jon?" I blurted out: *"If you can't play with the big dogs, go piss with the puppies."*

In a moment of passion and vulnerability, fueled by pride and ego, I let a locker room phrase fly in front of the public. It made my team laugh—but it also made the paper. The next morning, I was called to the principal's office and asked to formally apologize to the press, my team, and our competitors.

That moment wasn't courage—it was arrogance.

And it taught me a profound lesson about humility and self-control.

MISSION WORK, MACHETES, & MIRACLES

Years later, I served as a missionary in the Philippines. For two years, I walked the streets of Manila in a white shirt and tie, standing out like a sore thumb. It was one of the most courageous things I've ever done—not because I was fearless, but because I was filled with faith. I saw things most people never see.

One afternoon, my companion and I were walking down the street when a violent commotion broke out ahead of us. A man emerged with a machete and began attacking another man in the street. It all played out in slow motion.

We sprinted away, found a security guard, and pleaded with him to intervene.

He shook his head and said, "It's not our problem."

That moment haunted me. I thought, "If I were him, I'd risk my post to help." Maybe it's because of how I was raised. Perhaps it's because I've always believed we should step in when others need us.

But I also knew that if I got injured or involved, I'd be sent home, and I wouldn't finish the mission I was called to do.

Courage, sometimes, is choosing to stay on course—when your heart aches to do more.

FACING THE GUN

In another instance, walking down the street, a man stepped out from an alley and pointed a gun straight at my head. My mission companion froze. I looked at him, touched his shoulder, and calmly said, "Turn around."

Together, we turned our backs on the man and walked away.

I smiled. I whispered a prayer. And I believed—deeply—that everything would be fine.

The man didn't fire.

We walked away unharmed.

That was courage—not because we weren't afraid, but because we chose to believe. We decided to trust—and we walked in that trust, even while looking down the barrel of danger.

THE POWER OF CHOICE IN THE FACE OF FEAR

I've learned that courage is choosing to do what's right, even when fear is screaming at you not to.

It's not about being fearless. It's about being faithful.

I don't share these stories to sound like a superhero—I'm no bullet-dodging phenom from *The Matrix*. I share them because we all have moments when we feel like we're up against our own Goliaths.

And in those moments, you have a choice.

Even through fear, you can choose to act. And those actions can change your life—and someone else's.

You don't know who's watching. You don't know how far the influence travels.

But you can choose to be courageous.

To this day, I think about those moments. I still wonder if I could've done more.

But what I do know is this: I'm still here, I'm still breathing, and I'm still walking forward with faith.

TETHERED TO TRUST: COURAGE ON THE CLIFFSIDE

As a climbing instructor, one of the most powerful metaphors for courage came into my life.

Climbing—especially rappelling—is not just about ropes and rocks. It's about trust. It's about learning to lean backward into fear and believing that someone below is watching out for you. That they've got your back.

Your voice trembles when you're standing at the edge of a cliff, peering down with sweaty hands and a pounding heart. But you still have to speak the command sequence.

I yell down, "On belay?"

And I wait.

From below, I hear it: "Belay on!"

That simple phrase means: *I'm here. I'm watching. I've got the rope.*

But here's the thing—not to literally catch me. A belay partner doesn't catch a falling climber with their hands. That would destroy you both. Their job is to manage the slack in the rope and operate the braking system. They keep tension. They watch for signs of distress. When the climber slips or loses control, the belayer tugs on the safety rope—triggering the belay device to lock up and stop the fall.

It's a dance of physics, friction, and faith.

The hardest moment is that first lean. You're standing tall, toes at the edge, and you're told to *"Lean back."* Trust the harness, the device, the rope, the partner... Trust it all.

Courage lives right there—in that first lean.

As your weight shifts off the cliff, you feel your life transfer into a system of tension. One end of the rope tightens, keeping you secure to the anchor above. The other side, the "slack" side, runs down to your partner.

Want to stop? Pull down.

Want to descend faster? Loosen your grip.

But at every moment, you must trust. You must believe it.

Even after hundreds of climbs and rappels, that moment still gives me chills. And yet, it's a feeling like no other.

When I became an instructor, I had to learn how to teach others how to face that exact fear. I had to find words—not just commands—but real, calming encouragement.

When you see someone frozen in fear, staring at the abyss below them, courage isn't yelling, "Just do it!"

It's looking them in the eyes and saying, "I've got you. And I'll be right here until you're ready."

Watching a beginner face that ledge, lean back trembling, and then break into a smile halfway down the rock wall... that's one of the greatest gifts I've ever experienced.

It's not just the thrill of the climb—it's the transformation that happens when they trust the process, choose faith, and step into courage.

That's the moment they go from surviving their fear... to thriving.

Courage is not about fearlessness—it's about choosing to walk anyway. Sometimes trembling. Sometimes trembling with faith.

But always... stepping forward.

JON KOVACH JR.

Jon Kovach Jr. is an award-winning and international motivational speaker and global mastermind leader. In his work as an accountability coach and mastermind facilitator, Jon has helped and coached thousands of professionals achieve their goals with his Irrefutable Laws of High Performance. Jon is the Founder of Champion Circle Professional Development Association. He is also the featured Mastermind Facilitator and Team Leader of the Habitude Warrior Mastermind and the Global Speakers Mastermind & Masterclass series.

Jon is a 28x National #1 Bestselling Author. He is a featured keynote speaker on *SpeakUp TV*, an *Amazon Prime TV* series, and a TEDx speaker, delivering his signature speech, "Getting Unstuck." Jon's motivational messages have been viewed by over 1 million people, and his voice has trended and been used by global brands on TikTok, YouTube, and Instagram, including: Red Bull, Michael Bublé, Powell Books, GoDaddy Studio, Canada's Wonderland Amusement Park, the LSU Cheer Team, and the NHL.

Author's Website: *www.SpeakerJonKovachJr.com*

Charity Awareness: *www.Wish.org*

ANGÈLE LAMOTHE

THRIVING WITH COURAGE THROUGH THE POWER OF CHOICE

When I recall the endless hours spent in hospitals and the many medical challenges surmounted over the last few years (supporting my son's health journey), tears flow not from a place of sorrow, but from a profound acknowledgment of the beauty that exists in the midst of chaos.

I understand now that I am forever changed—not just as a mother, but as a human being capable of resilience, love, and exponential growth in the face of adversity. Life may not always go as planned, but within the chaos, courage and strength can emerge, and for that, I am eternally grateful.

Let me take you back in time. During quiet moments, when the machines hummed softly in the background, I took time to reflect. I remembered the hugs I had received, the support from friends and family, and the kindness of strangers. These moments opened my heart fully to the myriad of experiences, individuals, and lessons that have shaped my family's journey—the good, the very challenging, and everything in between.

The days turned into weeks, and while the journey was far from over, I found strength in each day that brought a new challenge and new opportunities for growth. My heart and mind opened to embrace the unpredictable nature of life. I learned to sit with discomfort, to breathe through it, surrender, and let it transform into something more meaningful and much bigger than me.

As my son began to recover, I realized this journey had been a profound teacher and healer. The lessons of acceptance, resilience, and unwavering love became deeply ingrained in me. I learned that while I could not control this experience, I could choose to infuse my journey with purpose and deep, meaningful change.

I have grown exponentially through my experiences and built courage and resilience beyond my human years. I now feel the freedom that comes with that acceptance. As I released the emotions stored within me, I could hear the universe reassuring me that the support, love, and kindness of others had been instrumental in walking this path. But more importantly, I realized that it was my own decisions—my choice to approach adversity through a different lens, my choice to focus on gratitude and to empower myself through every moment—that had transformed my experience.

The power of growth through challenges has shifted my entire frame of reference. It's not just about accepting what is but actively choosing to embrace this journey as a sacred one. I understand now that the essence of life lies not in the quest for control but rather in surrendering to the process and realizing the inherent power that's already within and that life is always happening for you.

In hindsight, I understand that these moments faced were just steppingstones on a journey that would allow me to inspire others and share this newfound perspective on resilience and exponential growth through challenges.

What if this is exactly where you need to be? What if you embraced the idea that every moment, no matter how difficult, serves a purpose in your life's perfect unfoldment? The more you try to control it, the more you will feel out of control and out of alignment with who you truly are.

Challenging moments can feel uncomfortable because they generate fear, anxiety, and a loss of control. Life is constantly changing, but that doesn't mean that it's out of our control. I felt a radical loss of control at times during this journey, but I remembered that monumental challenges are still within my control. I can control how I respond to situations—and in every moment, no matter what—and that is the ultimate definition of courage.

I realized that these challenges had not only shaped me but had also transformed me—my values, my priorities, and my perspective on life itself.

I had learned to embrace growth and view setbacks as catalysts for exponential growth. I understood that every hardship was a lesson, every obstacle an opportunity for self-discovery and transformation. I had witnessed my child's strength and resilience and, in doing so, had uncovered my own. It was a reminder that we are far more capable than we believe.

"Change is inevitable. Growth is optional and intentional."
~ John Maxwell

Change, I learned, is inevitable, whether we embrace it or resist it. Growth is what's optional; it only happens by choice and when you make the conscious and courageous decision to grow through challenges. By choosing to welcome transformation with open arms, you harness exponential growth—not just for yourself but for those around you. My eldest's journey catalyzed a shift within me, allowing me to become a spark of inspiration for others. Every moment is a new moment and an opportunity to try again and again!

Hardship often prepares ordinary people for an extraordinary destiny! What if these obstacles and difficult moments for me and my family were just a simple path leading me exactly to where I was supposed to be?

What if obstacles and challenges were just moments of monumental changes that we can embrace, accept, and use to propel us forward? Every challenge is a useful experience and a moment of tremendous self-growth. Life challenges test you to become stronger and to face things head-on, not to live on the surface, but to dig much deeper.

You can call upon that internal strength and resilience to change what you want and desire. That inner strength, inner peace, and reserve are what keep you strong.

What I discovered is that our relationships flourish when we lead with authenticity and openness. As I strive to be a better mother, daughter, and partner, I carry forward the lessons learned—moment by moment, breath by breath, and day by day.

In the end, it is this internal journey that shapes our external reality. By focusing on what I can control within myself, I honor the possibility of growth and the essence of gratitude as guiding forces. After all, I am not merely a victim of circumstance; I am the architect of my own life, designing a reality infused with strength, abundance, and love. And with that realization, I venture forth with courage, ready to embrace whatever comes next.

This journey transformed me, fostering resilience that felt beyond my years, and I found myself yearning to give back generously. It was from this deep well of gratitude and empowerment that my quest began. I began sharing my story not as a narrative of hardship but as a testament to the transformative power of resilience and support.

What most transforms our relationships is our courage and willingness to learn, heal, grow, and positively influence the lives of others through our experiences!

Learning from our obstacles, taking responsibility, and moving out of shame and guilt help us shift into empowerment and create monumental change. Taking responsibility means re-inventing, creating solutions to obstacles, and taking ownership, which generates huge power and change in your life.

Anyone can choose courage and empowerment; every person has that option in every moment.

Empowerment, resiliency, and growth through changes are conscious choices. Taking responsibility means re-inventing, creating solutions to obstacles, and taking ownership, which generates huge power and momentum in your life.

There is so much freedom and power in choosing courage as a way of living and being. In what vibrations are most of your thoughts? When you spend more time in joy, love, abundance, and gratitude, you will become a magnet for those frequencies.

You are the creator of your life, and you decide how you'll respond to life's challenges. Your life is created by design, and you always have a choice; you are the creator of your reality. You have the power to choose how you'll respond in every single moment.

What if this challenge was merely a moment of monumental change, one that I could embrace and use to propel myself forward? Every challenge, I realized, presents itself as an opportunity for tremendous self-growth if we choose to view it that way. While it is easy to feel overwhelmed in the heart of adversity, we possess the power to control our reactions and maintain an empowering outlook, thus inspiring real change in our own lives and in the lives of others.

We all encounter challenges; it's an inherent part of our human experience. But in those difficult moments, I want to remind all who are reading: The universe, after all, only gives us what we can handle—a testament to our inner strength, courage, and resilience!

Sometimes, in the depths of despair, it can feel almost impossible to grasp the true meaning of our journey and understand why this is happening to us. Let me remind you that the challenges we face do not define us, but rather refine us, shaping us into better human beings, mothers, daughters, sisters, friends, and partners.

How will you choose to face your challenges and shape the life you dream of?

ANGÈLE LAMOTHE

Angèle Lamothe is a high-vibrational leader who lives a heart-centered life and whose mission is to help raise the consciousness of our planet and transform the world. She is a mom of three, a triathlete, an author, and an empowerment coach who works with high-performing leaders to help them create abundance and develop their intuition, enabling them to live their richest life.

Angèle works in an acute care hospital and is obsessed with people's transformational journeys and how the power of the mind, when aligned with purpose and action, can create miracles.

Angèle leads a high-performance lifestyle and has the joy, energy, and time to do things she deeply enjoys. She can support you in developing tools to help you connect with your intuition and unleash your full power within so that you can lead a balanced and abundant life that is full of gratitude! To find all my links, visit: *www.linktr.ee/AngeleLamothe.*

Author's Website: *www.AngeleLamotheCoaching.com*

Charity Awareness: *www.DareToBeVulnerable.com*

BILL GOOD

OF COWS & BUFFALO: THE COURAGE TO CHANGE

- -

*"I have told you these things, so that in me you may have peace.
In this world, you will have trouble. But take heart! I have
overcome the world."*
~ John 16:33

*"And I remember what she said to me
How she swore that it never would end
I remember how she held me oh-so-tight
Wish I didn't know now what I didn't know then
Against the wind. . .
I'm still runnin' against the wind
I'm older now but still runnin' against the wind."*
~ Bob Seger, "Against the Wind"

"We cannot direct the wind, but we can adjust our sails."
~ Attributed to Dolly Parton

Former CBS News anchor Dan Rather famously signed off his
nightly newscast in 1986 with just one final word, "Courage!" He
only used it for one week, though, as the practice met with parody
within a broadcasting community unable to countenance such a
display of sincere emotion.

However, he did once again return to it at the conclusion of his final broadcast on March 9th, 2005, after sharing a heartfelt message to the nation, urging resiliency in the face of calamity, saying, "And to each of you—courage."

The root of this word, "courage," comes into our language from the French word, "coeur," meaning "heart." The concept of courage stems from perceiving that pulsating organ as the birthplace of emotions and feelings, which we draw upon to conjure up notions of inner strength and spirit. It is this connotation that underlies Jesus' imperative to his followers to "take heart" in the face of the challenges we will inevitably face in a world incognizant of the values in his teachings.

Brene Brown wrote, "Courage originally meant, 'To speak one's mind by telling all one's heart.' Over time, this definition has changed, and today, courage is more synonymous with being heroic... I think we've lost touch with the idea that speaking honestly and openly about who we are, about what we're feeling, and about our experiences (good and bad) is the definition of courage... Ordinary courage is about putting our vulnerability on the line."

She concludes with an observation that is as unquestionable as it is insightful: "In today's world, that's pretty extraordinary."

Just think about the heroes who are lionized in our TV shows and movies. Few of them are esteemed for their vulnerability and deep relational skills. Instead, they are applauded for their physical strength, emotional fortitude, and single-minded desire to go it alone. From John Wayne to James Bond and Captain America to John Dutton, from Katharine Hepburn to Scarlett Johansson and Wonder Woman to Ellen Ripley—these are the idols who bring the box office. We like our heroes short on transparency and long on whoop-ass. If it's not exactly the American Dream, it's most certainly the American Way.

Here, in this culture, it was once commonplace that "children should be seen and not heard." This means that generations of children were raised in families where they were taught that displaying their honest feelings and emotions was not something to be countenanced.

In the home in which I grew up, for example, opinions were fully the province of the adults. Youthful attitudes were completely unwelcome. Neither disagreement *with* nor disobedience *to* parental authority was countenanced in the least. To display either, no matter to what small degree, was to be relegated to the position of Emotional Outcast until such time as my sister or I was held to have "learned our lesson." I was well into adulthood before I was able to transcend the effect of this experience and truly live into my relationships by speaking up and standing up.

The point is this: these are "lessons" we need desperately to unlearn if we're to live whole and healthy lives, fostering whole and healthy relationships. Ms. Brown is precisely on point in remarking on the link between courage and vulnerability. If the first is rare in our society, it's because the second is not appropriately valued. In fact, it's downright countercultural.

Transformation is necessary here in order for emotional and spiritual maturity to follow. We get to shake off the fetters of survival and release ourselves into the freedom of thrival. We get to become better humans inspiring other better humans. This work takes courage.

So, if you've read this far, I want to ask you, do you find yourself stuck in patterns of just "going along to get along?" Does that describe your manner of being? If so, I challenge you to think about the aspects of your life in which you get to cultivate courage:

• Is it in venturing true intimacy by risking your authentic self (where you're afraid you might suffer rejection if others *really* knew you)?

- Is it in speaking the truth in love to those you care for who need to hear it?

- Is it in standing up for those too weak to stand up for themselves in circumstances where to do so may well jeopardize your own personal peace?

- Is it in becoming a "truth teller" in situations where it is unwelcome?

- Or is it in something else entirely?

In short—where, exactly, in your way of life do you need to manifest the courage to *change?* Where do personal responsibility and emotional authenticity call you to go, in the words of Bob Seger, *"runnin' against the wind"*? In spiritual evolution as in physical development, resistance—no matter how discomforting —is key to progress.

In the late 1980s, the University of Arizona constructed a three-plus-acre facility in Oracle, Arizona, which became known as Biosphere 2 and which remains the largest closed ecological system ever created. The structure provided a lush botanical environment perfectly regulated to promote growth. It was intended "to demonstrate the viability of closed ecological systems to support and maintain human life in outer space as a substitute for Earth's biosphere."

But, in relatively short order, the trees grew weak, began to fail, and lost their natural ability to produce fruit. Their branches actually began to droop and shrink in size. Why? Because the design of the artificial air conditioning failed to consider the beneficial effect of wind in promoting vital arboreal growth. In nature, trees grow and gain strength by standing against the wind. Absent this dynamic resistance, they become frail, listless and unproductive.

And so it is with human faith and life. If we allow ourselves to live untried and unchallenged by the winds of this world, our growth becomes stunted—just like the trees in Biosphere 2.

Courage is critical here, as is the willingness to change one's life patterns from survival to thrival.

Have you ever watched a herd of cows in a storm? Do you know how they face it? The answer is, they don't! They gather together, flank-to-flank, in a tight community marked by heavy breathing and wet-nosed nudging for closer position. Finally, as a group, they turn their collective backs to what they sense to be the cold and threatening wind—only to remain thus until the storm blows over. This is the pattern which characterizes survival.

On the other hand, consider their bovine cousins, the American Bison. When the ferocious wind-blown snowstorms of the Montana and Wyoming winters visit their midst, buffalo will turn directly into the oncoming weather and stand individually to meet the wind and snow head-on. Often their huge, furry heads and bare faces will be completely encased in snow, but still, they stand as if directly rebuking all the opposition nature has to offer. This is the pattern which characterizes thrival.

So, when those scary winds of change blow through your life, how will you identify—as a cow or a bison? How will you stand? Your decision, of course, is dependent upon your commitment to courage—*the willingness to put your vulnerability on the line.*

Will you allow yourself to be blown hither and yon at the whim of social pressure and conformity? Or, even as the herd blows hot breath on your back and seeks to nudge you in the direction of the ever-vacillating breeze of culture, will you reach deep into your true self, turn toward the truth, and go "runnin' against the wind?"

Some years ago, I found a small plaque in an airport bookstore that has occupied space on my desk ever since: "We cannot direct the wind, but we can adjust our sails." Good practical advice for sailors. Good functional faith for those navigating the winds of change.

Courage!

BILL GOOD

Bill Good is a Speaker, Teacher, Bestselling Author, and Counselor. Bill Good is passionate about implementing world change through personal transformation and relationship recovery. He is dedicated to creating a pathway to healing and leading beyond the ordinary to living a life without limits. Bill holds a Master's of Divinity from Fuller Seminary and is retired from Pastoral Ministry. He currently teaches at Grand Canyon University. He also received advanced certifications in Christian Reconciliation and Peacemaking, is a Graduate of Transformational Leadership Training, and holds a Master's in Leadership. He is also the CEO and senior counselor of Path to Peace, which provides conciliation services to organizations and individuals seeking to overcome trauma.

But Bill's first love is encouraging hope through his writing and speaking. A four-time Amazon Bestselling Author as well as a Speaker Hearts and TedX speaker, he is presently preparing a trilogy of books for publication: *Between Sundays: A Practical Study of Jesus' Reconciliation Ministry; From Here to There: A Collection of Autobiographical Reflections on Spiritual Development; The Good Factor: A Functional and Life-Giving Perspective on Manifesting the GOOD Life, a Way to a Better Way.*

Author's Website: *www.TheGoodFactor.com*

Charity Awareness: *www.PhoenixRescueMission.org*

BRIAN SWANSON

COURAGE: WILL I HAVE HAIR?

While walking down the path known as life, we all must take a moment to realize that every step is a step of courage. We step outside our front door and face the weather. It takes courage to step into a car and drive down the highway. Even turning on the furnace requires courage.

We do not recognize that overcoming these fears is courageous, because we know from experience that all these things are safe. We have gone outside thousands of times and not experienced any negative recourses. We have driven from our home to a destination just as many times. But if we look deeper, it was overcoming fear and the desire for a driver's license that allowed us to step into a car for the first time.

Like many, I joined the military after I graduated high school. There, we were taught courage. It was a lesson that if we encountered an enemy, we would have to have bravery to keep us alive. In basic training, they put us through an obstacle course where we crawl on our stomachs under barbed wire while gunfire soars over our heads. It can be dramatic. Some would say it requires nerves of steel. How did I have the courage to take on these tests? I told myself that the instructors would not shoot me and that thousands of people before me had made it out alive.

I treated numerous situations in my life in the same manner. I jumped from airplanes, road rollercoasters, got married, had children, skied down mountains, water skied, and even swam with sharks. There were always others who survived these challenges. But one challenge I was not prepared for was stepping out and facing the journey that came with looking for my biological parents.

I was adopted at three days old and was raised by my adoptive parents. I was told at a very early age that I was adopted, and if I ever wanted to find out who my biological parents were, my adoptive parents would help me search. However, because I was raised in a caring family, I had no overwhelming desire to begin the search until I was an adult, married with children, and wanted to know my medical background.

The idea of searching for one's birthparents is scary. It is facing the unexpected. After all, it can be a life-altering experience. It is about wondering if these newly found parents will accept you. So many questions run through one's head. The questions themselves are frightening, but some of the answers are terrifying. Are they rich? Are they poor? Are there siblings? Are they healthy? Will their medical background affect my children? I could go on with the hundreds of questions that will shake your nerves. But it comes down to one main fear that must be overcome with courage: The fear of the unknown. All these questions are the great unknown.

I faced the fears with the attitude that many adoptees before me had gone through the same scenario. They had searched and sometimes found their biological parents. While some had terrible experiences, others had positive experiences that instantly added to their own families. I stepped out, started searching, and spent hundreds of hours looking through the internet and other resources. In the beginning, a friend of my mom found my birthmother using public records. Then it was a matter of using the information I received to find my birthfather to put together the puzzle pieces of the mystery. It was a ten-year voyage through numerous resources.

My experience was positive while giving me a new extended family. However, going into it, I had what could be considered a couple unique perspectives. First, I figured I had numerous friends and, of course, some people who did not like me. With that thought, I asked the question, "What's one more person who doesn't like me?" That attitude is as simple as it can get.

Another fun perspective always crossed my mind. I was raised in a small town in Indiana. In my teenage years. I had a large interest in girls. I dated many. Not knowing who my biological parents were, it was always a curiosity if I ever dated my sister. You will be glad to know that this never happened. Once I found my biological mother, I did discover that my older half-sister and I went to the same school for a short period during elementary school. Surprisingly, this humorous curiosity was not beyond the realm of possibility.

Side note: I also wanted to know if I would have hair once I got older. Yes, today I am aware that male baldness is typically from the mother's genes, but I didn't know that then. When I met my father, he had hair! That made me very happy, and to this day, I have all my hair.

When we analyze the unknown, we always make up questions. Some questions are viable while others are not even possibilities. Along with those questions come answers. Those answers are directly from our own learned perspective. These questions and answers are what give us feelings of fear. Many of us think we have no imagination, but let me impress upon you that we all have an imagination. Our imagination, which we put up against fear of the unknown, is there to protect us. We must use the positive side of our imagination to overcome those fears. There is nothing wrong with making up a positive when all the negatives are made up, too.

While deciding to look for my birth parents, there were tons of negatives running through my head. As with all questions and concerns, there comes the attachment of emotions. It can be scary or exciting. But my creativity turned the search into a game, and doing that helped me overcome my fears.

At the time, that is all it was, a game. I tried to find them as fast as I could. I compared photos I found to myself. I even asked friends, "Does this guy look like me?" However, looking back, it was courage that kept me going. I can now say that I was courageous in searching for my biological parents. It was courage that allowed me to meet them. It was bravery that gave me the opportunity to open my heart to a whole new family.

This has been a story about the courage I had while searching. I cannot forget that it was not just my courage that made it all possible. It was both parents who, I am sure, had many of the same fears that they had to overcome. From their perspective, they might have wondered, "How healthy is my child? Was he raised to be a respectable and responsible man? Will he like me? Will I like him?" Again, there are hundreds of questions and answers. All are fictitious until proven fact.

One thing I do know: The parents who raised me had their questions, too. Who are these people who gave their child away? Why did they give the baby away? Once found, will these people replace us, especially since we raised him? There are more and more questions and answers. It is not easy for either party to be involved in a complicated parenting scenario.

Life constantly involves courage to move forward. We do not think of these everyday challenges involving courage, because we have forgotten what it was like the first time. For some of us, there is a fear of putting on headphones. It can give us a feeling of loss of control within our environment. But that fear is conquered when we use them and realize that we do not have to have that control.

More serious challenges can require focusing on something else to conquer. Forget about the negatives. Find the positives. Try changing the challenge into a game. Keep focused on the goal.

There is an ancient Italian saying that can help you through, "Que Sera, Sera." Translated, it means, "Whatever will be, will be." So, let it be, because the more we question, the more we imagine the answers, which can ignite fear.

We do not always label it as courage at the time, but once we look back, we realize that not everyone would have made it through the fear of the unknown and moved on. That is, by definition, courage.

BRIAN SWANSON

Brian Swanson is a dedicated entrepreneur, podcaster, bestselling author, and business owner. His specialty is within the world of learning, teaching, and business building. His experiences include working in restaurants, bars, finance, construction, as a comic bookstore owner, disc jockey, website creator, marketer, graphic editor, and owner of GalaxyFest (a popular local Pop Culture Convention). Brian has a passion for sharing his skills and experiences through writing, speaking, and co-hosting a long-running podcast, *Denim and Pearls.*

One topic he loves to share is his experience of searching for his biological parents. Finding them was a positive experience, and his willingness to share has helped many adoptees conquer their fears and begin their quest to find their parents. If he is not behind the computer or orchestrating an event, you can find Brian hosting or performing karaoke at numerous venues around the state any day of the week—that is, assuming he is not traveling around the world. Learn more about Brian here: *www.Facebook.com/ DJWildLife* and *www.DenimAndPearlsLive.com.*

Author's Website: *www.GalaxyFest.com*

Charity Awareness: *www.SurvivalToThrivalSeries.com*

CHRISTOPHER MUSIC

THE QUIET POWER OF COURAGE

. . . .

Courage is one of those unique qualities that quietly shapes the course of our lives. It's more than a dramatic moment or an extraordinary feat—it's a steady, often silent force that moves us through fear and into growth. Most of us associate courage with superheroes—those larger-than-life figures who defy danger, confront evil, and triumph against overwhelming odds. We applaud their bravery, as we should, because their choices reflect something timeless and powerful: the ability to rise above fear.

Nearly every blockbuster film celebrates this trait. The protagonist stands firm in the face of chaos, makes a hard choice, and emerges changed, stronger, and freer. But while these cinematic displays of valor are exciting and meaningful, they can inadvertently cause us to overlook the quiet, personal acts of courage we ourselves perform daily.

Sometimes, courage shows up not in the grand battle, but in the private struggle—making a phone call you've been avoiding, choosing honesty over comfort, or simply showing up when you'd rather run away. These seemingly small moments define our character just as much as any bold stand against adversity. They mark turning points. Milestones. They're indicators that we're evolving.

One such moment remains vivid in my memory: my first day of kindergarten in the summer of 1974. I was raised in a quiet

~ COURAGE ~

German farm town nestled in central Ohio. We didn't have preschools back then. My only structured exposure to other children had been Sunday school—held conveniently next door to our house because my father was the town minister. That building was safe. Familiar. The world beyond it, however, was not.

So, when my mother took my hand and walked me toward the schoolyard, a place full of noise, strangers, and the terrifying unknown, I froze. The playground buzzed with energy—kids laughing, racing to the jungle gym, spinning wildly on the merry-go-round. But I wasn't laughing. I was hugging my mother's leg, paralyzed by a fear I couldn't explain.

Then something happened.

A boy walked over. A classmate. He looked at me and simply said, "Come play on the merry-go-round with us." Just like that. A small gesture. A child's voice. And something in me shifted. I took a breath, let go of my mother's leg, and ran with him toward the chaos.

That small step was monumental for me. I still remember it clearly because it was my first conscious act of courage. And it taught me something essential: that pushing through irrational fear, even in a small way, can unlock an entire new world.

For many of the other kids, going to school was routine. They weren't scared. But for me, it took everything I had. That's the nature of courage—it's relative. What terrifies one person might seem insignificant to another. But what matters is the breakthrough—the moment you decide to move, despite your fear.

At its core, courage is the willingness to be uncomfortable—to willingly enter what feels like danger, knowing that what lies beyond it might be freedom, growth, and even joy. It's not the absence of fear—it's the decision to act in spite of it.

Throughout life, we face countless opportunities to summon courage. But among them, one stands out as more significant than the rest: the decision to live by your own truth.

This act—choosing to follow your own voice, your own sense of right and wrong, even when it conflicts with the wishes or expectations of others—is the most profound display of courage any of us will ever make.

It may begin subtly: choosing a career path different from what your parents wanted. Deciding not to marry, or to marry someone others don't approve of. Living in a place or a way that defies cultural expectations. These aren't just decisions—they are declarations of sovereignty.

When we choose to live by our truth, we step outside the collective comfort of group agreement, and that can be deeply unsettling. We may lose relationships, face criticism, or question our own sanity. But on the other side of that discomfort is a new life—a life built not on compliance but on authenticity.

This isn't about rebellion for its own sake. It's about alignment—aligning our choices with our soul. Aligning our actions with what we know, in our deepest being, is right for us.

Yes, it may look like defiance. But it is, at its root, devotion—devotion to integrity. Devotion to growth. Devotion to the part of us that refuses to settle for a life of quiet compliance.

In this way, courage is more than a moment. It becomes a practice, a way of being, a daily commitment to listen to that still small voice within and honor it, no matter what the world says.

And when we do? We don't just change our own lives. We give others permission to do the same.

That is the quiet power of courage. And it begins, always, with a single step.

CHRISTOPHER MUSIC

Christopher Music, MBA, RFC, CBEC, is a thirty-three-year veteran of the personal financial planning profession. He has owned, built, and sold two firms since 1992, resulting in the improvement of the financial destinies of thousands of families in the US. He is a Wall Street Journal/USA Today bestselling author and an award-winning international speaker on financial topics. A Certified Business Consultant, Registered Financial Consultant®, and Certified Business Exit Consultant®, he is committed to expanding his knowledge and expertise in the fields of personal finance and economics for the ultimate benefit of small business owners.

He has shared the stage and/or collaborated on projects with Grant Cardone, Forbes Riley, Steve Forbes, Brian Tracy, Erik Swanson, Robert Allen, Rudy Giuliani, Mel Robbins, and other leading coaches and consultants. Christopher currently lives his life virtually as a digital nomad, traveling the world full-time and working with healthcare practice owners as The Professional's Prosperity Mentor. He can be reached at CM@ChristopherMusic.com.

Author's Website: *www.ChristopherMusic.com*

Charity Awareness: *www.TheWayToHappiness.org*

CLEVELAND AUZENNE

THEY TRIED TO BURY ME, BUT I GREW ROOTS

I LEARNED TO HEAR THE SILENCE

In 2008, I stood in the police station in Church Point, Louisiana, holding court-ordered custody papers in my hand. Not because I did anything wrong, but because I had to prove I had the right to see my own son. His mother stood there, her mother beside her, and my son stood silently between them. My boy was crying while standing right next to his mother. I stood alone.

That moment broke something in me—but it also awakened something: courage.

Between 2008 and 2011, I spent more time in courtrooms than most people will in a lifetime. I wasn't fighting for attention or ego—I was fighting for time, for presence, for my son to know his father loved him enough to fight. Each time I walked in, I felt dismissed. Even when the law was on my side, the pain of rejection hit harder. I remember thinking, "This isn't right." But I kept coming back.

Napoleon Hill said, "Every adversity, every failure, every heartache carries with it the seed of an equal or greater benefit." I didn't know it then, but that quote was becoming my truth. Even through the setbacks and sleepless nights, I was being refined by fire. That fire? It was courage.

I didn't grow up seeing things like this. My mom and dad were both in my life. I had structure. I had stability. And I had a father who made time to show me the world. I'll never forget the trips he took me on as a kid—how those experiences opened my mind and shaped my imagination. That's why I wanted the same for my son.

But instead of packing for a trip, I had to beg—beg just to take my own child on vacation. Imagine being a father who wants to bless his son and having to ask permission like he's a stranger. I wanted my son to see the world like my dad showed me—not because it was fancy, but because it was foundational. A child needs that exposure. A son needs his father—just like I couldn't imagine my life without mine.

But the system didn't make it easy, and neither did my own blood. People I trusted went behind my back, siding with the mother of my child, a family member I loved. Instead of support, I was betrayed. That pain cut deep, but I didn't let it define me. I let it fuel me.

And then came the day that shattered me from another angle. My son was seven years old. I was on the phone with him. He didn't know it, but I could hear the programming in his voice—words he didn't come up with on his own. He said, "Daddy, you're dumb. You're stupid. You're black and ugly." That moment wasn't just painful—it was spiritual warfare. My own flesh and blood had been turned against me.

Still, I kept showing up. I kept working—two jobs, sometimes three—whatever it took—not just to pay bills but to build something worth passing down. My son didn't see it then, but one day, I hoped he would know what it cost to be courageous.

There were even months I didn't see him—and guess what? He only lived twenty-five minutes away. Crazy, right? That kind of distance isn't measured in miles. It's measured in heartbreak.

Even when I had the court order in hand, my son sometimes didn't want to come. That kind of rejection will test your manhood. It'll test your soul. I remember one of those days, standing in the yard after being turned away again. My wife looked at me and said something I'll never forget: "Trust God and put it in His hands." That moment demanded a different kind of courage. Not to fight harder—but to surrender. And for a man like me, who sees his son as his seed—his one and only—that surrender was one of the hardest things I'd ever do.

Hill said, "Persistence is to the character of man as carbon is to steel." That's how I survived—not with noise but with quiet persistence. I showed up, even when it hurt. I kept working, even when no one noticed. I kept believing, even when my prayers felt like they were hitting the ceiling.

There were no welcome signs. No medals. Just a whisper in my soul that said, "Don't quit."

I never got to see my son get on the bus—I never had that option —but I never stopped praying that he'd ride farther than they ever expected. I wanted him to know, even if he couldn't say it yet, that his father never walked away.

My anthem became "Lose Yourself" by Eminem. "You only get one shot..." I clung to those lyrics like scripture. Because that's how it felt: I had no choice but to make this count.

This chapter of my life—this story—is about courage. The kind that doesn't roar. The kind that shows up quietly, day after day, even when the door gets slammed in your face. The kind that takes a deep breath when your child calls you ugly and says, "I'll still be here tomorrow."

Looking back, I wouldn't trade the lessons for anything. The tears, the silence, the distance—they planted something in me. Roots.

So, now I ask you, reader: What does courage look like in your story? When was the last time you showed up even when you weren't welcomed? Have you ever loved something so much that you had to let it go just to keep your peace?

I didn't find peace because anyone apologized. I found peace because I chose to create it for myself. They tried to bury me. But I grew roots.

And now? I'm a business owner, a mentor, and a speaker. I live my life to help others find the courage they need—just like I once did. When they feel buried, I remind them: Maybe they're not buried. Maybe they're planted.

CLEVELAND AUZENNE

Cleveland Auzenne is the proud owner of IRIDE Transportation, a company dedicated to providing safe and reliable non-emergency medical transportation services. As a Certified Instructor with the Napoleon Hill Foundation, he empowers others through the timeless principles of success, mindset, and purpose. Serving as Vice President of the Southwest Louisiana Black Chamber of Commerce, Cleveland is a passionate advocate for economic growth, small business support, and community advancement.

A devoted husband to his incredible wife and a loving father, Cleveland leads with integrity, faith, and a deep love for people. He is committed to uplifting those around him and helping individuals align with their highest potential—both personally and professionally. Whether mentoring entrepreneurs, volunteering locally, or speaking on the power of mindset and perseverance, Cleveland believes that service, gratitude, and love are the true currency of success. His mission is clear: to build, serve, and inspire from the inside out.

Author's Website: *www.IRidesTransportation.com*

Charity Awareness: *www.SurvivalToThrivalSeries.com*

DR. CURT COLLINS

FAITH OVER FEAR, EVERY TIME

"Have I not commanded you to be strong and courageous? Do not be afraid; do not be discouraged, for the Lord your God will be with you wherever you go."
~ Joshua 1:9

It is in the moments of gut-wrenching pain and soul-level challenge that we discover what we're truly made of. Few escape this life without facing more than one crossroads moment. These moments don't just test us; they completely alter the trajectory of our lives.

"I have bad news." I could instantly feel the change in the atmosphere as I focused on my wife, who had Dr. Chang on speaker when his unexpected call came through while we were enjoying a rare lunch together at home. Time stood still as I took in the words and felt the panic and fear that was showing through my wife's beautiful blue eyes. For me, one such moment came with a single word: cancer. A diagnosis that shook our world and flooded it with uncertainty.

My wife's life, our life, was suddenly suspended in a fog. Our days were quickly consumed by internet searches, scans, specialist visits, and difficult conversations about the new reality we faced. This created fear and anxiety in both of us that, at times, felt unbearable. The future, once so vibrant and clear, had been replaced with fear, doubt, and uncertainty. And yet, it was here in the thick of this storm that courage showed up—not with unwavering clarity or confidence, but as a quiet presence urging us to choose peace over panic, faith over doubt, and love over fear.

Dr. David Hawkins, in his transformative book *Letting Go*, maps out the levels of human consciousness. At the pivotal level of two hundred lies courage, the first energetic state where true personal power begins to emerge. Everything below this threshold— shame, guilt, apathy, grief, fear, desire, anger, and pride—is reactive. It is governed by survival, victimhood, and external control. Everything above it—willingness, acceptance, love, joy, peace, and enlightenment—is proactive, creative, and sourced from within.

Courage is the tipping point.

When we live below courage, life feels like it's happening *to* us. We're at the mercy of circumstances, struggling to hold on, reacting to everything, and creating very little. But the moment we step into courage, something profound shifts: we begin to take ownership of our experience. We see challenges not as punishments but as possibilities. We begin to co-create rather than cope.

I've experienced this shift firsthand numerous times during my half-century journey here on Earth.

I still remember that night vividly. Sitting in bed with my phone in hand, I made the mistake of Googling her diagnosis. What I read took sleep off the table and sent my mind racing into the worst-case scenarios. "The odds didn't look good" is an understatement. The future was uncertain, and our search for help filled us with more questions than answers.

And yet, in the midst of that storm, a different voice emerged. It wasn't loud or even hopeful at first. It was simply present. It whispered, "You don't have to have it all figured out. Just stay present. Take the next step. Choose love. Choose courage."

That moment marked the beginning of a different journey—not just one of fighting illness, but of choosing to live from the place of courage. We couldn't control the diagnosis, but we could choose how to respond. We chose to become conscious participants in the healing process. We chose gratitude. We chose faith. And every one of those choices required courage.

Hawkins describes courage as the gateway to transformation because it requires the surrender of excuses. It demands that we stop blaming the past or fearing the future and begin to engage with the present moment fully. It invites us to stop avoiding pain and instead feel it, learn from it, and move through it.

That doesn't mean courage is comfortable. In truth, it rarely is. In fact, it's often messy. It brings up old fears, exposes hidden insecurities, and sometimes causes temporary chaos before clarity arrives. But what it does offer is liberation and a return to personal power, grounded not in control but in consciousness.

In Hawkins' model, courage is also the level where responsibility reappears. We begin to say, "This is my life. And I'm not waiting for someone else to fix it." We stop outsourcing our peace to circumstances, relationships, or achievements. We begin to live *at cause* rather than *at effect*.

This is where we begin to thrive.

So, how do we cultivate this level of courage, especially when we're tired, afraid, or uncertain?

It starts with willingness. Not the kind that requires heroic effort or grand gestures, but just the simple willingness to stay with yourself in the moment. The willingness to stop and breathe when everything inside you is screaming "run!" The willingness to speak your truth when you really want to just hide in the shadows. The willingness to try again and again after you've given it your best and still failed.

Hawkins suggests that courage arises naturally when we practice surrender. This might sound counterintuitive. After all, doesn't surrender mean giving up? But in this context, surrender doesn't mean resignation. It means letting go of resistance. It means releasing the inner war and meeting yourself as you are, with compassion and honesty.

When we let go of suppressing or denying difficult emotions, when we stop pretending we're fine and start acknowledging the truth, something powerful happens. The energy we once used to resist life becomes fuel for change. We stop wasting strength on holding it all together and begin directing that energy toward growth and healing.

In my own life, I've seen this play out not just during crises but in the everyday decisions that shape who we become: having hard conversations, taking new risks in business, letting go of limiting beliefs, and saying yes to opportunities that are far beyond my comfort zone.

Courage doesn't eliminate fear; rather, it coexists with it and takes the lead.

That's why courageous people often appear calm or centered. It's not because they're not afraid. It's because they've made peace with fear. They've decided that fear is not their master. They've placed their faith in something greater. They turn to love, purpose, and trust in a higher power at work. They move fear to the passenger seat and move forward with the belief that, regardless of the outcome, they can rest knowing that they fought the good fight.

When you begin to embody courage, life starts responding differently. You notice new doors opening. You find allies you never expected. You gain clarity, not because the road is perfectly mapped out, but because you move forward despite the uncertainty. You act, and clarity meets you on the way.

From a physiological standpoint, courage also transforms your biology. It shifts your nervous system from survival mode into a more regulated state. You begin to think more clearly, breathe more deeply, and move more intentionally. Courage literally changes the chemistry of your body and brain, allowing you to perceive the world through a new lens.

Living a courageous life doesn't mean you won't feel fear again. It means you've trained yourself to respond differently when fear shows up. It means you've become someone who chooses faith over fear, love over control, and possibility over doubt.

It means you've decided not just to survive but to thrive.

And thriving is just what my wife is doing. She faced her life's biggest challenge with courage, overcame what was presented as an impossible task, and continues to shine her bright light onto the world.

CURT COLLINS

Dr. Curt Collins is a visionary chiropractor, regenerative medicine expert, and founder of Tomorrow Doctor. Since 2001, he has specialized in upper cervical chiropractic care and integrative wellness, blending time-tested principles with new innovative therapies. As Clinic Director at Envista Medical Neck & Back Center in Bakersfield, CA, he leads a multidisciplinary team dedicated to restoring health and relieving pain through advanced treatments, including stem cell and regenerative medicine.

Dr. Collins also co-founded Level 3 Consulting, where he mentors doctors nationwide to scale practices, automate operations, and create lasting impact without burnout. Grounded in faith and driven by purpose, he believes health is our greatest wealth, our networks determine our net worth, and service is life's highest calling. Whether in practice, on stage, or guiding groups, his mission is to awaken human potential, elevate frequency, and inspire others to live a higher quality of life filled with health, happiness, and success.

Author's Website: *www.TomorrowDoctor.com*

Charity Awareness: *www.AmericanDreamU.org*

CYNTHIA DEL ROSARIO
FOUNDATIONS OF COURAGE

Let me get personal.

The biggest challenge I ever faced happened when I was a teenager. My parents were fighting—loud, chaotic, painful. My father, who struggled with alcohol, wasn't himself anymore. One night, in the heat of it all, he put a gun to my head.

Just typing that gives me chills.

At that moment, you're not thinking about anything logical. You're not processing emotions. You're frozen. Your life flashes before you, and you wonder: *Is this it? Is this how it ends?* He threatened my brother. He threatened me. He told my mother he was going to pull the trigger. And to make it worse, he said he would shoot the kids first—so she could watch.

He was intoxicated and irrational, angry because he didn't get his way. And while I try to separate the man he was when sober from the man in that moment, it was a moment I can never forget.

That was the night I truly met fear. And courage.

Because somehow—after that night—I never looked back. I never told myself, *I can't.* I never said, *I won't.* I never believed *I'm not going to make it.* That terrifying experience became a turning point. My courage was born in trauma. But it didn't stop there. I learned how to use it every day of my life.

COURAGE IS A FOUNDATION

I often tell people: Courage isn't a one-time act. It's a foundation. If you've got that, you can do anything in life.

Later, I faced another defining moment—one that looked nothing like that traumatic night but required the same bravery. I was thinking about leaving a job. Money was tight. Bills don't pause just because your spirit is suffering. I was drained, exhausted, and unhappy.

My husband, who's my greatest supporter, looked at me and said, "If it's making you this unhappy, it's time to leave."

He didn't say it with judgment. He said it with love. Because when you're giving up your sanity, your health, your peace—for a paycheck—you're giving away something sacred. That takes courage to admit.

And so I left. Not because I had something better lined up, but because I believed I was worth more than staying stuck. You have to be willing to give up comfort to achieve clarity.

That's the kind of courage I teach my kids.

TRUST BEGINS WITHIN

I've taught my children that they can do anything. Literally anything. But it starts with them. Because if you don't trust yourself, how can someone else trust you? How can anyone believe in you if you haven't stood in the mirror and declared, "I believe in me"?

You must first build that internal foundation.

Then, you surround yourself with people who will catch you when you fall—not people who say, "I told you so," but those who say, "Let me help you up."

That's what my husband and I do for each other. We catch each other. When I'm down, he's there. When he's struggling, I lift him. We don't wait for the fall—we anticipate it, and we're already reaching for each other before it happens.

PARENTING WITH COURAGE

My daughter is only twenty-one, and she's already traveled to over twenty-eight countries. Australia, New Zealand, Singapore, Korea, Japan, Spain, Poland, France—she's seen the world, and she's done much of it alone.

People say, "She must be fearless."

No. She's courageous.

Fearlessness is a myth. Courage is what happens when you move forward *despite* the fear.

I think back to my aunt, who couldn't even fly to the Philippines alone. My mother had to drive her to Maryland just to get on a plane with her. But my daughter? She gets on planes alone with confidence and a curious heart.

She's aware of her surroundings. She's smart, grounded, and fearless in the way that only someone raised to trust themselves can be.

That's the legacy I wanted to give her. Not wealth. Not perfection. Not protection from the world. But *courage to face it.*

My son, too, had his moment of courage. At just twelve years old, we sent him to Ireland to work on farms. Yes—by himself. That decision wasn't easy for me. But I reminded myself: I'm near and far at the same time. I'm always with them—even when I'm not physically present.

They've inherited my courage. Not because I told them to be brave, but because they *watched me live it*.

COURAGE IN LEADERSHIP

In my business, I'm blessed to lead an incredible team—most of them women. I make it a point to infuse courage into our culture. Whether we're discussing strategy, tackling sales, or navigating uncertainty, I remind them that our value doesn't come from price tags. It comes from knowing our worth.

I often share this story: There was a massive ship that had broken down. Ten different mechanics tried to fix it, and none of them could. Finally, an older gentleman came in, tapped one tiny section of the ship with a hammer—and it came to life.

He submitted a bill for $20,000. The captain was outraged and said, "You were here for five minutes."

And the mechanic replied, "$100 was for the tap. $19,900 was for knowing *where* to tap."

That's what experience, wisdom, and courage look like. Courage isn't just taking bold action—it's knowing your value in that action.

So, when we talk about sales, strategy, or leadership, I always say: Know what you're worth. Don't downplay your experience. Don't shrink your impact.

WHAT COURAGE FEELS LIKE

Courage is a state of mind.

It's not bravado. It's not ego. It's not loud. Sometimes, it's quiet. Sometimes, it's walking away from what's familiar. Sometimes, it's saying, "I need help."

But always, it's trusting that your next step—however uncertain— is worth taking.

And I'll be honest. Even now, when I see my daughter planning another trip, or my son asking to take on something new, I still have those mom nerves. I want to say, "Wait!" But then I remember: *I raised them for this.*

Because I showed them what courage looks like—not just by surviving, but by thriving.

FINAL THOUGHTS

From a terrifying night as a teenager to a thriving life as a mother, wife, and leader, my courage wasn't gifted to me. It was earned, tested, and shaped.

And every time I felt like shrinking, I expanded.

I don't have all the answers. I don't always know where the path leads—but I've learned to move forward anyway. That's courage.

And that's the foundation I offer to you.

If I could survive that night… you can survive *this* one.

If I could thrive despite fear… you can thrive *because* of it.

Let's build that courage together.

CYNTHIA DEL ROSARIO

Cynthia Del Rosario is a visionary leader whose steadfast integrity and inspiring spirit fuel her dedication to serving communities and developing innovative solutions with lasting impact. With over forty years of industry experience, Cynthia's career spans a broad spectrum of content creation, marketing, production, distribution, talent and rights management, and business affairs. She has collaborated with some of the world's leading brands, including Verizon, GE Capital, Procter & Gamble, Pfizer, IBM, Pepsi, and American Express.

As founder of 7 Mile Global Ad Solutions, LLC, she leads efforts to transform how branded intellectual property is managed, creating platforms such as IP360 and the 7MG Academy. Alongside her husband, Patrick Neville—an Iraq War veteran and 9/11 First Responder—she owns a popular bar and restaurant, Whiskey River NY, that fosters connection, community, and memorable conversation.

Her proudest achievements are her two children, Kayla and Aidan.

Author's Website: *www.7MilesGlobal.com*

Charity Awareness: *www.T2T.org*

DANIEL KILBURN

FROM KILL ZONES TO CALLING: WHAT COURAGE REALLY LOOKS LIKE

It started on the third day after my seventeenth birthday.

I wasn't chasing a dream or escaping a nightmare—I was simply a teenage boy staring down the barrel of adulthood and watching my single mother buckle under the weight of raising two kids alone. Something had to give. And what gave... was me. I marched myself into a recruitment office, handed over my future with a handshake, and just like that—I was in the United States Army.

Some might say that was an act of courage. But at seventeen, courage didn't look like a medal or sound like a speech. It looked like getting up, signing a paper, and leaving everything you knew because someone else needed a break. It wasn't just brave—it was decisive. And that, I would later learn, is the very foundation of courage: the willingness to move before fear has a chance to catch up.

The military taught me a lot of things, but the lesson that stuck the most came during my time in the 101st Airborne. I was part of the Battalion Recon platoon—we were later called the Scout Platoon.

The Platoon Leader wore his qualifications like armor—Airborne, Combat Infantry Badge, Ranger, Pathfinder, Foreign Jump Wings. A living legend. One day, he dropped this truth bomb on us during a field training exercise. He said, "When the grenade goes off, move. The shrapnel has already passed you."

At first, that didn't make much sense. I mean, when something explodes, your instinct is to hit the ground and stay down. But he explained it with the calm certainty of someone who had lived through too many such moments: by the time you hear the blast, the danger has already moved past. The real threat is the hesitation that follows.

He wasn't just talking about grenades. He was talking about life.

Fear tells you to wait. Courage tells you to act. That single idea changed the way I thought about decision-making. It's not about being fearless. It's about being faster than your fear.

Years later, I found myself in Southwest Asia, riding in a Humvee through Improvised Explosive Device (IED) territory. The first explosion I experienced wasn't just loud, it was personal. I saw it. I felt it. The blast hit with such force that I could feel the shockwave ripple through my body. I was in the gun turret, and everything went silent for a split second. Dust filled the air. The world became a blur.

Instinct kicked in. I grabbed the radio and started shouting, "Move! Get us out of the kill zone! Move! Move! Move!" But the guys below me—my team—were frozen. Their eyes were wide, their jaws slack. They couldn't move. The explosion had stunned them into silence.

And I couldn't blame them. In that moment, everything in your body wants to shut down. But we didn't have time. If I had been setting up that ambush, I would've followed the IED with a heavy machine gun to finish the job. So, I kept yelling until they moved. We got out of there. We survived.

That kind of courage isn't flashy. It's not cinematic. It's muscle memory, grit, and the discipline to do what must be done when everyone else is still trying to understand what just happened.

I think about armor a lot. Not just the kind you wear on a battlefield, but the kind you wear every day. Emotional armor. Psychological armor. We all put it on. We think it protects us. And sometimes it does. But real courage isn't in the armor—it's in trusting that it works and stepping forward anyway.

For me, courage has never been a one-time act. It's a series of choices, some of them small, some life-altering. One of the biggest came just a few years ago.

I was working at a steady government job. Good pay. Good benefits. It was safe. Predictable. But it didn't feel like mine. I felt like I was coasting, living someone else's version of stability. So, I quit. I gave away almost everything I owned; I didn't even sell anything. I moved across the country to be closer to my eldest daughter and granddaughter, to start a new business, to do something that mattered.

People thought I was crazy. Maybe I was. Things didn't go the way I imagined. There were moments I wanted to pack it all up and crawl back into the comfort zone I'd just abandoned. But every time I thought about quitting, I remembered why I left in the first place.

Because there's something inside me that refuses to settle. I have a mission. People to train. People to learn from. I didn't come all this way to play it safe.

It's a truth I've come to live by: we're all here for one of two reasons—either to learn something, or to teach something. And usually, it's both. There's someone out there right now who needs to hear something only you can say. But to share it, you have to be willing to show up. To speak up. To be seen.

Every night, I ask myself, "Did I help someone today?" Not every day brings a yes. Sometimes I don't get the chance. Sometimes I miss it. But the point isn't perfection. The point is to keep asking. To stay in the game. To keep showing up with an open heart and the willingness to serve.

Today, I got a call from someone across the country asking if I could help them with disaster management planning. I jumped at the chance. Not just because it's what I do, but because it means I'm still doing what I set out to do when I walked away from that desk job. I'm helping. I'm showing up. I'm proving, over and over again, that courage doesn't end when the battle's over. Sometimes, it's just beginning.

And now I'll ask you: Where has courage shown up in your life?

Think back to the moments where everything in you screamed to sit still, to stay quiet, to wait it out. What did you do? Did you freeze? Did you run? Or did you rise?

Maybe you've never worn a uniform. Maybe you've never seen a battlefield, but you've faced battles of your own. The ones that don't make the headlines. The kind fought in kitchens and courtrooms, break rooms and bedrooms. And in every one of those moments, courage asked the same question: Will you move?

That's the heart of it, really. Courage isn't always loud. It's not always dramatic. More often than not, it's stubborn. Quiet. Foolish, even. But necessary.

I've learned that courage doesn't need an audience. It doesn't need recognition. What it needs is a commitment. A willingness to act even when you're scared—especially when you're scared.

So, here's what I leave you with: the grenade's already gone off. The shrapnel's already passed. You can stay down... or you can get up and move.

Because surviving is good. But thriving? Thriving takes courage.

FAQ: SURVIVING TO THRIVING THROUGH COURAGE

1. How Do You Know if a Decision is Courageous or Reckless?

Courageous decisions often align with your deeper values and purpose. Reckless ones are usually fueled by impulse or ego. Ask yourself why you're really doing it.

2. What's the Difference Between Fear & Intuition?

Fear screams; intuition whispers. Fear immobilizes; intuition nudges. Learning to tell the difference is a lifelong practice.

3. How Do You Build Courage Over Time?

By making small, brave choices daily. Say yes to things that stretch you. Speak up when it's uncomfortable. The more you act with courage, the more it becomes who you are.

4. How Do You Deal with the Moments when Courage Fails?

You reflect, recalibrate, and try again. Courage isn't perfection. It's persistence. Even pausing and breathing in the face of fear is an act of courage.

5. What if No One Sees or Appreciates My Courage?

Courage doesn't require an audience. It's between you and your conscience. True courage often goes unnoticed by others—but never by your own soul.

DANIEL KILBURN

Kilburn is a retired U.S. Army Senior Infantry Drill Sergeant, a seasoned speaker, and the founder of Emergency Action Planning LLC. With a heart for service and a mission to safeguard families and communities, Daniel dedicates his life to teaching the principles of resilience, preparedness, and financial literacy. His powerful voice and grounded wisdom stem not just from years of military discipline but from real-life experiences navigating natural disasters, personal challenges, and transformational growth. Daniel's work centers on helping people rediscover their sense of purpose and security, especially during life's most uncertain moments.

An award-winning Toastmaster and bestselling co-author, Daniel brings authenticity, clarity, and compassion to every page he writes. Through his words, he challenges readers to reflect, rise, and resonate on higher frequencies—starting with love and gratitude. For additional information, Daniel's contact information can be found here: www.linkedin.com/in/DanielKilburn

Author's Website: *www.EmergencyActionPlanning.com*

Charity Awareness: *www.WoundedWarriorProject.org*

DANIELE G. LATTANZI

WHEN COURAGE BEGINS WITH A MICRO STEP

*"Courage doesn't mean you don't get afraid. Courage means you
don't let fear stop you."*
~ Bethany Hamilton
(A professional surfer who lost her arm in a shark attack.)

FALLING FORWARD

Famous English business magnate Richard Branson once said,
"My attitude has always been, if you fall flat on your face, at least
you're moving forward. All you have to do is get back up and try
again." This quote perfectly sets the stage for what I'm about to
share.

Pause for a moment and reflect: If you suddenly experienced a
debilitating event, how would you react? Would you immediately
seek out every possible treatment, determined to recover? Or
would fear overwhelm you, driving you into isolation?

Would you reach out to others who've faced similar struggles,
forming a community of support? Or would you withdraw,
shutting out the very people who could offer strength?

WHEN LIFE THROWS A CURVEBALL

Picking yourself up and moving forward is not always that simple. Also, the answer to the earlier question isn't always black or white.

One thing I've learned from experience is that life has a way of throwing curveballs exactly when you least expect them. And when it does, the true test is how you respond.

I certainly wasn't prepared for the curveball life threw at me about fifteen years ago.

It started on an ordinary day. I'd been busy doing some physical work, lifting heavy objects throughout the day. By evening, I felt an odd sensation in my lower back. However, feeling tired and sore from the day's exertions, I didn't think much of it and decided to head to bed early. As I lay down, I remember thinking I probably needed to do more exercise—that the muscle aches were just a sign of me being out of shape or something.

However, when I woke up the next morning, reality hit me in a way I had never imagined possible. As soon as I tried to move, a sharp, excruciating pain shot through my lower back as if someone had stabbed me with a pointed knife. Instantly, I froze, every muscle in my body tightening in reaction to the intense pain. Even the smallest attempt at movement caused the pain to spike sharply, locking me in place.

I tried repeatedly to move, to shift even slightly—but every attempt brought the same sharp agony. With each failure, my muscles became increasingly stiff and unresponsive. What should have been a simple, everyday act—getting out of bed—quickly turned into a living nightmare.

Suddenly, cold sweat and fear washed over me. Panic set in. *Why couldn't I move? Why this intense pain? What had happened to me?*

SMALL STEPS FORWARD

A thousand thoughts raced through my mind. If I couldn't move, what would happen to my job? My family? Would I need constant care?

I realized that dwelling on those questions wouldn't help. I needed clarity, and that started with reducing the pain.

No movement = No sharp pain = Clarity.

I could finally begin thinking clearly by pausing to breathe, relax, and avoid further strain on the injury. While it was evident that something significant had happened to my body, I recognized that obsessing over the unknown wouldn't help. Instead, I decided to focus on small, achievable steps I could take immediately—I thought of them as micro-goals.

The first micro-goal was clear: I needed professional medical help. I knew I had to find a way to see a specialist doctor who could tell me exactly what had happened to my back and, more importantly, how I could heal.

A DIAGNOSIS I DIDN'T EXPECT

With the help of my family, I saw an orthopedic doctor and underwent an MRI. The results were something I didn't expect.

Two of the discs in my lower back were half their standard size. Based on the doctor's experience, he traced it most likely to a genetic issue. That alone would've been enough to process, but then came the real curveball—one I wasn't prepared for.

The scan also showed two large bulging discs pressing directly against my spinal cord. The pressure, the doctor explained, was not only the cause of my pain and immobility, but if it worsened, it could lead to partial or even complete paralysis.

The doctor gave me two options. The first was surgery to fuse the lower vertebrae—a quicker fix to address the structural issue. The second was a non-surgical approach: physical therapy, swimming, chiropractic adjustments, and tailored exercise. It would take time, discipline, and consistent effort, but it would avoid invasive procedures.

STANDING AT A CROSSROADS

Well, my friends, the truth is this: I was at a crossroads.

Based on the diagnosis, I knew that the decision I was about to make wouldn't just affect me—it would affect my future and the well-being of my family as well. It was heavy. I told the doctor I needed time to think before deciding.

I replayed the doctor's advice over and over. Surgery promised quick relief but at a cost. The natural route required patience and faith.

Each time I leaned toward one choice, a "but" crept in:

- "This part sounds good, but what if…?"
- "That could work, but suppose it doesn't?"

Welcome to the spiral of *analysis paralysis*.

Making a decision is never easy, but making a decision that could be life-altering? That's an entirely different level. The truth was, I was afraid. Not just pain or discomfort. I was scared of choosing wrong. Afraid of what might happen if I bet on the wrong path.

TURNING FEAR INTO DECISION

Winston Churchill once said, "Fear is a reaction. Courage is a decision." That quote perfectly captures what happened next.

So, how did I break free from the deadlock I was stuck in?

The answer was this: I realized that my fear and inability to make a decision weren't just emotional. It was rooted in a lack of precise data.

Instead of staying stuck in worry, I shifted gears and began asking myself better questions:

• What don't I know about this problem?
• What information would give me clarity?
• What are the potential consequences of each choice?

By asking those questions, I stopped reacting and started evaluating. I wasn't driven by emotion anymore—I was searching for factual data to make an informed decision.

With a clearer perspective, I chose the natural path. It would be more challenging, but I believed in my body's ability to heal with the proper support.

That decision marked the beginning of my recovery. Over time, I not only healed but also built greater strength and mobility.

Since then, many years have passed. The genetic issue remains, but I've learned to manage it. I'm healthier, stronger, and more resilient because of that choice.

THRIVING REQUIRES COURAGE, NOT PERFECTION

A fitting metaphor for this journey is, "You can't drive a car looking in the rearview mirror." If we fixate on past pain, fear, and setbacks, we lose the ability to move forward. My story isn't about perfection. It's not about having all the answers or feeling fearless. It's about learning that thriving doesn't require a perfect plan, but a willingness to keep showing up.

If anything, here are a few takeaways from my story:

- You don't need to feel ready—you need to be willing.
- Fear thrives on uncertainty; courage asks better questions.
- When you stop reacting and start evaluating, you reclaim your power.
- Information empowers courage. Confusion feeds fear.
- Your body is capable of healing, but it needs your belief and effort.

Thriving isn't a destination—it's a choice you make daily. And courage is the compass that keeps you moving forward.

DANIELE G. LATTANZI

Daniele G. Lattanzi is your Practice Growth Partner with over twenty-five years of experience helping small businesses and healthcare practitioners transform their activity into thriving, scalable companies. His entrepreneurial journey builds on extensive management, finance, marketing, e-commerce, and business development expertise. Fluent in four languages— English, Italian, Portuguese, and Spanish—Daniele's linguistic skills have been instrumental in his international coaching and business operations across Italy, Europe, and North and South America.

As the Co-Founder and CEO of Effective Practice Management and Holistic Health Solutions since 2016, Daniele has dedicated himself to empowering private practice owners and their teams to unlock their full potential by providing proven practice management training and coaching. Follow him at: *www.Instagram.com/DG_Lattanzi*

Author's Website: *www.EffectivePracticeManagement.com*

Charity Awareness: *www.SurvivalToThrivalSeries.com*

DAWNESE OPENSHAW

TWENTY SECONDS CAN CHANGE EVERYTHING

I'll never forget the first time I heard the movie line that opened my heart to a possibility beyond anything I'd imagined up to that moment. It was in the movie *We Bought a Zoo*, where Matt Damon's character looks at his son and says:

> *"Sometimes, all you need is twenty seconds of insane courage. Just literally twenty seconds of embarrassing bravery. And I promise you, something great will come of it."*

The truth of this statement resonated deep within me. Courage doesn't have to roar. Sometimes, it's a flicker—a decision made in a single moment that alters the course of your life.

WHAT IS COURAGE, REALLY?

Courage isn't the absence of fear. It's not about being fearless. Courage is *feeling* the fear and choosing to move forward anyway. It's the willingness to step into discomfort and uncertainty with resolve.

To me, courage means standing up in the drift we sometimes find ourselves in.

It means not letting life pull me under when things get chaotic, confusing, or hard. It means deciding to take radical responsibility for what's next. To choose my next action with intention.

And sometimes, that decision only takes twenty seconds.

HOW I LEARNED COURAGE

I remember sitting in my parked car outside the grocery store, hands gripping the steering wheel, eyes brimming with tears. Everything in my life looked fine on the outside—but inside, I was crumbling under the weight of expectations I no longer recognized as my own.

I spent years avoiding risk, staying small, trying to please everyone around me. At this moment, when everything felt like my life was crumbling, I knew I had a choice to make.

I had to find my voice. I had to learn to trust myself again and own my power.

I had to make a choice…a different choice. I was at a crossroads, where I could either let life happen to me and become a victim of it, or choose something different. I could choose to keep drifting, or I could choose to *shift*.

That was the moment I began to build my courage muscle—not in grand gestures, but in tiny decisions repeated over time. I started saying yes to opportunities I didn't feel "ready" for. I started speaking up when I would've stayed silent. I started taking action in the direction of my dreams, even if my knees were shaking and I felt like I wanted to vomit.

Each time I chose courage over comfort, something shifted. I grew more confident. More rooted. More aligned with my authentic self. Now I've found so much courage, I'm founding a global movement to "lead the change"—not only to be the change but to cause and create change in my life, in others' lives, relationships, families, workplaces, communities, and the world.

COURAGE BUILDS CONFIDENCE

Most people think confidence comes first—that you have to *feel* confident before you can act brave. But it's actually the other way around: Confidence is the result of courageous action.

The more you choose to do the thing that scares you, the more you realize you *can*. That's when your brain and body begin to trust you. That's when the fear loses its grip. That's when you remember: "If it is to be, it's up to me."

Courage is a muscle that grows stronger with use. The first time you speak your truth, it might come out shaky. But the second time is steadier. By the tenth time, you've become a natural at it.

FROM FEAR TO COURAGE

Everyone fears something—spiders, the dark, public speaking, to name a few. Fear is part of being human. But fear doesn't have to be in the driver's seat of life.

While our fear wears many faces, most of it stems from a few universal roots:

1. **Fear of Rejection/Not Being Loved**:

   The core human need is to belong. The idea of being excluded, unloved, or judged keeps many people from speaking up, showing up, or pursuing their dreams.

2. **Fear of Failure/Not Being Enough**:

   This fear whispers, "What if I try and I'm not good enough?" It paralyzes our action and convinces us to settle.

3. **Fear of the Unknown/Loss of Control**:

Not knowing what will happen can keep us stuck. We crave certainty, even when it costs us our growth.

Heaven knows I've felt these all before, and sometimes still do. Understanding these fears is the first step in moving through them.

Great things don't happen in your comfort zone—they happen when you step outside it. I invite you to try!

Take a breath, silence the doubt, and choose courage—just for twenty seconds. That's all it takes to choose to:

- Say the thing that's been on your heart.
- Make the phone call.
- Apply for the dream job.
- Leave the toxic relationship.
- Sign up for the thing that scares and excites you.

THE CORE OF COURAGE:
A RELATIONSHIP WITH YOURSELF

At the root of courage is *self-trust*—the kind that says, "No matter what happens, I can and will handle it."

When you strengthen your relationship with yourself, you stop waiting for permission. You stop outsourcing your power. You stop letting fear run the show. Instead, you come home to your heart and remember your dreams.

You begin to ask, "What do I really want?" You listen. You reconnect with who you were before the world told you who to be. You tap into childhood dreams, the things you've been putting off, the parts of you longing for expression. And you do one of them. Just one.

LIFE IS NOW

When I had my moment and looked at the life I had created, I realized I had been waiting—waiting for the right time, feeling, and permission. Something inside me stirred, and I knew I wasn't willing to wait anymore. This is the moment I chose to shift from living in survival to wanting to live—to thrive.

NOW IT'S YOUR TURN

The 20-Second Courage Challenge

1. **Create a list** of things you've wanted to do but have been putting off—because of fear, doubt, or timing. Big or small.

2. **Choose one**—the one that makes your heart beat a little faster, your palms sweat, and if it's big, it might want to make you vomit. That's okay; keep breathing.

3. **Give yourself twenty seconds of courage.** Just twenty seconds to begin. To take the first step. To say yes to you. To say yes to living the life of your dreams.

Maybe it's speaking your truth. Maybe it's enrolling in a course. Maybe it's asking for support or making a bold ask. Whatever it is, it starts with a choice—your choice, right here and right now.

Breathe. Inhale courage. Exhale fear.

Don't let hesitation rob you of what could be the moment (the twenty seconds of insane courage) that changes everything.

Eleanor Roosevelt said it so well: "You must do the thing you think you cannot do."

So, ask yourself:

* What am I afraid of?
* What is possible if I have the courage to move through it?
* What do I *really* want?

You don't have to be ready. You just have to be *willing*.

The next twenty seconds are yours. Take a breath.

And leap.

DAWNESE OPENSHAW

Dawnese Openshaw is a visionary leader, a master transformational and relationship coach, and a passionate advocate for conscious living and loving. As Founder of Lead the Change, she empowers individuals, families, and organizations to lead with emotional, social, and relationship intelligence. Dawnese is the co-creator of the Global Leadership Experience, a life-changing training for those ready to align with their purpose and live a vision-led life.

A lifelong student of leadership since reading Dale Carnegie's *How to Win Friends and Influence People* at fourteen, Dawnese shares her experience and wisdom gained from daily living and supporting individual and organizational growth for over thirty years.

She and her husband, Scott, are celebrating thirty years of marriage, are proud parents of three amazing adult children, and are brand-new grandparents. Dawnese believes that when people live in alignment with their values, relationships thrive—and when relationships thrive, *magic happens.*

Author's Website: *www.LeadTheChange.org*

Charity Awareness: *www.SurvivalToThrivalSeries.com*

DHARMI SHAH

PLOT TWIST: I'M STILL STANDING & I'M FABULOUS

THE COURAGE TO BEGIN AGAIN

Courage isn't just about running into burning buildings or standing on a battlefield—it's about picking yourself up when life throws you down, dusting off your dreams, and saying, "Well, that didn't go as planned... Now what?"

For the longest time, I thought courage was about being strong, about holding everything together no matter what. But I've learned that real courage isn't about never breaking—it's about breaking, rebuilding, and finding a way to move forward, even when forward looks nothing like you expected. It's about embracing discomfort and uncertainty, knowing that those moments of struggle are often where the greatest growth happens.

My journey has been one of heartache and reinvention, of saying goodbye to dreams I had held onto for years and learning to embrace the completely unexpected paths life put in front of me. It's been messy, unpredictable, and—believe me—there were plenty of moments when I wanted to hit the eject button. But the beauty in those messy moments is that they become part of the story that shapes you. In the end, courage is what got me here, and "here" turns out to be a pretty incredible place.

WHEN THE DREAM CHANGES
(WITHOUT YOUR PERMISSION)

Let's be honest—no one likes plot twists when they're happening in real life. I certainly didn't. I had a plan, a clear vision of how my life was supposed to go. I had checked the boxes, done the things, and expected the universe to cooperate.

Spoiler alert: It did not.

The dream I had—the one I held onto so tightly—fell apart. Not in one big dramatic explosion, but piece by painful piece. It was like watching a slow-motion car crash, knowing you couldn't stop it. Trying to start a family was supposed to be one of the happiest chapters of my life.

Instead, it became a chapter filled with loss, heartbreak, and questions I never thought I'd have to ask.

Losing that dream wasn't just painful—it was identity-shattering. When you build your life around something and then it's taken away, you're left standing in the wreckage, looking around, thinking, "So… what now?"

I didn't have an answer. Not for a long time. And that's where courage came in—not as some big, bold moment, but as the tiny decision to get up every morning and keep going, even when I had no idea where I was headed. In those dark moments, courage was a whisper, not a shout. It was a steady belief that something better was waiting, even when I couldn't see it.

THE ART OF NOT HAVING A PLAN

I used to love having a plan. I was the person with color-coded calendars, long-term goals, and a clear roadmap for the future. And then, suddenly, I was living a life I hadn't planned at all.

At first, the unknown felt terrifying. But then, something strange happened—I started to feel… free. Without a rigid plan to follow, I got to ask myself, "What do I actually want?" Not the me from ten years ago. Not the me who was desperately trying to hold onto a life that no longer existed. But the me now—the one who had been through hell and was still standing.

What I discovered was a version of myself that I hadn't known existed. I started exploring new possibilities, ones I had never considered before. I poured myself into my work. I reconnected with people who brought me joy. I started traveling again, not as an escape, but as a way to remind myself that the world was still full of beauty and adventure.

And guess what? One of those unexpected paths led me here—to writing! Me. An author. Who knew? I certainly didn't have "publishing my story" on my original vision board, but here we are. Apparently, courage also means embracing the unexpected... and adding "author" to my LinkedIn profile.

COURAGE LOOKS A LOT LIKE A HOT MESS

Let's talk about what courage actually looks like—because, for me, it wasn't some perfect moment of triumph. It looked like crying in my car, eating an entire pizza by myself, and then deciding the next day that I'd try again. It looked like signing up for things I had no business signing up for, just to see what would happen. It looked like showing up to events alone, forcing myself to meet new people, and hoping they wouldn't immediately regret talking to me.

It looked like making peace with uncertainty and learning to say, "I have no idea what I'm doing, but I'm doing it anyway." Courage isn't always pretty. Sometimes, it's messy, awkward, and full of moments where you second-guess everything. But I started to realize that the mess was part of the process. The mess meant I was still moving forward, even if I was stumbling.

But the trick is to keep going anyway.

REBUILDING A LIFE THAT FEELS LIKE MINE

Slowly, I started to see that my life wasn't ending—it was just changing. And instead of clinging to the past, I had the chance to build something new. I started chasing experiences that made me feel alive again. I embraced friendships in a way I never had before, realizing that love comes in many different forms. I found joy in the little things—laughing until my stomach hurt, trying new things just for fun, rediscovering the parts of myself that had gotten lost along the way.

There was beauty in the brokenness, a rawness that I had never allowed myself to embrace before. And the more I let go of the idea that my life should look a certain way, the more I realized how incredible it actually was. Sometimes, the best things in life are the ones we didn't plan for.

UNEXPECTED WINS
(& ONE SLIGHTLY OVERPRICED CANDLE)

You know what's wild? When you stop gripping onto the life you thought you wanted, amazing things start showing up--like the fact that I built a business that lights me up. Or that I found an entirely new sense of purpose in helping others. Or that I discovered the pure joy of spending ridiculous amounts of money on candles that make my house smell like a fancy spa (zero regrets).

But more than anything, I've learned that courage isn't about having all the answers—it's about trusting yourself enough to keep moving forward, even when the path isn't clear. It's about knowing that even after the hardest chapters, there's still so much more ahead. And that's where I choose to live: not in the past, not in fear of the unknown, but in the belief that I am strong enough to handle whatever comes next.

The truth is, the life I live now is more authentic and fulfilling than the one I had ever imagined. And that's something I wouldn't trade for anything. It took courage to let go of the idea of perfection, to embrace the mess, and to step into the unknown. But it was all worth it.

COURAGE IN THE EVERYDAY

People always talk about courage like it's this huge, dramatic thing. But real courage? It's in the small moments. It's getting out of bed when you'd rather stay under the covers. It's making a new plan when the old one didn't work out. It's believing in yourself, even when you're not totally sure what you're doing. It's laughing at yourself when things go sideways (which they will). It's trusting that even when life doesn't go according to plan, something good is still ahead.

It's the quiet moments of reflection, where you allow yourself to simply be. And if I've learned anything, it's this: The unknown isn't as scary as it seems. Because in the unknown, there's also possibility. And in possibility, there's hope. So, maybe life didn't go according to the script... but this plot twist? It turned out to be the best chapter yet.

MY RECIPE FOR COURAGE

- A handful of resilience (because you will need it).
- A splash of humor.
- A whole lot of faith (even when you have no idea where you're going).
- And a dash of adventure—because sometimes, the best things happen when you least expect them.

DHARMI SHAH

Dharmi Shah is a globally recognized award-winning entrepreneur, celebrated for her transformative leadership and exceptional impact across industries. As the visionary founder of The Corporate Experience, a cutting-edge marketing firm, Dharmi curates unparalleled experiences that help businesses grow and thrive, all while forging lasting bonds that drive sustained success.

She is also the mastermind behind Refresh and Revitalize, an award-winning coaching brand dedicated to empowering women, cultivating a powerful community where they uplift, inspire, and support one another to reach their fullest potential.

Dharmi founded Evenings of Elegance, an elite event production company that spent over two decades creating extraordinary, high-profile events, leaving a lasting impression on every client. A culinary connoisseur, Dharmi finds pure joy in the kitchen, believing that the dinner table is where cherished memories, laughter, and joy come together, building profound connections with every shared meal.

Author's Website: *www.DharmiShah.com*

Charity Awareness: *www.TinyHeartsRememberedInc.org*

DIANNE SUSI

AFTER THE HOUSE WAS BROKEN, WE BUILT A LIFE

I can still feel the cold air of that afternoon, the sting of betrayal sharper than the wind against my face. I stood outside a house that wasn't mine, my husband's car parked neatly in the driveway, his crisp white work shirt visible behind the glass door. My hands trembled as I rang the doorbell, my heart pounding so loudly that I could hear it in my ears. The door cracked open, and there he was.

In that instant, the life I had built, the home I had poured my soul into, felt like it was crumbling beneath me. They locked the door before I could push it open, and I turned away, retreating to my car, swallowing the heartbreak that threatened to consume me. That was the moment I knew: I could no longer survive this way. Courage would have to be my new foundation.

Meeting Bobby had felt like the beginning of a dream. I was a senior in high school when my best friend introduced us at the local bowling alley. He was handsome, a football player, and everything my teenage heart could have wished for. We dated, and in time, he moved into my parents' home to escape the chaos of his own. We married, and though life wasn't perfect, I embraced it with open arms. We had simple joys—one car, walks through the neighborhood, and, eventually, the news of a pregnancy after months of hope and effort. When Natalie was born, I left work without hesitation, determined to devote myself to raising her.

For a time, it seemed like enough. We were making it work. But underneath the surface, small cracks began to show. Bobby worked nights and was rarely home. Strange phone calls became frequent. A name—Sue—began to surface, first innocently, then with a chilling familiarity. I dismissed it, clinging to the life I wanted to believe in. Until one day, I didn't. Until one day, I decided to follow him.

What I discovered shattered the illusions I had so carefully maintained. Infidelity, lies, financial betrayal. He had lent $25,000 of our savings to Sue without telling me. The tangled web grew darker: calls from Sue's husband confirming what I feared, finding our daughter's car seat in his car parked outside another woman's home. It wasn't just a betrayal of me; it was a betrayal of our family.

The unraveling reached a terrifying climax the night he returned home in a blinding rage after Sue revealed too much. His black, rage-filled eyes, the sound of him destroying our home, the fear that surged through me as I fled the house with our young daughter—these are memories etched into my bones. That was survival mode at its rawest.

But survival wasn't enough. Not for me. And not for Natalie. It took every ounce of courage to face what needed to happen next.

I told him to leave. No more negotiations, no more second chances. He asked if he could live in the garage, if he could bring his clothes by. I said no. I set the boundary that would save us.

In the aftermath, reality set in: divorce, financial uncertainty, and raising a child alone. For a time, we lived on welfare. I started a housecleaning business with a friend, scrubbing other people's homes while rebuilding the pieces of my own life. My parents, steadfast and loving, became my rocks. My mom cleaned with me, and my dad helped fix our house after it was destroyed. Family held us up when my own courage felt thin.

But even in those hardest days, I made a decision—a decision rooted in courage—to focus on what mattered most: Natalie. I refused to let bitterness poison our home. I never spoke poorly of Bobby to her. I never made her feel like she lacked anything. Our life wasn't extravagant, but it was rich in love, laughter, and support.

There were days when fear crept in, when grief over what had been lost felt suffocating. I cried at times, alone in the quiet when Natalie was asleep. But even in those moments, I chose to see what we *had*, not what we had lost. We had a home, we had family, and we had each other.

Slowly, life began to heal. Courage built momentum. We didn't just survive; we created a new life.
And then, as if placed on our path by grace, came Claudio—the kindest, gentlest soul I had ever met. In our very first conversation, he said, "You can bring Natalie." His heart was wide open, not just to me, but to my daughter. In Claudio, we found not just a partner, but a father, a friend, and a source of steady, unconditional love.

Our happily-ever-after wasn't flashy. It was built on kindness, on small daily acts of love, on the quiet courage it takes to keep choosing hope after heartbreak.

LESSONS LEARNED

Courage, I learned, isn't about grand gestures or fearless action. It's about the quiet, everyday decisions:

• The courage to believe you deserve better, even when it's painful to walk away.

- The courage to prioritize your child's emotional well-being over your own heartbreak.

- The courage to ask for help and to rebuild, brick by brick, when everything has fallen apart.

- The courage to stay open to love, even after betrayal.

If you are in survival mode right now, know this: You are stronger than you feel. Courage doesn't erase fear—it just chooses love over fear, one tiny choice at a time.

Today, I look back at that broken woman standing outside that house, and I am so proud of her. She didn't know how she would make it. But she chose courage anyway. And because of that choice, we didn't just survive.

We thrived.

DIANNE SUSI

Dianne Susi is a service-driven advocate with a passion for helping others live with dignity, stability, and compassion. She began her career as a claims examiner at an insurance company and later spent thirty-three years in the financial department of a major hospital. Her job was to ensure that every patient left with their claim paid, so they could focus on healing without financial stress. She took great pride in making sure every file that crossed her desk was handled with care, accuracy, and humanity. Alongside her professional work, Dianne also built a housecleaning and home organizing path that allowed her to raise her daughter, Natalie—and simply have fun.

Later in life, after her husband Claudio started a pet-sitting business, Dianne became a devoted animal lover, helping walk dogs and welcome them into their home. Their first dog, Primo—a fiery little Maltese all of seven pounds—ruled over every animal who entered their house, but grew to love the familiar ones. Since retiring from the hospital, Dianne now spends her days gardening, caring for backyard birds, and keeping their dog Richie happy and healthy. She often says that if she ever came into great wealth, she'd devote it entirely to rescuing and supporting animals in need. Follow Dianne on social media: *@DianneSusi*

Charity Awareness: *www.BVSPCA.org*

EILEEN E. GALBRAITH

WHAT DO YOU WANT? A JOURNEY INTO COURAGE

Are you captivating the world with your gifts? Are you waking up each morning filled with a sense of purpose, eager to create, to serve, to live boldly?

It took me years to realize that courage wasn't about being fearless—it was about feeling the fear and doing it anyway. It was about showing up, again and again, even when you don't feel ready. Especially when you don't feel ready.

Growing up, I often felt invisible. Seven months after I was born, I had a severe case of whooping cough, and, as a result, I not only had a crossed eye, but I also lost sight in that eye, which made me feel deeply self-conscious. Kids can be cruel, and I was the quiet, scared child who tried to disappear into the background. I longed to be seen, but I was afraid of being noticed. I wanted to feel loved. I wanted to belong. But most of all, I just didn't want to get hurt.

When I was nine, I overheard a doctor tell my mother something that shaped the rest of my childhood: *"If she ever gets hit in the head, she could go totally blind."* That sentence didn't just land in my ears, it imprinted on my identity. Suddenly, life wasn't something to be lived—it was something to be avoided. That fear followed me everywhere.

In seventh grade, I faced one of those "everybody's watching" gym class moments. We had to vault over the horse, the kind where you run, jump, grab, and flip your legs over. The gym teacher pushed me to try it, and after coaxing enough, I gave in. I ran. I jumped. And then my toes caught the edge.

I flipped—literally—and landed upside down, dangling and humiliated, paralyzed by fear. I didn't cry, but my whole body trembled. The thought raced through me: *If I hit my head, I could go blind.*

Kids laughed. I hated gym class after that. I hated the spotlight. I hated risking anything.

But then came my mother, my silent cheerleader. She didn't scold me. She didn't baby me. She *believed* in me. She nudged me toward something unexpected: cheerleading.

At first, I resisted. But eventually, I tried it out and I discovered something I didn't expect: I liked it. I wasn't afraid of the cheers or the crowd. I was still scared, but I was also inspired. For the first time, I saw myself differently. I wasn't just surviving it, I was becoming.

Over time, I realized that being a cheerleader wasn't just a junior high experiment. It became a metaphor for my life. Today, I am a cheerleader—for women who are ready to rise, for entrepreneurs finding their way, for people on the edge of believing in themselves. I created a framework called G.A.P.—Genius Aligned with Purpose—to help others bridge the space between potential and performance.

Courage isn't always about climbing mountains. Sometimes, courage is making a call or sending an email. Maybe it's as simple as trying again after failure. Standing up after your fall. And the riskiest, bravest thing I've ever done? Starting my own business. It's not for the faint of heart. It takes grit. It takes vision. But more than anything, it takes courage.

And still, that wasn't the hardest thing I've ever had to do.

The hardest thing? Learning how to love again.

After going through a rough divorce and surviving a failed suicide attempt, I faced a darkness deeper than anything I had known. I had been broken—not just by a relationship, but by the complete collapse of trust, identity, and hope. That moment didn't just test me; it stripped me bare.

It took me over a year to rebuild not just my life, but also my spirit. It took years to recover.

What surprised me most in the healing process was this: Vulnerability was the key that opened the door.

I used to believe that vulnerability was weakness, that if people saw the real me, with all the cracks and scars, they would judge or reject me. But in my lowest moment, I realized something powerful: Trying to pretend I was fine was exhausting. And more importantly, it kept me from healing.

So, I started being honest. I let the tears come. I spoke the truth out loud.
And slowly, the fear started to lose its grip. I learned that vulnerability isn't the opposite of courage—it's the birthplace of it.

When I let others in, not just to the polished parts but to the messy, aching places, I found something I never expected: connection. People don't walk away. They lean in. They support. They relate. My vulnerability became a bridge, not a barrier.

When you lose trust in someone you once loved, you begin to see everything through a fractured lens. Life feels uncertain. People feel unsafe. Your own decisions feel suspect. Fear starts whispering lies that feel like truth: *You're not worthy. You're not lovable. You'll never get it right.*

Being courageous in the face of that pain felt impossible. But every day, I made the smallest choices to try again—to get out of bed, to show up for myself, to believe that something better was possible even when I didn't feel it yet.

Courage doesn't always roar. Sometimes it's the quiet voice that says, *"I will try again tomorrow."*

People think courage is loud. But I've learned that some of the boldest acts of bravery are quiet whispers in the dark: *What do you want?* That question has been a lifeline for me.

It started when I was little, pulling at my mother's sleeve, pestering her for something, attention, affection, a moment of her time. When she finally snapped in frustration and asked, "What do you want?" I had no idea how to answer.

As adults, we still don't. We complain about what we don't like. We focus on what's missing.

We say things like, "I don't want to feel stuck," or "I don't want this job," or "I don't want to be alone."

But have you ever sat down, really sat in silence, and asked yourself: "What do I want?"

It's not a silly question. It's not selfish. It's a sacred invitation to dream again.

Maybe you want freedom. Or connection. Or to live boldly in your truth. Maybe, just maybe, you want to love yourself enough to take the next brave step.

Here's the truth: You are allowed to want. You are allowed to be seen. And you are allowed to be courageous even if your voice trembles.

Today, I still ask myself that question: "What do you want?" And when I answer it, I write it down. I capture it. I believe in it.

Courage, after all, isn't about being fearless. It's about answering the call, even when fear is in the passenger seat.

So let me ask you: What do you want?

And more importantly…

Are you willing to be courageous enough to go after it?

EILEEN E. GALBRAITH

With an innate talent for connecting with others, Eileen champions a philosophy rooted in dialogue, believing fervently that communication is the linchpin of a better world. Throughout her journey, mentors consistently hailed Eileen's joy in service, her intuitive grasp of people's desires, and her aversion to conventional sales tactics. For Eileen, sales were never about coercion; they were about understanding needs and offering solutions with sincerity and empathy.

However, it was adversity that propelled Eileen into the realm of entrepreneurship. Confronting personal crises, she discovered a reservoir of resilience and empathy within herself, prompting her to extend counsel to other women facing similar challenges. Thus, her accidental foray into entrepreneurship birthed two ventures in the early 2000s, now united under a single banner. Today, Eileen is not just a sought-after speaker and multi-time Amazon Bestselling Author; she is the visionary behind "Implement to Impact," a coaching enterprise dedicated to empowering women entrepreneurs with a focus on fostering time freedom, wealth creation, and a supportive community.

Author's Website: *www.ImplementToImpact.com*

Charity Awareness: *www.SurvivalToThrivalSeries.com*

ERIC D. JACKSON

CHOOSE COURAGE

. . . .

*"Survival lives in the past; courage creates life in the future,
a life of thrival."*
~ Eric D. Jackson

We all need reminders to be courageous. We all desire to thrive.

According to EtymOnline.com, the etymology of "courage" c.1300 is: "Valor, quality of mind which enables one to meet danger and trouble without fear" is from late 14c. In this sense, Old English... which also meant "zeal, strength," ... inner strength... brave heart... free will."

The etymology of "thrive" c.1100 is: "thriven, late 12c., "to prosper, flourish; grow, increase, mature," from a Scandinavian source... "to thrive," originally "grasp to oneself," ... "to clutch, grasp, grip, take hold of" (compare Norwegian triva "to seize" ... "advanced in growth."

In order to prosper, flourish, grow, increase, and mature—to grasp oneself, and to seize the life you want to live will require the courage, the inner strength, and a brave heart—your free will—to meet the dangers and troubles outside of your comfort zone.

"We cannot be victims if we are to be victorious!"
~ Eric D. Jackson

I almost reference weekly in some conversation I host or lead, that:

"We are living in an imperfect world, with imperfect people, making imperfect choices, getting imperfect results."

It's amazing to me that, as a species, we have survived at all, that we still get any good results when we keep multiplying less than whole numbers, and keep getting positive results. That ability we humans have, to do more against all odds, may be proof (at least to me) that there is something more to it than the simple math suggests. Perhaps faith and love in the world truly make a difference, and that is something we can find hope in as well.

As a species, we humans have survived thousands of years, overcoming tremendous odds and obstacles. For many people, it feels so much harder to do anything more than just survive, and we are wired to want comfort—balance, ease, rest.

We have to overcome not only the external imperfections of this world, but also our own internal complications, in order to **thrive**.

"We are complicated and flawed."
~ Ryan Leak

As human beings, you can always count on us being focused on our own self-interest, our *survival*. Yes, we can be selfish, too, but those two are not the same thing, and we need courage to be better people. It takes courage to set aside our self-interest because we cannot thrive alone.

Thriving happens in community, and we cannot thrive if we stay alone in our comfort (and our complicated) zones.

I know that I personally need reminders every day to choose courage. Fortunately, there are many ways to strengthen our courage, and I'll share five steps or skills to help with this at the end.

If everything we want (thriving, our *Thrival Zone*) is on the other side of our *comfort zone*, then let's say that survival is what keeps us safe and comfortable, and that is why we must **choose courage** to move us out of our comfort zone—*out of our Survival Zone.*

I've spent nearly my whole life in the Survival Zone—decades too long! Actually, this year, my theme word is "Thrival!" How fitting that this book opportunity presented itself to coincide with the turning of this new season in my own journey, and I hope you **choose courage** for your journey as well!

Most days can be a struggle. There can be a gravitational pull to stay comfortable. That gravity is like a heavy weight slowing us down and anchoring us to past patterns and programs we are already comfortable with, even if they do not fully serve us or our future. The heavier the weight of those patterns and programs, the more we can be anchored to the past, and the less prepared and agile we are to "move forward and upward" into the future we dream of living fully.

Survival is not a bad thing—it is just not a **thrival** thing.

We have survived for thousands of years because certain programs and patterns have helped us minimize dangers and increase comfort and security. But progress and opportunity have only ever happened in an environment of courage.

For some of us, and perhaps for most, the programs we continue to run have serious limitations. Depending on our upbringing, maybe those limitations have been crippling to our progress and ability to thrive.

That is why we must find it in ourselves to choose courage—so that we can begin to choose to also overcome, to take ownership, and to change the outcomes we are able to experience and intentionally create in our own lives.

It is in our human nature that we all capture, both good and bad, patterns and programs from birth. One of those programs, which might have sounded like good advice, may have been to "work on your weaknesses" and to "improve your shortcomings."

If you follow these patterns, perhaps "you'll be more comfortable, and feel better this way…" but solely focusing on improving our weaknesses only makes us more "average!"

Perhaps better advice for us would be to become more excellent in our areas of strength first, and then decide which areas we either want to improve, or need to mitigate, delegate, and/or collaborate in healthier ways.

That takes courage, also—to become the fullest, most complete version of ourselves.

Consider these five steps to improve your ability to make courageous decisions in your own journey:

1. It will take courage to let go of old patterns and programs.

2. It takes courage to stay put in the moment of impulse, to increase our own awareness and impulse control, and to improve our self-control between impulses and responses.

3. It will require courage to move forward and upward, to create new patterns and programs—ones that help you thrive.

4. It may take the most courage to be accountable for the outcomes you produce, and especially the outcomes you don't. When you fail, when you fall, do it forward. Learn from your mistakes, your tests, and your experiments, mastering something new.

    This requires the most courage because we grow when we become really uncomfortable—when we have to be honest with ourselves and acknowledge, accept, and even agree that we are who we are, do what we do, and have what we have, because of our own selves. We are where we are because of how we have responded to life so far, and the great news is we can change that for the better! We can each change tomorrow, and even our own destinies, in this place of accountability.

5.   When we find—or better yet, when we choose courage, we choose to take agency back in our lives. We can be present, aware, or neutral. We can let go of the anchors. We can embrace the now—we can even embrace the very best of us, the most noble of us, even perhaps the eternal. We can forge a new future—**the future *us* that yearns to thrive!**

Say this for yourself,

"There is an old truth that used to be me. And the present truth is I am who I am today. I am choosing courage, to take agency of myself, because I am becoming the future version of me that THRIVES in ALL that I am."

Courage allows us to look into the mirror and see ourselves clearly where we are at right now, to accept ourselves up to this moment in all the good, bad, and the ugly… and to choose what steps we need to make next to move us forward and upward into the life we want to thrive in.

That same courage allows us to see others as they are—and more importantly, it allows us to accept others, extend grace to others, to show others dignity, respect, and even honor—to give them space to be who they are, and encourage them in their journey of choosing courage—from survival to thrival.

Thrival is not just for ourselves alone, and it is not solely material or superficial expressions of success. Thriving is living in a mindset and an environment of abundance and significance that allows us to honor the space for others to thrive as well. Thrival means sharing, working, and collaborating with others. Thrival allows us to extend blessings to others—to see others, care for others, and elevate others as we each make our journey beyond merely survival and self-interest.

Thrival means to prosper, flourish, grow, increase, and mature—to grasp oneself, and to seize the life you want to live with the required courage, the inner strength, and a brave heart—your free will—to meet the dangers and troubles outside of your comfort zone so that you can realize the excellent expression of who you are uniquely destined to be, and help others realize their destinies as we journey together.

Cheers to your journey forward and upward, thriving courageously!

ERIC D. JACKSON

Eric D. Jackson is dedicated to aiding business leaders in achieving the transformations they desire in life, work, and finances. As a speaker, coach, and trainer affiliated with the Maxwell Leadership Team and SCALE Architects of Predictable Success, Jackson showcases his expertise in leadership and finance. Additionally, he manages his own insurance and financial services practice and is eagerly anticipating the release of three book projects.

In his role as a Financial and Leadership Coach, Jackson assists leaders in expanding their influence, strengthening their teams, and amplifying their impact. He is a certified Coach, Trainer, and Speaker with Maxwell Leadership, a licensed SCALE Architect by Predictable Success, and a Licensed Financial Services Partner with certifications as CLU and MLO. Jackson is the principal and recruiter for Leadership Life Finances LLC, offering commercial benefit solutions for business leaders through "It's Your LIFE," catering to their insurance, financial, and training needs. He also serves as the Principal at Transformational Leadership & Culture Intn't LLC. Jackson is also an established publisher, known for his journal/planner and success series, *Forward & Upward.*

Author's Website: *www.ItsYourLife.com/links*

Charity Awareness: *www.KidInTheCorner.org*

GENESIS GOMEZ

FINDING COURAGE WHEN NO ONE IS CHEERING

They say courage looks like standing tall, sword raised, fearlessly charging forward.

But real courage—at least in my life—looked a lot less glamorous.

It looked like whispering "just keep going" to myself after another door slammed shut. It looked like fighting back tears in my car after a setback, and still walking into the next meeting with my head high. It looked like leaving behind relationships, jobs, and even family dynamics that were hurting me—even when it meant stepping into the unknown completely alone.

For much of my life, survival was the goal. Get through the day. Keep food on the table. Smile even when it hurt. Pretend everything was fine because breaking down wasn't an option.

There were moments when it felt like no one was cheering for me —when people who said they loved me became my biggest critics. When I started stepping out of survival mode and daring to dream bigger, it wasn't met with applause. It was met with suspicion, resentment, and sometimes outright sabotage.

But somewhere deep down, something stronger than fear grew: Courage.

Courage isn't the absence of fear—it's the refusal to let fear drive. It's standing up, dusting yourself off, and saying, "Not like this. Not anymore."

When I walked away from toxic relationships—when I left behind spaces that dimmed my light—it was one of the loneliest seasons of my life. But it was also the most pivotal. For the first time, I wasn't surviving for someone else's approval. I was choosing to thrive—for myself, and for the life I wanted to model for my children.

Starting my own businesses—from mortgage brokering to building Reigning Resilient Queens—didn't come from a place of "I have it all figured out." It came from a place of "I'll figure it out because I have no other choice."

And stepping into modeling, writing books, and speaking on stages? That wasn't about chasing fame. It was about reclaiming every part of me that had been silenced, hidden, or doubted. It was about standing tall and showing other women what's possible when you choose yourself and refuse to shrink.

There were failures, humbling lessons, moments when I questioned everything, and times when I almost gave up because the weight felt too heavy to carry.

But every time I thought about quitting, I remembered the girl who used to dream of standing on stages, sharing her story. I remembered the woman who needed someone to show her it was possible to rebuild from nothing. And I kept going—not because I always felt brave, but because I had decided that fear would no longer have the final say in my story.

Thriving isn't a finish line you cross with fireworks and fanfare. It's a quiet, sacred thing you build every day—in the choices you make when no one is watching. In the way you speak to yourself after a failure. In the way you get back up, again and again, believing that, somehow, your story is still worth fighting for.

Today, I see courage in every chapter of my life—even the ones that broke me. Especially the ones that broke me.

Because courage isn't born in comfort. It's born in the battle. And thriving isn't about arriving—it's about deciding, every single day, to live from hope instead of fear.

If you are in the middle of your survival story, I want you to know: You are already courageous. You are already braver than you realize. And there is a thriving life waiting for you—not because everything gets easier, but because you get stronger.

Keep going. Keep believing. Your next chapter isn't just survival. It's your legacy.

GENESIS GOMEZ

Genesis Gomez is a speaker, author, entrepreneur, and the founder of Reigning Resilient Queens, a movement committed to helping women rise through life's hardest chapters with strength, self-worth, and vision.

With a career spanning the worlds of modeling, public speaking, financial services, and end-of-life planning, Genesis brings compassion and clarity to every space she enters. Her journey reflects what it means to rebuild, to lead with heart, and to use every experience—personal and professional—as fuel for a deeper purpose.

Featured in national media and recognized for her authentic voice, Genesis continues to empower others to grow forward with grace and grit.

Author's Website: *www.GenesisGomez.com*

Charity Awareness: *www.ElevatingConnections.org*

JAMI LAH

THE COURAGE TO ASK DIFFERENT QUESTIONS

Life has taught me that courage often doesn't announce itself with fanfare. Instead, it whispers through the questions we dare to ask when everything around us seems to be falling apart.

The journey from survival to thrival requires different forms of courage: the courage to change our questions, to offer value without being asked, to say yes despite uncertainty, to reassess what we truly love, and to transform our perspective through the power of inquiry. My own story illustrates how these different faces of courage can transform a devastating setback into an unexpected path forward.

THE COURAGE TO CHANGE THE QUESTION

One pivotal moment of my life occurred during the 2008 financial collapse. I was working in commercial real estate when the market didn't just slow down, it stopped completely. The projects I had been working on for months were suddenly placed on indefinite hold. The timing couldn't have been worse; I had recently divorced and was responsible for supporting my three beautiful children. In those first few shell-shocked days, the questions that ran through my mind were the ones most of us ask when disaster strikes: "Why is this happening to me? How will I survive this? Why now?"

These questions initially left me feeling anxious, but something inside me—call it survival instinct or divine guidance—nudged me to try a different approach.

As I contemplated what's next, I consciously shifted my question from "Why is this happening to me?" to "Why is this happening for me?" This subtle shift wasn't about denying reality or forcing positivity. It was about opening myself up to possibilities I couldn't see when I was stuck in a mindset of scarcity.

It was my first real act of courage, choosing to believe that even in this collapse, there might be an opportunity I couldn't yet recognize.

This new question began to reshape not only my thinking but also how I responded to others' dreams during this challenging time. Around this same time, my daughter approached me about participating in a study abroad program called Semester at Sea.

My immediate internal response was, "There's absolutely no way we can afford this right now." But instead of shutting down her dream, I found myself saying, "You can go, but you'll need to find financial aid, get a scholarship, and work to make this happen."

In the midst of financial uncertainty, I was somehow encouraging my daughter to pursue an educational opportunity that was financially out of reach at this time. But something in me recognized that limiting her potential because of my fear wouldn't serve either of us. This realization led me to consider how I might contribute to making both our dreams possible.

THE COURAGE TO OFFER VALUE
WITHOUT BEING ASKED

As my daughter worked on making her dream a reality, I asked myself another question that would prove transformative: "How might I contribute to this same program, you see? It was also one of my dreams to take my children around the world and expose them to different cultures and experiences."

This question shifted my focus from what I lacked to what I could give. I reached out to Semester at Sea and asked if there was anything I could do to help them, explaining that I had unexpected time available since my real estate projects were on hold. I learned they had a program for "Lifelong Learners" who joined students on voyages.

What an incredible experience for people of all ages to explore the world together during a semester on the ship, not just the students! So, I began sharing information about this program with groups that might be interested in lifelong learning opportunities. I wasn't doing it with any expectation; I just felt a strong instinct to help where I could add value.

This act of giving without expectation created an opportunity. Semester at Sea offered me a position as their Communications PR Coordinator for an upcoming voyage.

THE COURAGE TO SAY YES WHEN YOU DON'T HAVE
ALL THE ANSWERS

When this opportunity arrived, I faced another moment that required courage. While I had the skills for the role, the timing and circumstances presented their own challenges. I didn't know what this journey would mean for my future career path or financial stability. There was no clear picture of how I would manage the complex logistics of traveling around the world. I did know that this would give my daughter the experience of a lifetime and that I would be able to take my other two children around the world while serving in this role. A unique experience for all of us.

Despite these uncertainties, I recognized that meaningful experiences are an essential part of life, even during times of professional transition. This is where another question transformed my path: "Am I making this decision out of fear or love?"

This powerful filter helped me see my choices with clarity. I realized that saying "no:" would come from manifesting a variety of fears: fear of the unknown, fear of stepping away from conventional career paths, fear of embracing uncertainty. Saying "yes" was truer to my core and where the essence of love is omnipresent—specifically, my love of connection, new experiences, and personal positive growth.

The decision to follow my core made more sense. I said, "Yes."

This "yes" opened doors I couldn't have imagined. Before that voyage began, I learned that TED was launching its TEDx program, allowing independently organized events under the TED banner. Something in me lit up. I used my skills to connect TEDx with Semester at Sea, as it seemed like an amazing opportunity for the students and lifelong learners who would be on the voyage and for TEDx.

That decision, made without a clear roadmap and without certainty of success, changed the entire trajectory of my life. For the past fourteen years, I've been producing TEDx events and have worked with over 500 speakers, helping them share ideas that matter.

Looking back, I can see that what appeared to be a devastating career collapse was actually the universe's way of redirecting me toward work that aligns perfectly with who I am—a connector who loves shining light on people and their ideas!

THE COURAGE TO REASSESS WHAT YOU LOVE

The financial collapse didn't just change my circumstances; it forced me to examine my life's direction at a fundamental level. When the financial collapse hit, I was forced to step back and reassess what truly mattered to me. This wasn't a luxury; it was a necessity. With my primary income stream suddenly drying up, I had to ask myself: "What do I truly love doing? Where do my natural talents lie?"

This process of self-examination revealed truths that had always been there, waiting to be acknowledged. The answer was clear: I love connecting people. I love creating spaces where ideas can be shared. I love shining a light on others and helping them communicate their unique gifts to the world. This clarity didn't immediately translate into a paycheck, but it gave me a compass to navigate by when everything else seemed uncertain. Eventually, following this compass led me to work that sustains me both financially and spiritually.

THE POWER OF TRANSFORMATIVE QUESTIONS

My journey from survival to thrival wasn't just about external circumstances changing—it was about the internal shift that happened when I changed my questions. As a result, I have found that these Universal Transformative Questions that helped me can help anyone, depending on their situation:

- **From Limitation to Possibility:** "I can't do this." → "How can I do this?"
- **From Victim to Creator:** "Why is this happening to me?" → "Why is this happening for me?"
- **From Frustration to Innovation:** "Why doesn't anything work?" → "What can I do differently?"
- **From Scarcity to Abundance:** "What am I losing?" → "What might this make possible?"

- **From Taking to Giving:** "What can I get from this situation?" → "How might I contribute value here?"
- **The Decision Filter:** "Am I making this decision out of fear or love?"

These questions don't magically solve problems, but they reorient my mind toward possibility rather than limitation. They help me access the courage that's always within me, even when circumstances feel overwhelming.

A TAKEAWAY FOR YOUR JOURNEY

If you're facing a moment that requires courage, whether it's a career collapse, a relationship ending, a health challenge, or simply the courage to pursue a dream, I invite you to experiment with changing your questions. Notice the questions you habitually ask when facing challenges. Are they questions that empower you or disempower you? Do they open possibilities or close them? Do they come from love or fear?

Try taking just one disempowering question and intentionally reframe it. See what shifts in your perspective and the actions available to you.

Remember that courage isn't about having all the answers or feeling completely confident. It's about being willing to ask different questions and follow where they lead, even when the path isn't clear.

Sometimes the most courageous thing you can do is to stop asking, "Why me?" and start asking, "What now?"

In my experience, when you change the question, you change what's possible. And that small shift might just be the first step on a journey from merely surviving to genuinely thriving.

JAMI LAH

For more than twenty years, Jami Lah has built international strategic partnerships that create exponential impact and brand awareness in the United States and abroad. As an innovator and connector, she leverages her vast network of CEOs, investors, and thought leaders in commercial real estate, technology, and start-up sectors to facilitate global change. She is currently the Founder and Executive Director of TEDxStGeorge and Producer for TEDxSanDiego. She has also produced TEDxOnBoard, TEDxCincinnati, and TEDxSemesterAtSea. Through these platforms, Jami has created numerous immersive events whose talks have garnered millions of views, advancing ideas on sustainability, health, wellbeing, AI, and emerging technologies.

Through her Lifelong Learning Worldwide initiatives, she creates transformative experiences, curates educational travel opportunities, champions powerful storytelling, and explores AI applications that empower individuals globally. Jami's exceptional ability to identify synergies between stakeholders establishes her as a trusted innovation catalyst, while her strategic vision transforms possibilities into tangible outcomes, benefiting organizations and communities alike.

Author's Website: *www.Jami-Lah.com*

Charity Awareness: *www.SurvivalToThrivalSeries.com*

LADY JEN DU PLESSIS, DC
POKING HOLES IN THE MIRROR

. . . .

"The wound is the place where the light enters you."
~ Rumi

As an only child until the age of twelve, I grew up surrounded by thirty-six first cousins who all had built-in best friends. Even with a large extended family, I often felt isolated. My father's alcoholism and my mother's verbal abuse shaped much of my early life. There was no one to lean on, no sibling to share secrets with, or to help process the chaos around me. I had to figure it out alone—and in doing so, I learned to wear armor. The kind of armor you don't even realize you've put on until it becomes heavy and familiar.

My home wasn't filled with peace and protection; it was a battleground of unpredictable emotions. My dad wasn't a bad man. He just had demons he never dealt with. He was a fun drunk until things got triggered, and then it became dangerous. I learned to anticipate the change in his tone, to gauge how bad the night might get based on how much beer was in the fridge or how my mom looked at him.

Despite the dysfunction, I became a high achiever. I was determined to rise above the story that others had written for me. I became a state tennis champion, a symphony flutist, and runner-up Miss Colorado. I even started college on a pre-med path to become a cardiologist. Later, I changed gears and studied Architectural Design and Construction Engineering.

After thirty-five wonderful years in the financial services industry, I would fund over $1 billion in mortgage loans and became one of the top two hundred originators in the country. But no matter how far I climbed, I still felt like that little girl trying to be seen—still trying to prove I was more than "Jenny, who ain't got a penny."

The unique thing about this is that after Brian and I got married, I remember asking him to clean off the top of the refrigerator. He didn't do it right. I could still see dirt on the edges. I think he used Windex. I didn't talk to him for two weeks. He kept asking, "What's wrong?" And I kept saying, "Nothing, nothing, nothing." Finally, I broke down and told him it was because he left dirt on the refrigerator. He laughed while I was crying.

That was the moment I realized I didn't know how to argue. As an only child, I hadn't learned to fight or disagree—there was never anyone to practice with. I had built up so much inside of me, so many unspoken feelings and frustrations, that something as simple as dust on a refrigerator broke me. That's armor, too. Silence. Avoidance. Isolation.

But I started to find my voice. I began to let people in.

With a nickname like "Jenny, who ain't got a penny," at first, I thought it was funny. I even put a penny in my shoe so I could laugh along with everyone. But then, one day, my uncle said something I'll never forget. He told me, "Jenny, you'll grow up to be just like your parents. You're going to be poor. You're going to be like your dad, an alcoholic. You're going to be like your mom, a verbal abuser."

I brushed it off—until the day I walked in and saw my dad holding a shotgun to my mom's head. I ran into the field behind my grandparents' house, just like Jenny in the movie Forrest Gump, sobbing, praying I wouldn't hear a gunshot. From that moment forward, my life became a mission to prove myself to everyone. I thought perfection could fix the pain. If I excelled, maybe the yelling would stop. Perhaps the drinking would stop. Maybe I would be enough.

So, I did everything I could to make them proud. For example, I became one of the few women in the country to fund over a billion dollars in mortgage loans. Yet, through all of that, I still didn't feel seen. Not by the people who mattered. I was still "Jenny, who ain't got a penny."

Years later, when I was asked to speak at a luncheon for an organization called Sterling Women, I realized just how tightly I'd been wearing that armor. While I had been speaking and presenting for years, I had never spoken publicly about my childhood—not like that. And I had invited people to attend the luncheon. What was I thinking?

As I started to write that speech, I cried. I was miserable. I wrote about the fear of being truly seen. If people knew the truth about me—where I came from—how would that change the way they thought about me or worked with me? They might judge me. They might whisper, "Who does she think she is?"

But I kept writing.

After that speech, women came up to me in tears. One said, "That's my story, too." Another said, "I've never shared it with anyone, either." In those moments, I knew I could never go back. I was always going to share my "Jenny-Penny" story.

I realized something: I could poke holes in the armor—just small ones. And when I did, my light came through. People started to see me—not for what I looked like, not for what I had achieved, but for who I really was.

And the more I poked, the more we connected.
Even with the remnants of armor still clinging to me—because some of it never comes off completely—I had discovered that

vulnerability was my strength. That authenticity was abundant. That courage wasn't just surviving—it was sharing and thriving!

And let me tell you about podiums.

I despise them.

They constrict me. I've spoken behind one only three times in my career—twice at Sterling Women and once at the National Press Club. But during that first speech, the podium was my shield. It allowed me to remove the armor while still protecting me. It gave me permission. But now, I don't need permission. I don't need the podium. I've already stepped forward into the limelight.

One cold winter night during my childhood, my mother woke me up to go find my father after he had been on a fire call (he was a volunteer fireman), because he didn't come straight home after the fire call. He was drinking again. That night, she made me get out of the car and go into the bar to get him. I was around seven. I didn't want to go, but she said, "Then walk home."

I walked into that dark bar, yanked on his jeans because I was too small to reach his knees while he was sitting on the bar stool, and begged him to come home. And I'll never forget what he said when he looked down at me and asked, "Who are you?"

That moment—like so many others—left a mark.

But every mark tells a story.

Every scar is a place where the armor cracked.

Today, as a mastermind leader, business mentor, and producer and host of my own TV show, and three podcasts, I continue to guide others through their own breakthroughs—helping them remove their armor one layer at a time.
That's where your light shines.

You might be reading this and thinking, "I've built some armor, too." Maybe yours looks like perfectionism, silence, or perhaps it's people-pleasing. Or maybe, like me, it's a blend of all three.

But here's what I want to leave you with:

You don't have to rip the armor off. Just poke one hole.

Let one beam of light shine through.

Say one true thing to someone you trust.

Share one story you've been scared to speak aloud.

The journey from survival to thrival isn't always loud. Sometimes, it begins with a whisper. With a small crack. With a story shared.

You're not alone. You never were.

Keep reading. Keep sharing. Keep showing up.

And maybe one day, you'll stand where I stood—on a stage, behind a podium, or simply in front of someone who needs your truth—and say, "I used to wear armor, too."

Because the more you share, the more we all heal.

The more you shine, the more others will find their light. Let that be your legacy.

Let that be your first step—from hiding to healing.

From surviving to thriving. One story at a time.

JOURNAL PROMPT

Where have I worn armor in my life, and where am I ready to let the light in?

LADY JEN DU PLESSIS

A dynamic leader renowned for transforming powerhouse businesses into companies that run smoothly without the need for daily intervention by its leader, Lady Jen Du Plessis, Dame Commander, is known as The Team Building & Scaling Architect who boasts over forty years in finance and over $400 million in revenue generated. She knows exactly how to build wealth through strategic team scaling, sustainable systems, and high-impact leadership, and has helped over 8,000 entrepreneurs leap from practitioners to thriving enterprises to achieve the pinnacle in their business.

She is a celebrated 22X Amazon #1 Bestselling Author, podcaster, and TV host who delivers real transformation, not just fast profits, so her clients achieve both business success and personal fulfillment. She cherishes her life in the countryside, enjoying local wineries, ballroom dancing, humanitarian efforts, boating, and quality time with family.

Author's Website: *www.JenDuPlessis.com*

Charity Awareness: *www.SurvivalToThrivalSeries.com*

JOANNA RUSSELL

FROM SURVIVAL TO THRIVAL: A JOURNEY OF COURAGE

Courage isn't something we're born with—it's something we cultivate, often in the face of heartbreak, fear, and uncertainty. It's not about being fearless; it's about standing in the storm and choosing to move forward anyway.

My story is not one of ease, but of transformation because I've refused to let adversity define me. Instead, I've allowed it to shape me into someone who is resilient, resourceful, and determined to thrive.

From leaving home at sixteen to crossing the Atlantic after my mother's death, and from navigating the unfamiliar landscape of American social work to reinventing myself as an executive coach, my journey has been marked by one constant: the courage to keep going, even when the path ahead was shrouded in uncertainty.

THE FIRST LEAP: COURAGE AT SIXTEEN

When I was no longer able to live at home at the age of sixteen, I was a bundle of emotions—scared, heartbroken, angry, and in total disbelief. At that age, I didn't understand the full picture. I was vulnerable, raw, and angry, unable to comprehend that my mum was battling her own demons, fighting depression, and emotionally unavailable in ways I wouldn't fully grasp until I was much older. All I knew then was that I was suddenly on my own.

Even in my most vulnerable state, something inside of me refused to give up. Looking back, I see now how courageous it was to keep living my life, to go on when it would have been so much easier to let despair swallow me whole. I put myself through college—not once, but twice—working tirelessly to create a future for myself.

When I became a young parent, the stakes grew even higher. Suddenly, it wasn't just about surviving for me—it was about creating stability for my children. There were moments of deep doubt, loneliness, and fear, but every time those feelings threatened to pull me under, I found a way to push back harder. It was almost like the challenge created an energy that propelled me forward.

Looking back, I see that leaving home was a pivotal turning point. It forced me to become even more independent and helped me build resilience. Those qualities were already within me, and yet through the adversity of my situation, they almost became my superpower. I am so grateful for that experience now, even if it took time to appreciate it.

COURAGE TO START OVER:
MOVING ACROSS BORDERS

Moving from the United Kingdom to the United States was already a leap into the unknown, but doing so only a month after losing my mum made it one of the most challenging chapters of my life, requiring every ounce of courage I could muster. Though grieving deeply, I knew I had to keep moving forward. Starting over while mourning her loss felt like trying to rebuild a house during a storm—but I reminded myself why I had made this leap: for growth, for possibility, for courage.

Landing in the US, everything felt unfamiliar. The air was different, the streets were wider, and the sense of starting from scratch was overwhelming. I remember the first time I stood in a grocery store, staring at shelves full of brands I didn't recognize, feeling like a stranger in my own life. There were moments when I felt like an outsider, moments when the grief of losing my mother would hit me out of nowhere. But through it all, I kept focusing on what lay ahead rather than what I had left behind.

COURAGE TO PIVOT: REINVENTING MYSELF

The next challenge that presented itself was the landscape of social work in the US. It was not just different—it was almost unrecognizable to me. In the UK, my work was rooted in law, policy, systems, budgets, and corporate collaboration; in the US, it was more rigid, specialized, and medicalized. The opportunities to make the kind of impact I cherished seemed scarce. This realization could have left me feeling defeated, but instead, it sparked something new.

With a diverse background in social work with significant leadership responsibility and the unique perspective gained through my marriage to a CEO, I had developed a deep understanding of leadership principles, strategic thinking, and the nuances of organizational culture. These experiences provided me with a comprehensive view of effective management across different sectors. I'd seen firsthand how powerful effective leadership could be—not just for the bottom line, but for the well-being and growth of people. My passion for leadership had always run deep, and I knew that my next chapter was calling me to step out of the systems I'd known and build something of my own.

Pivoting wasn't easy. It meant facing uncertainty, taking risks, and starting from scratch. But it also meant freedom—the freedom to work in a way that was true to my values, to empower others, and to create positive change. The skills I had developed—empathy, listening, seeing the bigger picture—became the foundation for my next chapter. Transitioning from social work to coaching wasn't just a career move; it was an act of courage. It required me to trust myself, embrace vulnerability, and lead with purpose. I'm grateful for every lesson, every challenge, and every moment that demanded bravery.

THE EVERYDAY FACE OF COURAGE

Courage isn't just about grand gestures or dramatic leaps. More often, it's found in the quiet moments of decision-making, in the willingness to step into uncertainty, and in making promises to ourselves that we're not sure we can fulfill. It's about facing fears, taking action despite doubt, and pushing through obstacles to achieve a desired outcome. The courage to keep going—especially when the outcome is unclear—is what drives personal growth and resilience.

In my experience, courage is a mindset, a way of life. It's about being willing to risk failure, to try again after setbacks, and to keep moving even when the path is difficult. It's the foundation that makes growth, transformation, and authentic living possible.

LESSONS IN SELF-LOVE & RESILIENCE

There have been moments in my life—moments of true grief, loneliness, and fear—when I could have given up. But instead, I chose to fall in love with myself. I am incredibly proud of who I am and what I've built. I know now, in a way I could not have known at sixteen or even at thirty or forty, that if you are ever at a crossroads, doubting whether you can do it, I want you to know you absolutely can.

It's a choice—whether we live, or whether we let life take us down. I am glad I found the courage to live my absolute best life and to be grateful for every step, even the hardest ones.

FORTUNE FAVORS THE BRAVE

If there's one mantra that has carried me through life's darkest times, it's this: Fortune favors the brave. These words have served me well when fear threatened to hold me back—when everything felt impossible, but courage whispered, "Keep going." I encourage family, friends, and clients alike to dig deep because the resources they're looking for are almost always within—they just need to trust themselves enough to find them.

As I've learned through my own journey, courage is not the absence of fear, but the decision to move forward despite it. It is the cornerstone of every transformation and the foundation of every story worth telling

EMPOWERING OTHERS THROUGH COURAGE

Sharing this story isn't just about reflecting on where I've been; it's about showing others what's possible when they tap into their own courage and determination. If you're reading this, wondering whether you have what it takes to move from survival mode into thriving, to overcome whatever challenge lies ahead, I want you to know this:

You don't need all the answers right now; you don't need guarantees or perfect conditions before taking that first step forward. All you need is courage, the kind that whispers, "Persevere," even when everything around you feels impossible.

Because if I could do it, if I could leave home at sixteen with nothing but determination; if I could start over in a new country after losing my mother; if I could reinvent myself professionally after two decades—you can, too.

Thriving isn't just about where we end up; it's about the path we choose to take and, in turn, who we become along the way.

JOANNA RUSSELL

Joanna Russell is a Senior Executive Coach and founder of Ajile LLC, recognized for expertly blending traditional leadership development with holistic coaching to drive organizational transformation and strategic growth. With nearly two decades of high-level experience in the UK healthcare sector as a Specialist Senior Social Worker, Joanna distinguished herself by managing complex cases, navigating intricate legal frameworks, and overseeing significant budgets—demonstrating advanced business acumen and operational leadership. Her transition from senior case management to executive coaching marks a natural evolution in her commitment to developing leaders and fostering organizational excellence.

Now based in the U.S., Joanna partners with high-achieving professionals to restore motivation, elevate performance, and enhance leadership effectiveness. She also leads peer advisory groups and has served as Director of Coaching for a personal development company, designing impactful coaching frameworks. Joanna's warm, relatable, and deeply empathetic approach guides clients through sustainable transformation, helping them reconnect with purpose, set healthy boundaries, and thrive at the highest levels of leadership.

Author's Website: *www.AjileLLC.com*

Charity Awareness: *www.ThistleFarms.org*

DR. JOEL PARKER

A BLINDSIDE MOMENT

. . . .

COURAGE

The Oxford Dictionary defines courage as "the ability to do something that frightens one; strength in the face of pain or grief." It's a simple yet profound idea—a fitting preface to the story I'm about to share, one that reshaped my understanding of courage as both a mindset and a lifeline in a dire moment.

A BLINDSIDE MOMENT

Have you ever been cruising through life, building your family, business, and dreams, only to be hit by a *WTF* moment that comes out of nowhere? If you haven't, count yourself lucky. I wasn't so fortunate last year. It felt like getting T-boned at an intersection by a distracted driver on their phone, blowing through a red light.

BAM. It hit, and it hit *hard*.

I was running a management consulting company with my partner, helping independent veterinary practice owners create time and financial freedom. That freedom meant they could run thriving practices while still having space for family and personal passions. Veterinarians, often Type-A personalities, pour themselves into their work, risking burnout and sacrificing their health and family life. Our mission was to help them find that balance.

My routine was solid—flying between our west and east coast offices, eating organic, hitting the gym with a personal trainer two

179

or three times a week. Sure, my sugar intake was higher than recommended, but at sixty-eight, I felt like a thriving thirty-year-old. I was cruising, not tapping into much courage, just living the good life.

Then, BAM—it hit.

THE MOMENT OF SHOCK

I had a heart attack.

I'd been preparing for a trip and stopped to pick up a Sherpa dog carrier I'd found on Facebook Marketplace. I was walking back from picking it up when, out of nowhere, a crushing pressure erupted in my chest. Imagine the worst heartburn from too much Indian food, then dial it up by a hundred. That's what it felt like.

Disoriented, I stumbled back to the car, dodging oncoming traffic, and slumped into the driver's seat. "I don't want to scare you guys," I said to my wife and son, "but something's not right." My wife, a trained veterinarian, sprang into action, assessing me and calling an ambulance.

Minutes later (though it felt like hours), the ambulance arrived. They gave me a baby aspirin, hooked up an IV, ran an ECG, and rushed me to the hospital. Not wanting to confront the gravity of the situation, I even joked with the cardiologist, "Just send me home with a jumbo bottle of Pepto-Bismol!"

I spent the night in intensive care. The next morning, I was wheeled into the cath lab for an angiogram, which revealed an 80-90% blockage in my Left Anterior Descending Artery (LAD). The surgeon quipped, "We call that the widow-maker."

A sobering, *WTF* moment? Absolutely. A brutal, in-your-face, screeching halt to life as I knew it. Was I frightened? Hell yes.

THE MOMENT OF REFLECTION

Staring at the ceiling in the recovery room, you've got nothing but time to think. Thoughts and questions swirl around in your head —Why me? What happened? How do I lie still for an hour so the

180

femoral catheterization site can heal? And the bigger one: What's next? Fear, uncertainty, and a dark cloud of emotions settled over me.

Twelve hours later, I walked out of the hospital with six new medications and a radically altered view of life.

THE MOMENT OF COURAGE

The reality sank in over the next forty-eight hours. *What now?* A heart attack? Me? I felt vulnerable, exposed, and in denial. One question loomed largest: What does this mean? Was my life over? Should I play it safe, coast to the finish, live in fear of another attack?

Amid the fear and uncertainty, a realization hit: courage. It would take courage to push through, to park the fear and face the situation head-on. The Oxford Dictionary defines "confront" as "to face up to and deal with a problem or difficult situation." From Latin *con* (with) and *front* (face), it means handling something directly, without flinching. That takes courage—a strategic, fearless resolve to tackle the problem.

This moment of courage, this direct confrontation, sparked a deeper insight: a *WTF* moment isn't just a crisis. It's a crossroads, a chance to make a decision. It's an opportunity to ask yourself:

* What truly fuels you?
* What do you love doing?
* What lights you up?

THE "WHAT'S TRULY FULFILLING" MOMENT

In that moment, I realized I had the power to pivot. A *WTF* moment could become a *What's Truly Fulfilling* moment. My purpose wasn't just about cruising along—it was about doing what set my soul on fire.

I started asking myself: If I only have twenty years left, in the final quarter of my life, how do I want to spend them? What would my final symphonic movement, my last operatic act, look like?

Looking back, the answer was clear.

I've always loved helping others build what I call *Standing Ovation Practices*™—businesses that deliver such extraordinary experiences that clients walk away thrilled and rave about them without prompting. You can't buy that kind of loyalty with discounts or freebies. It's about creating a purpose-driven team that crafts and delivers an exceptional experience, like a flawless musical performance or a Michelin-starred meal. It doesn't happen by accident; it's carefully designed, delivered, monitored, and refined.

RESTART BUTTON

So, I made a bold move. I hit the restart button. I sold my company and started something new, stepping fully into what lights me up: guiding others to create their own *Standing Ovation Practices*™. I left the old behind and embraced a path that felt true to my purpose. I felt an unexpected, wonderful surge of energy flow through me.

We all face *WTF* moments. Some are massive, like a heart attack. Others are quieter but no less significant—yet they all have that nagging feeling that you're meant for something more, that it's not time to hang up your hat and coast to the finish. Not yet.

When those moments hit, you have two choices:

• Let fear take the wheel, play it safe, and live cautiously, coasting to the end.

• Use it as a wake-up call to discover and pursue *What's Truly Fulfilling*.

And here's the kicker: You don't have to wait for a *WTF* moment to wake up. You don't need to be sixty-eight, lying in a critical care bed, staring at the ceiling, and grappling with mortality to start living fully.

Better yet, you can skip the *WTF* moment entirely and choose a *What's Truly Fulfilling* moment *now*. You don't have to wait for life to shake you awake.

That future? It's yours to create. Have the courage to start living that life that truly lights you up and feel that surge.

DR. JOEL PARKER

Dr. Joel Parker, a veterinarian since 1984, became a private practice owner in 1986. He grew his practice, guided by solid management principles, into a Standing Ovation Practice™—a practice that delivered an above-and-beyond expected experience. He later founded Veterinary Endoscopy Solutions and Canine Equipment™. After fifteen years, he sold the businesses and started Veterinary Practice Solutions in 2004, a veterinary management consulting firm, innovated with "Whiteboard Wednesdays" on YouTube, and early online webinars. In 2024, he launched Parker Business Systems (PBS), a boutique-style consulting firm specializing in transforming privately owned veterinary practices into Standing Ovations Practices™.

He, above all, leads a purposeful life, helping others achieve time and financial freedom.

He lives with his family between Clearwater, FL, and Vancouver, BC. He enjoys sports cars, great coffee, strumming a ukulele, and playing with his unique, small, weird dogs.

Author's Website: *www.TheStandingOvationPractice.com*

Charity Awareness: *www.TheWayToHappiness.org*

J.S. KOVACH

THE HUMAN POTENTIAL

"To speak of the human potential is to speak of the chances for enriching the quality of human life as well."
~ Unknown

My passion is encouraging people to get outside and facilitating empowering, emotional experiences with nature. While this passion could lead to opportunities such as interpreting at National Parks or similar settings, I especially enjoy working with children and individuals with disabilities.

As a child, my family regularly went camping and explored the outdoors. As my six siblings and I were all homeschooled until college, my family was able to vacation during the off-season when most kids were still in school.

Many of these vacations were spent exploring the vast National Parks in Utah: Arches, Bryce Canyon (after which my brother was named), Canyonlands, Capitol Reef, and Zion. Right after public school started and right before it ended, the Parks were nearly devoid of tourists, and this made me feel as if my family owned the parks. "This land is my land" was very real to me at a young age—it was like the National Parks were my personal playground. It wasn't until I grew older and started planning my own trips, when I had time off work or the long weekends during college semesters, that I experienced the Disneyland effect of Zion in the summer.

185

I was a very perceptive child, and I wasn't very old when I began noticing how our family camping trips or hikes affected my dad. My dad has had depression and anxiety as long as I can remember, and was never a very "touchy-feely" or personable dad —except when we were outside.

My dad knows more about plants and animals than anyone I know, and he would come alive as he knelt down to show his kids various plants—he would have us touch them, feel their texture, smell them, or even lick them if that was relevant to the particular plant. I learned from him to savor the experience of a hike instead of rushing to the destination: We often stopped to watch and listen to birds, smell flowers, hug trees, and just enjoy the breeze.

Not only did my dad create immersive experiences in nature that captured my interest, but the simple fact that my dad, who was so often reserved and impersonable, softened his voice and took time to be with his children helped to develop in me a deep, irrepressible love for wild places. Nature was the healing balm for my dad's depression, and, later, for my own depression and anxiety as a teenager and adult.

My interest in working with people with disabilities began when I was a child and was reiterated when I was a teenager. When I was fifteen, I met someone who forever changed my life. I began helping a neighbor with cerebral palsy at my mom's request. Laura, my neighbor, used a wheelchair as she had spastic episodes, a damaged hip, and extremely limited mobility in her left side. I would help her sort her mail, pay her bills, clean up her apartment, and just chat with her. As a teenager, I wanted to be anywhere else than cooped up in that small apartment, "working for free," with a practical stranger.

However, Laura learned of my passion for writing, and she asked me to write her autobiography. After tidying up her apartment, I would open my laptop and transcribe as she shared her incredible life story. She was raised in a time when people with disabilities were social outcasts—her mother's pastor told her mother that she was a sinner and so God cursed her with a "useless, disabled" child.

Laura grew up believing she was just that—a mistake, a curse, a burden. She suffered physical and sexual abuse from her father, was neglected by her mother, and faced ostracism from her community. Her mother's neglect actually kept her from being institutionalized—as many people with disabilities were at that time—as her mother just didn't get around to it.

If you were to meet Laura, you would love her immediately. She's feisty. As an adult, she accomplished the impossible for someone like her at that time: She moved out on her own. She discovered a local equine therapy camp, signed herself up, and began to gain strength and confidence. Eventually, she helped establish a non-profit for people with cerebral palsy, started her own equine therapy program, and even became a diving instructor at the city pool.

She told me, frankly, that recreation saved her life. She had been in a very dark place before she realized she could do whatever she set her mind to. Today, she remains an activist and collaborates closely with her city council to develop accessible ramps, curbs, and elevators throughout her city. She is my absolute inspiration, and I hope to one day be a quarter of how awesome she is.

Since moving away from that area, I have volunteered with the Special Olympics and group homes; I've worked as an adaptive adventure guide, taking clients backpacking, canoeing, and rock climbing. My internship was at a summer camp located outside Yosemite National Park, where I served individuals with intellectual and developmental disabilities. I absolutely love helping people discover their abilities through recreation, and I wholeheartedly believe that people are much more likely to push themselves and have the courage to try new things when their senses are stimulated by the outdoors.

Whether in my personal life or my professional career, my passion is serving human potential. I have discovered my own potential through outdoor recreation and wilderness experiences, and my quality of life improves significantly when I am outside.

"If survival, if immortality, is out of the question, then of much more importance to each human being is the issue of how to make the most out of the time one has. And that is a question of quality."
~ D. Dustin et al., 2011

One of my closest friends is a woman with cerebral palsy whom I met at the summer camp outside Yosemite. During the pandemic lockdown, she often told me how much happier she felt when she was exploring outdoors. She struggled with the stay-at-home orders because her physical therapist was closed, her equine therapy was postponed, and all her summer camp plans were canceled for the foreseeable future.

Outdoor recreation is great for anyone, but it can be positively life-changing for those who have been told they could never lead a normal life. The first time they step into a climbing harness or get transferred into a canoe can be transformational.

For many of my clients, nature was a sensory experience through which they could feel, touch, smell, and connect with a power greater than themselves. Immersed in nature, they experienced a sense of belonging and purpose. The acquisition of new skills and knowledge boosted their sense of self-development and personal freedom.

Insofar as outdoor recreation can be extrinsically rewarding, prolonged immersion in a wilderness setting can engender mental, emotional, and even spiritual benefits. Nature provides a platform to learn new skills, make individual physical goals, and to discover and challenge new personal limits, while also encouraging recovery and self-care.

As a result of this self-confidence, my clients developed a belief in their ability to attain and excel in leadership roles. Furthermore, they dared to believe in their human potential to succeed in other aspects of life, including aspects that were once their constraints.

References

Dustin, D., McAvoy, L., Schultz, J., Bricker, K., Rose, J., Schwab, K. (2011). *Stewards of Access, Custodians of Choice.* Sagamore Publishing.

J.S. KOVACH

J.S. Kovach is an award-winning author and in-demand copyeditor with over two dozen bestselling books to her name, including collaborative works with celebrities such as Erik Swanson, Sharon Lecter, and Brian Tracy.

She wrote her first 80,000-word novel at the age of twelve, which garnered critical acclaim from top YA literary agents. She has since written four YA novels, multiple short stories, and was selected for publication in her university's Student Leadership Journal for her research essay, *Outdoor Recreation Increases Self-Confidence in Women*.

Her passion for writing, reading, and editing blossomed into a thrilling career in the editorial and publishing field, where she currently serves as Editorial Manager for Integrity Publishing.

When her nose isn't in a book, she is usually found outdoors hiking, kayaking, or camping with her husband and three dogs: a 90-pound Newfoundland mix, a 36-pound Borderspaniel, and their "foster fail" 9-pound rescue longhaired dachshund.

If you're looking for a copyeditor, please contact her at *Kovach.Edits@gmail.com*.

Author's Website: *www.JSKovach.com*

Charity Awareness: *www.ACLU.org*

JULIE DELGADILLO

BUILDING TRUST WHEN NO ONE IS WATCHING

COURAGE IN THE MIRROR

In my profession, in my life, and in every room I walk into—I know everything starts with trust.

Trust is not a checkbox. It's not a campaign. It's not even a deliverable. It's a relationship with your word. With your follow-through. With your integrity.

I work in the nonprofit world. That means building relationships —with donors, seniors who receive meals, volunteers, and colleagues who rely on you to do what you said you would do. And when you don't, people notice. People feel it. People depend on it.

It's not just about giving or receiving. It's about keeping your word on both sides. It's about being the steward of what's right.

My dad used to say, "You can dream, but don't quit your day job." And I get that. He wasn't discouraging me from going after big things—he was teaching me about responsibility. About showing up. About being someone that people can count on.

To me, integrity is doing what you say you're going to do, and doing it whether anyone sees you or not. It's not just for the show; it's not just when people are clapping. It's what happens behind the scenes. Are you the same person when the lights are off?

It's so easy to post on social media that you're feeding the poor or delivering meals, but if behind closed doors, you're out of alignment—that's not integrity. That's not trust.

I've always believed that leadership is about showing, not just saying. It's about being a do-leader, not a "tell-leader." Whether it's a mentee, a team member, a family member, or a friend, leadership is about showing them how—not pointing the way, but walking it with them.

And sometimes that walk is hard. Sometimes that walk asks you to stretch further than you thought you could go.

MY ROCK BOTTOM LESSON:
A MISSED MEAL, A BROKEN TRUST

I recall one day when we were preparing meals for seniors through Meals on Wheels. These are folks who rely on us for their food. This isn't just a service—it's their lifeline. We had a day where something failed in the delivery process, and meals didn't make it out. And let me tell you, this wasn't just a logistical problem. It was a breakdown of trust. A senior waiting for that meal—some of whom won't eat without it—that's not just a missed delivery. That's a missed promise. That's where accountability kicks in.

That day wrecked me. I felt like we failed the very people who counted on us most. I remember sitting alone in my office that night, crying. Not because of blame, but because I knew the weight of our word. I made a vow that day: I will lead with more than just passion. I will lead with precision. With action. With follow-through.

And here's the thing: practicing trust is like exercising. It gets easier with consistency. Like confidence, it's a muscle. You're not born with it. You don't wake up one day with it. You build it by showing up again and again—even when it's uncomfortable. Even when no one's cheering you on.

Even something as simple as saying, "I'm going to exercise," and then actually doing it—that's integrity. That's self-trust. That's the frequency at which you begin to vibrate. And the more you trust yourself, the more confident you become. You build congruence. You walk through life differently.

A QUOTE I LIVE BY

One of my favorite reminders comes from my own father, but it echoes what I believe to my core:

"You can dream, but don't quit your day job."

Not because you shouldn't chase your dream, but because your responsibility is part of your purpose. Your dream is only as strong as your discipline.

YOU'RE NOT BEHIND—YOU'RE RIGHT ON TIME

I've come to understand a big truth: You're not behind. You're not late. You're exactly where you need to be.

We put all these pressures on ourselves: "By thirty I should have this... by forty I should have that..." But those timelines? They're made up. The real question is, are you keeping your promises to yourself? Are you showing up the way you said you would? If yes, you're right on time. Every time.

That's the deepest form of trust—the one we have with ourselves.

A DEFINING DECISION: COURAGE TO SHIFT GEARS

For me, that courage became clear when I made a personal decision. I changed jobs—not because I wasn't doing well, but because I wanted to be closer to home, closer to my family, closer to the version of life that aligned with my heart. That shift required sacrifice. But it also brought clarity. I could feel my own frequency strengthening, my own integrity aligning.

OWN YOUR WANT, HUMBLY

I've also learned this: don't apologize for wanting something.

Recently, there was something I wanted deeply, but I was afraid of judgment. I worried about what people might think. And then I realized—if I keep living in that fear, I'm not being true to myself. I'm not living in my purpose. And if I'm not living in integrity with myself, then everything else is off.

So, I went for it. And even if I failed, I would have failed trying. That's courage. That's love. That's empowerment.

MENTORING MOMENTS: WHEN SHOWING UP IS ENOUGH

When it comes to passing this on—mentoring others, onboarding new team members, building leaders—I always say this: Don't be afraid to show up. Don't be afraid to connect. Don't be afraid to build relationships.

You don't have to sell yourself. You don't have to prove yourself. Just connect. Be real. Ask questions. Share your story.

I've sat with donors and never once talked about money. We just connected. We talked about who we are. We learned about each other. And that trust—that human-to-human moment—opens doors.

Sometimes, the door is for you. Sometimes, you're just the one meant to open it.

But either way, you must trust yourself. Believe in yourself. Even if it doesn't lead exactly where you thought it would, you will never regret showing up.

IF YOU WANT TO EMPOWER THE WORLD...

To me, empowerment is about staying coachable. Staying open and being willing to admit that maybe we don't have all the answers. It's about being willing to let someone else show us a better way.

We're all on the road trying to get somewhere, and we're all using the same freeway. We might be headed to different destinations, but the route is shared. The growth is shared. And the wisdom is available—if we listen.

But first, you have to be rooted in who you are. You've got to trust yourself before you ask others to trust you. You've got to walk your talk.

Every day, when you wake up and brush your teeth, make your bed, follow through on your word—that's where it begins. That's how courage is built: One small act of self-trust at a time, even on the days when you don't want to. Even when it feels easier to quit. Even when the world is quiet and you wonder if it matters at all.

It does.

Keep showing up. Keep doing what you said you would. And when you need to rest, rest. But don't quit.

Because this world needs your integrity. This world needs your courage. This world needs people who are willing to walk the walk.

And if I've learned anything, it's that your courage multiplies when you share it. When you give it away, it doesn't run out. It grows.

IMAGINE IF...

Imagine a world where every leader kept their word—a world where trust wasn't earned over years but built in moments of authenticity; a world where women walked into boardrooms, courtrooms, and classrooms fully themselves, unapologetically aligned.

That's the world I'm building—one connection at a time, one act of courage at a time.

Dear reader, please consider these challenges:

- What is one commitment you've made to yourself but haven't followed through on?
- Today, pick one small act of integrity—and do it.
- Journal this mantra: "I keep my word. I trust myself. I show up."

That's where courage starts. And that is how we move from survival... to thrival.

JULIE DELGADILLO

Julie Delgadillo is a confident, enthusiastic, witty, and sought-after passionate servant leader and award-winning mentor with over twenty years of experience in non-profit management, leadership development, and confidence coaching. Julie is the Director of Development for Meals on Wheels and the previous Executive Director of Corazón U.S. and Comunidad Corazón A.C., México. Julie is a firm believer in leading by example and actively engages in developing community leaders. It's not uncommon for her to roll up her sleeves and personally contribute to building spaces where children can learn, women can lead, and entire communities can rise through education and opportunity.

Julie's strengths and passions are rooted in empowering women to lead with confidence in every area of their lives. Julie has personally coached and developed teens and women from around the globe, serving as an International Ambassador for the economic development of women. Julie is an International Beauty Queen, the 2026 Ms. Global Icon Elite, and a long-time Hunger Relief Advocate.

Author's Website: *www.linktr.ee/SheConquersTheWorld*

Charity Awareness: *www.SurvivalToThrivalSeries.com*

JULIE JONES

THE COURAGE TO CONNECT: HOW ONE STUDENT CHANGED MY LIFE

After fifteen years of teaching, I thought I had seen it all—until one small school in South Texas showed me what true courage really meant.

As a general rule, my students and their parents liked me, and I liked them in return. When we moved to a rural town in South Texas, I was hired as a middle school math teacher. The principal asked me to serve as the new Department Head, because the school needed to raise test scores or face a state takeover.

I was honored and immediately went into "administrator mode," fueled by ambitions of becoming a district leader. Our math team spent the summer in workshops and working with consultants to design new lessons. We were excited and ready for the new year.

On the first day, I introduced myself and told the students this would be the year we turned the school around. But something was off.

My students didn't look like me. For most of them, English was a second language. I arrived dressed professionally, but they saw me as repressive. I skipped the icebreakers and dove right into the first lesson. We had a lot of work to do, so I skipped the pleasantries. Consequently, the students viewed me as cold and uncaring.

Behavior problems erupted. Some parents even pulled their children from my class. I became one of the most disliked teachers. I didn't understand—wasn't I trying to help?

At first, I blamed "these kids." I thought they didn't value education. I believed the problem was with them.

One day, while I was teaching, a substitute from the classroom next door knocked on my door. Standing beside him was Marco, a student whose parents had already moved him out of my class. Marco was glaring at me and was visibly upset.

The substitute asked for my help managing Marco's behavior. Judging by Marco's expression, I knew he wouldn't be receptive to me as a mediator. I suggested calling the office for help.

Marco clicked his tongue, rolled his head dismissively, and walked back into the classroom.

A few minutes later, the Assistant Principal and a police officer appeared at my door. Marco had announced to his class that he had a knife and intended to "cut that white b****."

Fear gripped me. They explained that Marco would be sent to an alternative school. Although I tried to stay strong, I was shaken to my core.

In the weeks that followed, things calmed down. I focused on teaching, but wondered why I was struggling this year. I feared facing Marco again—after all, he had wanted to hurt me.

After Christmas break, I learned Marco would be returning. Initially, the principal planned to move him to another track and give him a fresh start. But that didn't happen.

"He's going right back to the class next to you," he said. "I suggest you find a way to build a relationship with him."

Fear raced through me. I considered resigning. I wondered about my safety and my rights. It didn't seem fair.

That night at home, I looked at myself long and hard in the mirror. Marco was smart and well-liked by other teachers. I was the only one who had struggled with him. Maybe the problem wasn't with him.

Maybe it was me.

"You are the adult," I said to myself in the mirror.
The next day, I had a knot in my stomach the moment I woke up. I knew I would have to face the person who hated me and vowed to cut me.

I knew I'd see him during passing period. When the bell rang to end fourth period, my heart began to pound. I went to the hallway to monitor the students and greet the ones entering my classroom.

When Marco appeared, he didn't make eye contact. I took a deep breath and said, "Hi, Marco. Welcome back."

He slowed, looked at me strangely, and asked, "Why?"

"Because you belong here, not there," I replied.

He nodded slowly and entered the room. My body was still shaking, but I had made it through the first encounter.

The following days, I kept showing up. Marco would glance at me. I'd smile and greet him casually. Gradually, the wall between us began to come down.

After a few days, Marco responded with brief answers. "Yeah." "Good." "Okay."

Weeks turned into months. Our conversations grew longer. We talked about baseball, families, and weekend plans. I learned about his dreams, his struggles, and the challenges he faced outside of school.

By spring, Marco and I had built a real teacher-student relationship, one based on mutual respect and trust.

On the last day of school, as we chatted in the hallway, he said, "You know, I used to not like you."

"I know," I smiled.

He grinned. "I've learned that you're not so bad. You might even be one of my favorites."

I fought back tears. In that moment, all the fear, hurt, and uncertainty melted away.

Marco finally saw me—not as cold, but as someone who cared.

The difference wasn't Marco.

It was me.

I had found the courage to let go of pride and ambition and become the teacher Marco needed. Even though he was no longer my student in the classroom, he was still mine in the hallway. Every child on that campus was my responsibility.

Marco taught me more that year than I had learned in fifteen years of teaching. He taught me that courage isn't always about standing tall in the face of danger. Sometimes, courage is humbling yourself. It's reaching out to someone who pushed you away. It's believing that connection is still possible, even when everything inside you screams to run.

Courage isn't always loud. Sometimes, it's the quiet decision to smile when you're afraid, to extend kindness even when it's risky. It's the decision to replace judgment with understanding.

It's about lifting others up, even when it's hard. It's about believing in people, especially the ones who seem the hardest to love. Courage is looking in the mirror and realizing that you have the power to change your relationships. YOU have the power to change your life. It can be scary. But finding the courage to show kindness and love will change not only your life, but will also impact the lives of others.

And ultimately, that's what we are on this earth to do.

JULIE JONES

Julie Jones is a Dallas-based business protocol and etiquette expert, corporate trainer, and sought-after public speaker. A certified graduate of the renowned Protocol School of Washington®, Julie brings a unique blend of experience as both an educator and entrepreneur. She spent fifteen years in education before building and successfully selling a plumbing company—proving her ability to lead, teach, and build from the ground up. Her passion lies in addressing a critical gap in today's professional world: the development of soft skills. Julie believes that success requires more than degrees or determination—it's about building trust, communicating with confidence, and forming lasting relationships.

Julie now works with professionals of all ages to refine their business image and interpersonal skills. Her client roster includes major corporations such as American Airlines, JW Marriott, and Grant Thornton, as well as prestigious universities like SMU, Texas Tech, and Tulane. She also coaches student-athletes, emerging professionals, and high school leaders, preparing them to thrive in the modern workplace.

Author's Website: *www.TodaysProfessionals.com*

Charity Awareness: *www.SurvivalToThrivalSeries.com*

KIMBERLY STEVENS
NEVER GIVE UP

. . . .

I was alone in the middle of San Francisco Bay, surrounded by nine-foot waves of freezing, dark water. The shore was a mile away, barely visible through the thick San Francisco fog. The 54-degree water cut through my wetsuit, making my entire body ache.

I had a decision to make—swim or be swept under the Golden Gate Bridge and out to sea.

The current was stronger than I expected, pulling me off course, dragging me closer to the Golden Gate. I knew this was coming. I had trained for it. But in that moment of cold darkness, none of my training seemed to matter. The waves weren't stopping, the cold wasn't letting up, and the shore wasn't getting any closer on its own. I was alone, afraid, and cold.

During the race briefing that morning, two thousand other swimmers and I were given one crucial instruction: When you're lost out there in the fog and waves, find and follow the orange buoy to the shore. And now my survival depended on my ability to follow that simple advice.

Swimming Alcatraz wasn't the first time I had faced a moment where I had to decide whether to push forward or let the current sweep me away to failure.

The first time I remember facing a moment like that was when I was ten years old. I had just finished my first swim meet, a "B" meet. Driving home from the meet, I was piled into my mom's station wagon with five other kids. They had all placed high enough to win ribbons, and they were all celebrating. I had nothing to show for my weekend of hard work.

It was a devastating feeling. The pain of sitting there empty-handed while the other kids celebrated was unbearable. I wanted to quit swimming. I wanted to walk away and never feel that pain again. But quitting wasn't an option. My parents had invested in me and, in return, I made a commitment to swim for one year. Since quitting wasn't an option, I decided to face the challenge.

After that day, I faced the pool and life differently. Thirteen years of competitive swimming later, I'd logged thousands of practice hours and countless miles in the pool. I ended up being the only kid from that car ride who won enough future races to become an NCAA Division One Hall of Fame Swimmer.

Swimming taught me discipline, endurance, and grit. It also trained me for something I could never have predicted: the diagnosis of citrullinemia in two of my three children. The pain I felt sitting empty-handed at ten years old was only a glimpse of the deep loss I experienced years later when my firstborn son, Braden, died at just fifteen days old from citrullinemia. That grief nearly broke me—but it also demanded a new kind of courage: the courage to believe in life again and to choose to have more children, knowing what might come.

The disease was so rare, even the prenatal testing that we did when I was thirty-five weeks along did not foresee the phone conversation I overheard when my daughter was three days old.

The conversation ended, and my husband hung up the phone and just looked at me. He was speechless, and so was I. No talking was necessary; we both knew we had to get our baby girl to the hospital immediately. Citrullinemia is a death sentence, and if history repeated itself, my new baby was going to die. I tore her from her grandmother's arms, wrapped my arms around her, hugged her tightly, and wept.

I threw some things in a bag, buckled Victoria into her car seat, sat in the back with her, and we drove to the hospital. It was deja vu with a twist. This time, I wasn't doing mouth-to-mouth to breathe for my baby; it was not the middle of the night, and we'd caught it early. This time, we knew what we were facing.

As we drove toward the hospital, I kept denying the diagnosis. No. God... no, no, NO!

We arrived at the hospital and were ushered to the ICU immediately, where doctors were already waiting for us. We got Torrey undressed, and nurses started digging for veins to draw a blood ammonia level and to start an IV. The familiar smells took me right back to Braden's hospital days, as they drew blood "stat" and hung medications on IV poles. I could not believe we were back in the hospital; this was a mistake.

How ironic that I was in the pumping room when the lab results came in. Victoria's ammonia level was 230 (normal is up to 60). With Braden, I had saved every drop of pumped milk, believing that when he got well and came home from the hospital, I'd be ready. That milk represented my hope. When he died, pouring it down the drain felt like I was pouring out my heart.

Once I heard Victoria's diagnosis, I panicked. I knew I would not survive losing another child to citrullinemia. I dumped the milk without thinking. I couldn't let myself believe again, only to have my heart broken all over again.

Then Janie, our pastor's wife, looked me in the eyes and said, "This is *not* Braden. This is VICTORIA FAITH. DO NOT GIVE UP ON THIS CHILD!"

Those were the words I needed to hear from God, although spoken through Janie. At that moment, I believed. I hoped. Somehow, I knew my baby girl was going to kindergarten, healed from Citrullinemia. Lord, I believe... "Help my unbelief," I said out loud, referencing Mark 9:24.

THE COURAGE TO BELIEVE AGAIN

Swimming trained me for this moment—to face uncertainty head-on. It trained me to step forward into the unknown of citrullinemia and believe Victoria would live. I believed God was for us and trusted Him for her healing. I hoped it would be soon, but until then, my kitchen became a laboratory and I became a mad scientist mama bear.

Back in San Francisco Bay, the current threatened to drag me under. But I fought my way back to the top of the waves, spotted the site boat and the orange buoy, gritted my teeth, and swam for dear life. Once I saw the orange buoy, there was no way I was letting it out of my sight. Tenacity drove me to shore the same way it drove me to fight for Victoria's life.

Twenty-five minutes later, I could clearly see the target beach and several orange buoys along the shore. I started sprinting and couldn't wait to get out of the cold water. Four minutes later, the water grew shallow and warmer. I stood up, ran through the chute, and heard the cheering crowd.

I couldn't quite make out what they were yelling until the water cleared from my ears, and then I heard it:

"FIRST WOMAN!"

Who, me? The one who almost drowned?

Yes. I was the tenth swimmer across the finish line and the first woman.

COURAGE IS DECIDING BEFORE
THE MOMENT COMES

When faced with uncertainty, fear, or the unknown, we don't have to start from scratch. We filter those moments through the baby steps we've already taken. I had already decided I was going to finish that race before I ever jumped into the water. That decision carried me through the waves, the cold, and the doubt.

After hard work and sheer determination, I survived and won—and so did Victoria!

Courage isn't the absence of fear. It's deciding that fear won't get the final word.

Courage is choosing to keep swimming when your body aches, your lungs burn, and the finish line feels too far away. It's standing beside a NICU bed when the numbers don't look good and holding on to the belief that your child's story isn't over.

Courage is trusting the decision you made before the storm came. It's holding onto your "why" when everything around you says, "Let go." It's choosing grit over comfort. Integrity over applause.

Hope over certainty.

Swimming taught me that persistence and grit win the race. And even after a defeat, I now know that the bravest thing I can do... is simply show up again.

Waves will come. Life will try to break me.

But I never give up.

KIMBERLY STEVENS

Kimberly is a results-driven keynote speaker who empowers teams to harness grit and gratitude to achieve their goals and exceed expectations. With a powerful personal story of resilience and a proven track record of success, she inspires organizations to take small, daily steps that create big, measurable outcomes—both professionally and personally.

As a record-holding collegiate athlete and an award-winning insurance agency owner, Kimberly understands the power of determination, adaptability, and strategic action. Her career began with sixteen years in pharmaceutical sales, helping patients navigate insurance complexities.

Her passion for turning challenges into opportunities led her *to Extend the Wav*e, a movement bringing hope, encouragement, and connection to children and families in hospitals nationwide. Inspired by the Hawkeye Wave, Extend the Wave ensures that families facing difficult medical journeys feel seen, supported, and are never alone. Through this initiative, Kimberly is proving that a simple act of kindness can create a ripple effect of impact across the nation.

Author's Website: *www.ExtendTheWave.org*

Charity Awareness: *www.ExtendTheRose.org*

LATONYA AUZENNE

THE COURAGE TO WALK AWAY

There's a moment in every survivor's journey where you stop just surviving—and you start becoming. For me, that moment came standing on the hill, holding my baby girl in my arms, blood running down my face.

They say your whole life can flash before your eyes. Mine didn't. Instead, I saw my daughter's.

I was just a teenager myself, living in the projects of Shreveport—what we called "the hill." It was a place where fights were entertainment, survival was a sport, and loyalty could turn violent in a heartbeat.

That day, two boys had gotten into it—one of them my nephew. As usual, it escalated. But this time, it got personal. A girl I thought was my friend decided she was going to "whoop everybody in the family." I told her, "No, not us. We're friends. That's kid stuff; they'll be playing again tomorrow."

But before I could finish the sentence, she hit me—with my daughter in my arms. I remember the shock. The sting. The blood. And the way my baby cried.

Something snapped inside me that day. Not in anger—but in awareness.

I realized I had been standing in a war zone, calling it community. I had mistaken trauma bonds for friendship. And worse—I had brought my child into it. Not because I was careless, but because I didn't yet believe I had a choice.

That day, I made one. I had the courage to walk away.

It didn't happen all at once. You don't just wake up one day and stop hearing the old voices in your head.

The voices that say:

- "You ain't never gonna be nothing."
- "This is just the way life is."
- "You better stay where it's safe, even if it's toxic."

Those voices had lived in me longer than I knew. I called them reality. But really, they were just echoes of pain I hadn't released yet.

I had to find the courage not only to walk away from people, but to walk away from the thoughts that kept me bound.

I call it "stinking thinking." That mental mold that grows in the corners of your mind when you've lived in survival mode too long. The kind of thinking that makes you play small, shrink back, and doubt everything good that comes your way.

I had to fight that voice with a new one.

One that said:

- "You are not your pain."
- "You are not your past."
- "You are powerful."

And let me tell you—it took courage. More courage than I ever knew I had.

Courage isn't always loud. Sometimes it's quiet. Sometimes it's a whisper that says, "You deserve better."

Leaving the hill wasn't just about changing my address. It was about changing my identity. I went from being a scared young girl who thought chaos was normal... to a woman who started imagining a different future. I started seeing visions of myself not just surviving but thriving—owning a business, helping others, speaking on stages, traveling, and living.

And today, that's exactly what I do.

But let me be real: breaking generational cycles takes serious courage. It means walking away not only from people you love but from *patterns* that feel familiar. It means getting misjudged, misunderstood, talked about—even by the people closest to you.

It's uncomfortable to be the one who breaks the mold. But I chose to walk away from the known—the noise, the cycles, the chaos— and into the unknown. I chose healing over hurt. Growth over comfort. Legacy over limits.

That's what courage looks like.

Today, I help others find that same courage. I speak. I coach. I support my community. And I'm proud to say I'm a certified instructor with the Napoleon Hill Foundation—teaching the same principles that helped me renew my mind and rewrite my life.

Because the truth is: courage is contagious. When you see someone who looks like you—sounds like you—who has been through what you've been through—rise up anyway. It shifts something. It gives permission.

That's why I share my story—not for sympathy but for strength. Not because I live in the past, but because I know someone else is still there.

And if my story can be a bridge for them to cross over from survival to thrival, then every tear, every scar, every setback was worth it.

If you're reading this and you feel stuck, hear me: You are not crazy for wanting more. You are not weak for walking away. You are not selfish for choosing peace.

That's not weakness. That's **courage**.

Courage is deciding to think differently. To love yourself enough to say, "No more." To believe, even if you've never seen it, that joy is possible.

You are not alone. You're not too far gone. And yes—you absolutely can.

If I can rise from the hill... You can rise from wherever you are, too.

And I'll be here, cheering you on every courageous step of the way.

LATONYA AUZENNE

Latonya Auzenne is a purpose-driven entrepreneur, certified Napoleon Hill instructor, and NeuroChange Practitioner dedicated to transforming lives through mindset mastery and business empowerment. As co-owner of IRIDE Transportation, she helps deliver safe and reliable non-emergency medical transportation across Louisiana. Latonya is also a passionate speaker, author, and direct sales leader, using her voice and personal story to inspire others to rise above adversity and reclaim their power.

Raised in Shreveport and now rooted in Lafayette, she brings a deep commitment to faith, integrity, and community impact. Latonya serves as Secretary of the Greater Southwest Louisiana Black Chamber of Commerce, where she champions minority-owned businesses and economic equity. Through workshops, coaching, and public service, she equips others with the tools to live their dreams and create lasting success. With a heart for healing and a bold vision for the future, Latonya is living proof that with belief and action, transformation is possible.

Author's Website: *www.CEOLatonya.com*

Charity Awareness: *www.CasaStLandry.org*

LAURIE K. SCHWARTZ

THE COURAGE TO SUCCEED: MY DAUGHTER'S STORY

We have three bright, beautiful children. My husband and I are so blessed. Our first son has a photographic memory—an excellent student. Our second son is also a bright student and excels academically. Then there is our long-awaited daughter. We were so excited to have her. I was awake during her delivery, eagerly anticipating the birth of my beautiful child. When the doctor announced, "It's a girl," I nearly jumped off the delivery table to do a dance. That would have been rather messy, however, since I delivered her.

Our little girl is so sweet, so adorable, so lovable, and very sharp. As she grew, she consistently could run circles around her brothers in intuition and common sense. From a very young age, she showed exceptional emotional intelligence, awareness, and critical thinking that set her apart—traits no standardized test could ever measure. Her strength of spirit was unmistakable, even then and still today.

So, how is it possible that this darling, competent child, now in the third grade, brought home the results of the California Achievement Test (CAT) with scores that didn't reflect her abilities? Her father and I were baffled, not because we didn't believe in her, but because the test results didn't align with the bright, curious learner we saw every day.

Determined to understand, I scheduled a meeting with the school counselor, someone I also trusted, having known her outside of school. She provided possible explanations, and I left somewhat reassured. Our daughter completed third and fourth grades successfully. Her teachers praised her work ethic and eagerness to learn. Her report cards were consistently solid.

Then came fifth grade, and the CATs returned. Again, the scores were not representative of the engaged, capable student we knew. I met with the school counselor once more. That's when we learned how much weight the CAT scores carried. Despite her classroom achievements, these scores would determine her placement in middle school, a new and different environment.

When our daughter began middle school, she was understandably confused. She had been placed in a lower academic track, away from her friends. She was assigned to a class that, to the best of my memory, was part of a program where students sampled both Spanish and French before selecting one. While the setup was intended to be exploratory, it was reserved for students in lower tracks. We questioned why this opportunity wasn't offered to all students.

Our daughter noted that the students in her class were not performing at the same academic level as she was. Once again, I found myself advocating for her in the counselor's office. The counselor explained that placement was based solely on CAT scores, not report cards. I stood firm, asking for a placement that reflected her true performance. Eventually, the counselor agreed, with the caveat that I would take full responsibility if she struggled. I gladly accepted.

She didn't struggle. She thrived! Once again, I want to praise my daughter for showing such strength and resilience to succeed.

Most people would have quit by now, and I am so honored to learn from a child who would never quit.

Through sixth, seventh, and eighth grades, she excelled. But then came the CATs again in eighth grade. Unfortunately, the same pattern repeated. Despite great grades and a growing and glowing list of accomplishments, the test results threatened to misplace her once again. This time, I didn't wait. Much like when I was awake through my daughter's birth in the delivery room, I would stay awake through this whole process to make sure we delivered a successful outcome. Before high school even began, I made an appointment with the new principal, who was also at a new school.

The principal was a military man, formal and precise in his demeanor. He wanted to know why I requested a meeting before school began. I explained our concerns and shared her academic track record. He listened carefully and agreed that her class placement should reflect her abilities. True to his word, she was placed appropriately and succeeded. She was later invited into the National Honor Society.

By eleventh grade, we were optimistic. She had earned her place among the top students. When it was time for the PSATs, we felt hopeful that the testing would finally align with her performance. But when the results arrived, we were again stunned. Her combined score was much lower than expected. We knew she was more than a number, but we also understood the implications of these scores.

At this point, we shifted our focus to understanding rather than reacting. A good friend recommended a specialist from a private school known for assisting students with learning differences. We scheduled a meeting, and he agreed to work with her and evaluate the deeper cause of the disconnect.

We also consulted an Educational Psychologist. After a series of evaluations, we received insights that finally clarified everything.

The most enlightening discovery was how our daughter's brain processed information. You, too, may have a child who faces challenges when it comes to testing, and these challenges may stem from learning processes. Unlike the traditional linear structure that standardized tests rely on, her mind operated in a circular, holistic fashion. Imagine brainstorming with a topic at the center, surrounded by subtopics, which in turn connect to more ideas—a dynamic web of thoughts rather than a straight line.

This unique processing style was a gift. It allowed her to make creative and intuitive connections, but it also meant that she needed more time to organize her thoughts in the rigid formats required by standardized tests. She didn't lack intelligence—she needed a different structure and pace.

We provided these insights to the tutor, who now had a clearer understanding of how to prepare her for success. With the right tools, the right pace, and the right strategies, she had what she needed for the SATs.

In twelfth grade, she was granted the opportunity to take the untimed SATs in an environment that honored her learning style. For the first time, she walked into a test with a sense of empowerment. This wasn't just about scores. It was about embracing how she learns and knowing that she had the right to succeed in her own way.

And that's truly what courage looks like in an individual.

Courage is continuing to believe in yourself even when the world measures you unfairly. Courage is showing up, again and again, even when the system doesn't understand you. Courage is discovering who you are and owning it unapologetically.

This is her story. This is her triumph.

And yet, this was only the beginning. Just when we thought the greatest battles had been fought, an unimaginable twist tested everything we had learned. From misplaced SATs to administrative hurdles and another round of advocacy, the journey ahead would show us the true power of persistence and perspective. But in every setback, we uncovered strength. And in every delay, we found purpose. The courage that carried us through the CATs would now face the institutions that hold the keys to higher education.

These experiences shaped my daughter's college path and changed my life as a parent. They became a defining lesson in advocacy, faith, and forgiveness. If you're a parent or student reading this, may you find strength in this story and feel empowered to advocate courageously.

You truly have the courage to succeed. I believe in you.

LAURIE K. SCHWARTZ

Laurie Koller Schwartz is a passionate advocate, devoted mother, and accomplished business leader. She is a graduate of the University of Baltimore in Maryland. She and her late husband, Michael, moved to Scottsdale, Arizona, where she rehabilitated and sold homes. Prior to that, she was a member of the Board of Directors of the International Association of Near-Death Studies (IANDS) and later the founder of NOVA—the Network Of eVolutionary Advancement. In both of those capacities, she coordinated national and international conferences on death, near-death studies, and reincarnation. Her professional strength is matched only by her fierce dedication to her family of three children, daughter-in-law, son-in-law, and five grandchildren.

Laurie strives to inspire readers with themes of resilience, courage, and the power of persistence. Her contributions to *The Book of Survival to Thrival* spotlight her belief in fighting for what's right—even when the system falls short—and her commitment to empowering others with compassion, strategy, and unwavering love. She lives by the principle that true success is measured by the lives we lift along the way.

Charity Awareness: *www.HOV.org*

DR. LÉ SANTHA NAIDOO

FORGED IN FIRE

Trust isn't just a word—it's a lifeline. This truth hit me with startling clarity one night when the line between survival and death became razor-thin, and courage was the only currency that mattered.

As an Emergency Medical Technician in Lawrence, Massachusetts, I'd seen my share of emergencies. But nothing prepares you for the moment when you become part of the danger you're supposed to be managing.

Lawrence wasn't just any city—it was a place of stark contrasts, where vibrant Hispanic communities existed alongside glaring disparities in wealth, significant violent crime, and a bustling interstate cutting through decades-old neighborhoods. It was vibrant yet gritty, filled with stories of struggle and perseverance.

The call that night was for a gunshot wound. Standard procedure: Assess for scene safety, assess the patient, stabilize, and transport. My partner and I arrived to find what appeared to be a controlled scene—tense but manageable. The police who arrived before us gave the all clear that the scene was safe. The initial panic had subsided, giving way to that fragile calm that settles after chaos. We were focused, ready to do what we'd been trained for. Save lives. That was the plan, anyway.

Then came the shots. Two distinct cracks that tore through the air and shattered our illusion of safety. In that instant, everything changed. This wasn't just about treating the wounded anymore. This was about survival—ours as much as theirs.

I locked eyes with my partner. No words were necessary. Our silent understanding spoke volumes: We need to watch each other's backs. In that moment, I understood the weight of trust between EMTs and the police who were supposed to be protecting us with a clarity that no training manual could ever convey.

The scene was hellish. Blood pooled beneath the wounded, gushing from gunshot wounds, we had to triage with precision and speed. We moved through the chaos like clockwork, controlling bleeding, protecting ourselves from exposure, and assessing whether patients were even alive. The screams, the metallic tang of blood, the flashing lights—it was a surreal, high-stakes nightmare.

There was no room for hesitation, no margin for error. Every movement was deliberate, every decision a race against time. I felt the weight of lives in my hands, quite literally, as I applied pressure to wounds, knowing that seconds could mean the difference between life and death.

What I remember most vividly was the paradox of it all: the overwhelming urge to run away and the absolute conviction that I couldn't. Wouldn't. That's what courage is, I realized. Not fearlessness, but action in the face of fear. Moving forward when every instinct screams retreat.

In those moments of crisis, something fundamental shifts inside you. The world narrows to what's directly in front of you. Your senses heighten. Time simultaneously speeds up and slows down. And somewhere in that twisted reality, you find a version of yourself you didn't know existed—one capable of functioning amid terror, of making life-or-death decisions when your own life hangs in the balance.

That night changed me. It wasn't just the violence or the intensity. It was the raw, unfiltered realization that in this line of work, your partner isn't just a colleague—they're your lifeline. You trust them with your life, just as they trust you with theirs. In those moments of chaos, that bond becomes unbreakable, forged in the crucible of shared danger and unspoken understanding.

For years afterward, I carried the weight of that night. The sounds, the smells, the fear that had coursed through my veins. But I also carried something else: the knowledge that I hadn't broken. That when faced with mortal danger, I'd stayed. I'd done my job. I'd chosen courage over fear.

This is the untold story of emergency medicine—not just the high-stakes medical interventions, but the inner battles we fight while performing them. The struggle to remain calm when your heart is pounding out of your chest. The discipline to follow protocols when instinct urges you to flee. The humanity to see the person beneath the trauma, even as you fight to save them.

I've come to believe that this is the difference between surviving and thriving: the courage to walk toward what scares you, to understand that fear isn't something to avoid but something to move through. That night in Lawrence could have broken me. It could have been the end of my career, a traumatic event that sent me running from medicine forever.

Instead, it became a cornerstone of my identity—not because of the danger, but because of how I responded to it. I discovered a reservoir of courage I didn't know I possessed. I learned that when put to the test, I could function under pressure that would cripple most. This wasn't bravado or recklessness; it was the quiet confidence that comes from facing your worst fears and finding yourself still standing on the other side.

The journey from survival to thriving isn't about eliminating fear or hardship. It's about developing the capacity to face them head-on. It's understanding that courage isn't the absence of fear but the triumph over it. It's recognizing that our greatest growth often comes from our most challenging moments.

Years later, as a physician, I draw on that night regularly. When faced with difficult diagnoses, challenging patients, or my own moments of doubt, I remember the EMT who stood her ground when bullets flew. I tap into that same courage—the courage to stay present when it would be easier to distance myself, to engage fully with suffering when it would be simpler to detach.

This is how we move from merely surviving to truly thriving: by recognizing that our hardest moments don't define us—our response to them does. By understanding that courage isn't a quality reserved for heroes in extraordinary circumstances, but a muscle we can develop through daily acts of bravery. By knowing, deep in our bones, that we are capable of far more than we imagine.

That night in Lawrence taught me that thriving isn't about avoiding the fire—it's about walking through it and emerging transformed. It's about trusting the process, trusting others, and most importantly, trusting yourself. Because when you know you can face the worst and remain standing, nothing can stop you from living your best.

LÉ SANTHA NAIDOO

A revolutionary force in medicine, Dr. Lé Santha Naidoo transcends traditional healthcare with her triple board certifications and visionary approach to wellness. As founder of Avyanna Wellness Institute and "The 100 Club," she delivers bespoke health optimization to an exclusive clientele, transforming lives through personalized and precision care. Rising from adversity to international acclaim, her journey to becoming a pioneering physician and her health advocacy captivate audiences worldwide on major television networks (*NBC*, *ABC*, *CBS*, *FOX*) and global stages. Her bestselling memoir, *Fat to Fabulous*, stands as a testament to her extraordinary resilience.

Receiving many honors for her community service, leadership, and ranking as America's Best Concierge Physician, Dr. Lé Santha's brilliance extends beyond medicine—she's a fierce mentor, philanthropist, and catalyst for human potential. Her unique blend of medical mastery and profound compassion creates not just physical healing, but profound life transformation.

Author's Website: *www.LeSantha.com*

Charity Awareness: *www.MercyChefs.com*

LISA CANNON

BEHIND LOCKED DOORS

....

The year was 1996. I was thirty-one, living in England, and temporarily staying with family. It was supposed to be a fresh chapter—a new beginning in a country I'd always wanted to explore more deeply. I had taken a job at a therapeutic school that served children from the foster care system, ages eleven to nineteen, many of whom were dealing with severe behavioral and emotional challenges. I saw it as an opportunity to make a difference. I believed in the resilience of children. I still do. But I wasn't prepared for what would happen next, or how deeply it would shake me.

The school operated in shifts, and staff were periodically required to stay overnight with the students. It was my turn to stay the night. The building was structured more like a home than a school, with individual offices that were always locked and common areas where staff and students shared meals and time together.

That morning, after a long and emotionally charged night, I walked into the office to grab some paperwork. The hallway leading to the office was quiet. Too quiet. As I turned the corner, a young boy—probably no older than fifteen—was standing outside the office door. He had apparently been waiting for me. The staff had mentioned he wanted to apologize for something he had said to me the day before. I took a deep breath and approached him, reminding myself that he was just a child who had been through more than most adults could imagine.

He reached out his hand, and I took it cautiously, ready to receive his apology. But instead of a handshake, he yanked me toward him with terrifying force. His grip was vice-like—too strong for me to pull away. His face twisted into an expression I can only describe as angry, entitled, and consumed. He began using graphic, vulgar language while rubbing himself against me, sneering into my face, enjoying my terror (which I later learned was called Frotteuristic disorder).

I froze.

In that moment, I wasn't a professional. I wasn't a caregiver. I wasn't even a woman who knew how to protect herself. I was simply scared—paralyzed by disbelief, unable to react fast enough. My breath caught in my throat. My heart raced. I couldn't scream, only whisper, "Stop," which seemed to empower him even more.

The next few seconds felt like years. Then, suddenly, another teacher—a male staff member—came through a locked door into the hallway and saw what was happening. He shouted and pulled the boy off me. I stumbled backward, ran into the nearby office, and locked the door behind me. I collapsed onto a chair, shaking and gasping for air, trying to process what had just happened.
I had never felt so powerless in my life.

What followed should have been a supportive debriefing, an investigation, a show of solidarity. But instead, it was silence. The school's psychiatrist told me not to make a big deal out of it. He said, "These things happen here. The boys have been through so much—they act out. Just try to move on."

But how could I?

I did what I was taught to do in moments of distress: I documented it. I wrote down everything—every word, every movement, every feeling. I poured it out onto a piece of paper inside the staff incident ledger, cataloging my fear, my trauma, my shame. It wasn't just a report—it was a lifeline. My truth laid bare in black ink.

But the next day, I found out that the page had been torn out.

They erased my experience. They silenced my truth.

I didn't return to work for more than two weeks. I couldn't eat. I couldn't sleep. Every time I saw a teenager on the street, I would cross to the other side, trembling, haunted by the memory. The boy's face would flash before my eyes. I'd relive the moment over and over again, wondering what I could have done differently, blaming myself for not being stronger, louder, faster.

Eventually, I filed a police report. I couldn't stay silent any longer. I needed to reclaim a piece of myself. I never returned to that school again.

Later, I learned that the same boy had attacked three other women before and at least one after me.

That truth devastated me.

Not just because of what he had done—but because I knew that if the system had listened, if they had acted when these women came forward, more women might have been spared—I may have been spared. My voice could have prevented more pain. But they ripped my words out of the book. They chose the comfort of denial over the courage of accountability.

For a long time, I felt broken. I didn't know I was suffering from PTSD. I just thought I was weak. That I couldn't "move on" like they said I should. I didn't talk about it with anyone except a few close friends. Shame wrapped around me like a fog—dense, inescapable, and quiet. I kept thinking, "It wasn't that bad. Others have been through worse." But that's the dangerous lie we tell ourselves when we're trying to survive.

It took years for me to reclaim my confidence—to trust myself around people again, to walk into a room without flinching at a sudden movement, to believe I was safe in my own skin. Healing didn't happen overnight. It happened slowly, in layers—through journaling, through therapy, through letting others in.

Looking back now, I realize the strength it took just to breathe through that trauma. To choose not to bury it inside me, but to face it and eventually use it to grow.

I share this story not to dwell in the darkness of that day, but to bring light to a truth many live with in silence: trauma doesn't just pass with time. It festers in the quiet if we don't give it voice.

So, to anyone reading this who has felt dismissed, silenced, erased—please hear me: your story matters. Your feelings are valid. And your healing is possible.

You don't have to carry it alone. Talk to someone. Write it down. Seek support. Seek justice if you can. But most importantly, seek peace for yourself.

We don't get to choose what happens to us, but we do get to choose what we do next. I chose to fight my way out of fear, to speak, even if my voice shakes, and to hold compassion for myself and others walking through similar storms.

And while I may never forget what happened in that hallway, I no longer live there. I've found the key to the door that once locked me in fear—and I've used it to set myself free.

Today, I stand as a woman who has weathered the storm—who turned wounds into wisdom and pain into purpose. I am a guide for those who have lost their way, a gentle voice reminding them of who they truly are.

I dedicate my time to supporting others with empathy and intention. It is my deep professional calling to guide individuals toward greater clarity and fulfillment in both their personal and professional lives.

Whether I speak to one heart or many, my message remains the same: there is a path beyond the struggle—a way through the fog —leading to joy, to purpose, and to a life fully awakened.

LISA CANNON

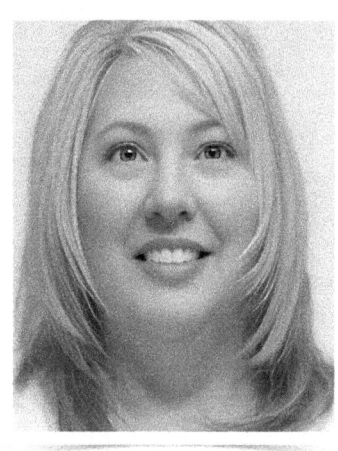

Lisa Cannon is the founder of 4SuccessU, a coaching and consulting company committed to helping women entrepreneurs build profitable, purpose-driven businesses. With over twenty years of experience in coaching, training, consulting, and public speaking, Lisa has empowered thousands of professionals to gain clarity, confidence, and direction through her signature blend of strategic systems, intuitive insight, and practical mindset tools. Having navigated her own share of personal and professional transitions, Lisa brings a deep, authentic passion for helping others step into their next level.

Her specialty lies in guiding clients through pivotal transitions—helping them shift from stuck to strategic, scattered to focused, and overwhelmed to thriving. Lisa's coaching style is straightforward and results-driven, yet always grounded in empathy. She's also a published author and widely respected for her no-fluff, heart-centered approach. Her motto? Life is short—show up boldly, lead with purpose, and become the greatest version of yourself.

Author's Website: *www.4SuccessU.com*

Charity Awareness: *www.SurvivalToThrivalSeries.com*

M.A. FULTS

COURAGE TO LIVE

FEAR & COURAGE

It is often said that courage is facing danger in spite of fear. I can't say I've been really fearful very often. There was once when I was around ten years old and I'd followed two brothers to a cliff face with a narrow track going up its side. The two of them quickly went up, but I stopped about halfway when the track narrowed to, what looked to me, about two inches. I'm sure it wasn't that narrow, but my mind said it was. I ended up backing down, too scared to continue.

Another time, around eight years old, I was watching a scary movie with my brother. It was the 1932 horror film *Murders in the Rue Morgue,* with Bela Lugosi. It scared me so much that I couldn't finish watching it that first time with my brother, but the next year, I faced my fear and forced myself to finish it, albeit with two other friends.

The final time when I let fear get the best of me was when I succumbed to claustrophobia, refusing to go into an MRI face down, requiring my face to be wedged into a cushioned hole. I'd developed a phobia of having my face covered, specifically my nose and mouth, during my time in the Navy. (Needless to say, the "mask mandate" was extremely difficult for me to follow.)

When stationed on a ship, all the sailors are required to have a gas mask at their General Quarters (GQ) station, specifically for use during drills. Even though the nation was not at war, we drilled and practiced for battle, including chemical and biological warfare. That meant donning a gas mask during drills.

At first, not a problem for me, but as time passed, as the bridge (my GQ station) heated up, as breathing in the mask seemed to become difficult... I developed a phobia of something covering my face and, seemingly, restricting my breathing. Face down in an MRI machine, with my torso completely surrounded, I felt as if my breathing was constricted. I tried a few times to go through it, but even with drugs, the claustrophobia won out, so each time I left without completing the procedure.

Fear got the best of me those three times. But each time, while I didn't immediately overcome the fear, eventually I persevered—I continued on, albeit back down the track, conquering the fear of a scary movie a year later and consenting to an MRI a few years later, although this time face up. But what about the times when fear rose its ugly head and I did not freeze, run from the room, or refuse to go forward?

DEATH & COURAGE

To most people in the world, cancer is one of today's scariest diagnoses—it is a "death sentence" and only "aggressive treatment" can prolong your life. While it is a terrible disease, cancer has been reversed and, for many people, cured through natural and supernatural means.

In 2012, I was diagnosed with Stage 2b (yes, "to be or not to be" did run through my mind) breast cancer... the big "C." Only I don't serve a God smaller than cancer, no matter how big the world sees cancer to be. That's mainly because death, or dying, doesn't frighten me. I've known since age twelve that I would die one day because my sixteen-year-old brother died in a car accident that year. I realized that if he could die that young, anyone could, including me. So, for me, the word cancer only meant that I had a fight on my hands. Thankfully, not one I would fight alone.

DOCTORS & COURAGE

I had four doctors involved with my fight, and they all were focused on "keeping me alive a while longer." When they saw and heard my smiling, unconcerned reaction, I think they all thought I didn't fully comprehend how serious this diagnosis was.

The young doctor who did the biopsy could tell that the cells were cancerous, though he couldn't tell me outright—I'd have to wait for the lab results. His face, though, did tell me. It was so serious, so concerned, and I felt sorry for him even as I chuckled. With a smiling face, I told him, "I am okay, and I am going to be okay, no matter what. I've known for decades that I would die someday. But I believe in a God who lives and who has made a way for me to live, even after this body dies. So, it's okay, doc."

The next doctor, an oncologist, was equally as serious. Again, I laughed and joked with her a bit, then told her much the same as I told the first doctor. She ended up smiling, too, because I think she knew that, yes, I was going to be okay.

The third was the surgeon who performed a lumpectomy. He was young and, as it happened, would be heading to the war in Afghanistan as a surgeon four months later. He remained focused on the surgery, with little thought beyond that, no frowns or concern on his face. Hmm, maybe that was just a surgeon's way —no emotion, no before-and-after, just complete the now.

The fourth doctor, the oncologist who would see me through the next seven years, was very serious. He treated my belief system as claptrap, a bunch of nonsense. For him, I needed to follow his instructions and prescriptions to the letter. If I didn't, I would die, or, at the least, die sooner. He wanted me to live, but that would only happen if I listened to him. He prescribed three different chemotherapy treatments, two for six treatments over eighteen weeks, and a third chemotherapy for eighteen treatments over one full year.

Having read up, ten years prior, on the effects of chemo, I hesitated, letting him know I was not comfortable receiving that toxic poison into my body. He continued to insist and even became angry. Finally, I told him I would pray about it, asking God that if I was to do the chemo, then He had to give me peace about it.

That Sunday, I asked for prayer, and as soon as the request for peace was made, I had it. It ticked me off because I really didn't want to go through chemo, but I had received absolute peace, so I agreed to the treatments. Surprised, but pleased, the oncologist helped me through the worst of the side effects with targeted medications.

LOVE & COURAGE

Fear can, and all too often does, overcome us. However, I learned long ago from scripture that "Perfect love casts out all fear" (1 John 4:18). Whether my aversion to chemo was based on fear or not, that perfect peace sustained me throughout that long year. And whenever fear began to raise its head, I turned to my Lord, saying to myself, "God is Love, His love, His Perfect love, casts out all fear." And that fear would be gone.

I fought cancer and have been cancer-free for twelve years now, but no one fights cancer alone. I was assisted in that fight by many doctors, multiple nurses and physician assistants, along with many loved ones, family, and friends. But I was sustained, carried through it all, by my faith in God: Father, Jesus, and Holy Spirit. The Three-in-One were with me, comforting and caring, loving and supporting. I believe that without them, I would not be alive on this earth today. Actually, without them, I wouldn't want to be alive, here and now.

The old hymn, *Because He Lives*, provides the why behind the courage I've had through my six decades of being a Christ follower. *"Because He lives, I can face tomorrow. Because He lives, all fear is gone. Because I know, I know, He holds the future. And life is worth the living. Just because He lives."* The "He" is Jesus, and millions have testified, and still do testify, that He lives within them. Gratefully, I'm one of those millions.

One short chapter cannot divulge all the trying times, pain, and grief that one person goes through in their life. Nor can it provide multiple good times, triumphant times, joyful, laughter-filled times. It's life, and we all thankfully go through it together. The blessed ones know this, embrace this, and do life, the laughter-filled and tear-filled life, with one another.

One day this body of mine will die, of that I'm certain. But my spirit and soul will continue to live, and that gives me the courage to face whatever may come my way. Yes, I will most likely have many more struggles, difficulties, and even tragedies to face and navigate through, but love, most notably God's love, will be my source, my root, my grounding. His love gives me the courage to live.

M.A. FULTS

Born into an Army family, and with thirty-nine years serving in and then working for the US Navy, Fults spent many years traveling and living in foreign countries, including four years in Tehran, Iran.

She holds a BFA in Drama Production from the University of Arizona and an MS in Management from the Naval Postgraduate School in Monterey, CA. After retiring for the second time in 2022, Fults continued her lifelong pursuit of learning while embarking on her newfound passion for heart healing, financial advising, and life coaching. She has been blessed with one son.

Charity Awareness: *www.Compassion.com*

MARANDA CARLILE

TWO ENDINGS, ONE FIRE, & THE COURAGE TO BUILD AGAIN

Sometimes the fire that burns you… is the same one that lights the path forward.

There are moments in life when you realize you've outgrown your surroundings, not because you're ungrateful, but because you're ready.

I didn't see it at first. I was working hard, juggling multiple roles: trying to build a wellness practice, doing aesthetics, integrative health, and offering medical marijuana cards as a side gig, working part-time in a rural clinic, and part-time in a pain clinic. I wasn't chasing recognition. I just wanted to make a difference.

Back in December 2019, I'd quietly started Astra Health and Wellness. I had big dreams, but the pandemic hit, and momentum vanished. I eventually began offering medical cannabis cards and neurotoxins in 2021, which helped fund a new opportunity that soon appeared.

I invested in a new venture with two entrepreneurs who were launching a clinic. Our conversations centered around words like "equal partner," "shared leadership," "partnership," and "independence." From the beginning, the language used led me to believe we were building something collaboratively.

When a proposal to join them was offered, I was clear: "I'm not interested in working for someone." I was assured that I'd be my own boss, responsible for what I earned, rewarded for what I built. A shared load between providers. The phrase "equal partner" was used more than once.

So, I jumped in, trusting and believing we shared a vision of co-creation.

I poured everything into that vision, financially, emotionally, and energetically. I sold assets, reinvested profits, and committed myself fully. I believed in the mission. I trusted in the people. But belief and trust aren't always enough. Because when things aren't clear in the beginning and laid out in a contract from the get-go, it turns into a "he said, she said."

As the months passed, things began to shift. Promises blurred, expectations changed. Conversations grew tense. My questions, once welcomed, became inconvenient. The "contract" I finally received wasn't a partnership agreement at all; it was a lease. Conversations shared in confidence among "the partners" and with the business in mind were later interpreted differently or relayed to staff in ways I hadn't intended.

That was the first fracture.

I left with grace, but not without grief. I had given so much to something that, in the end, wasn't truly mine. I negotiated my exit, minimized the damage, and turned inward.

That's when Astra started becoming more than a side gig. It wasn't just a business anymore; it was a reclamation. For the first time, I wasn't asking for a role. I was writing one.

But life wasn't done testing me yet.

Just as I was finding my footing after leaving that practice, I walked into a contract renewal meeting at the rural clinic I had served faithfully for over six years, through the COVID-19 pandemic and beyond. In the years leading up to that meeting, I had repeatedly asked to increase my hours, hoping to work and serve more. Instead, the practice manager hired another provider we really didn't need.

I'd worked there since 2017. I was part of the community. My patient outcomes were strong. I had never received a patient complaint. I mentored students, supported the team, and showed up every week with integrity and commitment, giving it my all, and expecting nothing but a chance to keep doing what I loved.

Instead, I was told, without notice, that my services were no longer needed and that my contract would not be renewed.

It was described as a "business decision."

There were no thank yous, no warning. No goodbyes to my patients or the staff I worked beside. Just a quiet walk to my car and the kind of silence that stings more than words.

I later learned that assumptions had been made about my future, conclusions drawn without my input, and conversations had without my presence. What I do know is this: the people I worked beside, the ones I had hoped would advocate for me, did not.

And interestingly, some of them experienced similar endings in the years after I left. But theirs came with softer landings, severance, and resignation.

Mine did not.

Two doors had closed within months of each other. And I was left staring at a blank page, wondering if I was the common denominator.

That's the thing no one tells you about these moments. You don't just grieve the loss of income or routine—you question your own worth.

You start to believe that maybe the problem... is you.

But it wasn't.

Sometimes, your light blinds people who were never meant to walk beside you. And sometimes it takes being pushed out of the old to step fully into the new.

Those two departures, one professional and one personal, became the fire that forged Astra into something real. Not just a name, but a mission. A declaration. A place where I could show up fully, as a provider, a leader, and a woman committed to root-cause healing.

It wasn't an easy season. I was grieving. I was afraid. I had to pull myself out of bed most days. But I also felt something new stirring: freedom.

I was no longer asking for permission.

I was creating my own table.

"Courage isn't loud. Sometimes, it's the quiet decision to begin again."

Thrival isn't born from comfort—it's forged in the fire of what you won't tolerate again. I didn't just rebuild. I reimagined everything.

I stopped trying to prove my worth to people who didn't value it. I stopped quieting my instincts in rooms that confused honesty with opposition. I stopped doubting myself every time someone else couldn't see my vision.

Instead, I got to work. Not just on the clinic, but on myself.

I took my pain and turned it into process. I mapped out the kind of care I had always wanted to deliver, care that listens, educates, and empowers. I studied systems, built protocols, and designed patient journeys that prioritized clarity, connection, and true healing.

My first few days in business were humbling. Some days I saw one patient. Some days, none. But I knew this work mattered.

I was finally serving from a place of peace, not pressure.

The patients who found me weren't just looking for another provider; they were looking for answers, and they were ready to do the work. I didn't need a packed schedule to prove I was on the right path.

The depth of the work validated the direction.

With every chart, every conversation, every follow-up, I was reminded: This is what it was all for. You don't need their validation when you've built something far greater.

I didn't need a lifeline; I needed a moment to realize I was already standing on solid ground.

Looking back, I don't carry bitterness, I carry boundaries. I didn't need closure because I found clarity.

And I don't regret those chapters. They refined me.

They taught me how to trust my gut, stand in my values, and never again trade peace for approval. I moved from grief to grit, from endings to empowerment. A true turning point in the new blueprint being forged.

Maybe your goodbye is still unfolding. Maybe you're in that quiet, uncomfortable space between what's ended and what hasn't quite begun. Maybe you've started to feel the nudge, an inner knowing that something isn't right anymore, even if you can't fully explain why.

You don't need all the answers to move forward. You only need one kind of clarity, the kind that tells you this no longer serves you. And that's enough.

Because the truth is: Your value doesn't diminish just because someone else failed to recognize it. Your worth is not dependent on their invitation, their validation, or their ability to see your vision.

What feels like failure might just be alignment in disguise. Sometimes the ground has to fall out from under us so we finally learn how to build our own.

"You're not too much. You're just in the wrong room."

"You're not crazy. You're clear. And that scares people."

"You're not difficult. You're discerning."

"You're not broken. You're just done shrinking."

If something no longer honors your value, you are allowed to outgrow it. And when you do, what you create next will carry your signature strength.

Mine did.

And it all started the moment I stopped asking for a seat at someone else's table and decided to build one of my own.

And if you're standing on that edge, wondering if it's time, wondering if you're ready, let me say this:

You are.

And when you step forward, not only will you rebuild…

You'll rise.

MARANDA CARLILE

Maranda Carlile, FNP-BC, is a board-certified Family Nurse Practitioner, TEDx speaker, international presenter, and founder of Astra Health and Wellness. She helps high-performing women and men rebalance hormones, heal the gut, restore energy, and reclaim their health through a personalized, root-cause approach. She serves as a cohort leader for the BHRT Academy, is recognized for her expertise in functional lab interpretation and gut health, and brings over fourteen years of trauma-informed care experience as a Sexual Assault Nurse Examiner (SANE). Blending science with deep empathy, Maranda understands how being dismissed when something feels off can affect your ability to show up—for yourself, your family, your relationships, and your career. She believes you deserve answers that go deeper than surface-level labs or symptom suppression.

As a wife and mother of three, Maranda knows the power of showing up fully—for yourself and those you love. Whether on stage or in the clinic, her mission is to take a comprehensive, whole-body approach to help you feel safe, seen, and whole again—through advanced lab testing, hormone optimization, and gut healing.

Author's Website: *www.AstraHealthAndWellness.com*
Charity Awareness: *www.NationalMSSociety.org*

MARIS SEGAL & KEN ASHBY

MEETING COURAGE

Ken: It was the kind of night that didn't just surround me; it pressed in from all sides. Dark. Cold. Heavy with silence, broken only by the hum of tires on asphalt and the occasional groan of the wind scraping across the high mountain pass. I was deep in the Rocky Mountains, somewhere between where I'd been and where I was going, neither of which felt like home. The sign had said Interstate 70 East, toward Denver, but in that moment, direction meant nothing. Because while I was high in the mountains, the truth was, I had never felt lower in my life.

A few hours earlier, I had left my sons standing on the side of the lawn next to the street at their university. It should've been a proud moment—seeing my grown sons at college, seeing them step into their future. But pride wasn't what I felt. Not even close. They were shouting—no, screaming, "We will never speak to you again!"

Their voices cut through me like knives through fabric, ragged, raw, and wounded. And I deserved every word. I had just told them that their mother and I were separating. It wasn't a shock—they knew things hadn't been great—but hearing it out loud, seeing their father drive away alone, that moment became a line in the sand they never asked for and never wanted. And me? I was already cracked, and this... shattered me.

I didn't have a plan. I had a car, a tank of gas, and a thousand-mile ache in my soul, stretching from California to Colorado. You can't outrun what's behind you if you keep putting it in front of you. The road may have been winding, but the thoughts in my head were relentless and straight: You blew it. You failed them. You failed her. You failed yourself. Courage? That wasn't anywhere near me and certainly not in my head. I didn't even think about it, and probably, in the shadow world around me at that moment, couldn't have even defined it!

The higher I climbed into the mountains, the darker it became—both outside and within. The air thinned, my chest tightened, the road narrowed, and the guardrails mocked me with their flimsy promise of protection. It felt like the world had hollowed out, and I was just a passenger in some cruel simulation.

That's when the thought came: You could end it now.

Just like that. Quick. Clean. A sharp turn of the wheel across the yellow line and disappear over the edge. The canyon below would welcome me in silence. No more guilt. No more pain. No more echo of my sons' voices ricocheting through my skull.

But then—another thought followed, just as quickly, just as powerfully: What if you take someone else with you? It was a whisper. Soft, but unshakable. What if, in trying to escape my own pain, I destroyed someone else's life? A stranger in the oncoming lane, just driving through the night, suddenly caught in my personal wreckage. And that's when I saw it.

A small, glowing sign up ahead: Scenic Pull Out. Nothing fancy —just a patch of gravel, a faded picnic table, and one flickering light that had no business still working in a place like that. But it called to me. Instead of turning left into the abyss, I turned right into the pause. I pulled in, parked, turned off the engine—and listened.

Silence. And in that silence, something unexpected happened: I breathed. Not the shallow, frantic breathing of panic—but something deeper. As if my lungs remembered their job. My heart slowed just enough to let something else slip in. A single, quiet thought: Choose life. It wasn't shouted. It didn't thunder from the heavens. It wasn't even poetic. But it was true. And it cut through the noise in my head like a blade: Choose life.

I leaned back in the seat, eyes heavy, body drained. The night wrapped around me like a blanket, and I drifted into something between sleep and surrender. And somewhere in that half-dream, I started to see things differently. Not what I had lost—but what I still had. The laughter of my boys when they were small. The sunsets I'd watched without ever thinking they might be my last. The music that had carried me through. Friends who had shown up when I didn't deserve it. The quiet moments. The loud ones. The messy, beautiful gift of being alive.

Gratitude seeped in like morning light. And when I opened my eyes again, the mountains hadn't moved—but I had. Not far. Just enough. That moment, though I didn't know it then, was where I met courage. Not the chest-thumping or sword-wielding kind. Not the kind that earns medals or makes headlines. No, this courage was quieter. More patient. It wasn't trying to save the world—just me. I'm not saying it got easier right away. It didn't. Healing is never linear. There were more hard conversations. More mistakes. More nights when I questioned everything. But I had made a choice. And that choice carried me forward.

I stand in gratitude for my courageous choice to turn right that night. It changed me! I imagine what would've been lost if I hadn't made that turn: the people I've met since, the redemption, the forgiveness, and the second chances at love. The fulfilling life we live now and the beautiful relationship I have with my sons were worth that moment of summoned courage to live.

Maris: My parents were married fifty years before my father passed away suddenly. They were a resilient duo who navigated life as it unfolded. They instilled in us the power of family.

My mother lived a truly courageous life! She was a wife, a mother, and an award-winning clinical social worker known for giving a voice to those who rarely had one. Her health issues never stopped her. From Cushing's disease to breast cancer, diabetes, and heart attacks, she was the ever-ready bunny always back to work after a health scare and known for her grace, grit, and style. Mom listened with her heart and with curiosity, and even my school friends counted on her wisdom.

My sisters and I gathered at my mom's house for a visit, each of us coming from our homes in Florida, Texas, and Virginia. We piled onto her bed on this cool January morning after ringing in the new year together just weeks before. I sat facing mom, and my sisters were snuggled close by. The room filled with loving energy and the kind of silence that speaks louder than words. We knew this moment was coming, yet nothing could truly prepare us. We chatted in between her naps and sang our favorite childhood songs. At the end of our last song round, breaking the silence, Mom said in a whisper, "Your father is calling me." This could not be happening!

We thought we had more time! In that moment, my sisters and I summoned our own courage gained from my mother's strength, and we encouraged her to go to him with open arms and dance once again. As I watched her take her final breath, her eyes went from mine to a subtle void. I saw peace where there had been pain from the lung cancer that took her from us.

My sisters and I held her and each other. An overwhelming wave of gratitude and grief crashed over me at once—raw, unfiltered, and inescapable. And now, without our parents to be the family nucleus, we felt a bit orphaned. Even in that beautiful, painful moment of recognition, something else was there. Love. The kind that doesn't fade, even as life does. The kind that holds you up when everything feels like it's falling apart.

My mom was a true role model even to her last breath. The courage we summoned wasn't about stopping the inevitable or pushing away the sorrow—it was about **staying present**, even when it hurt. It was about holding her hand, whispering our love to her to give her wings, letting her know she was not alone and that Dad would be waiting.

Ken & Maris: In those moments, neither of us would have called it courage. It felt more like survival—like we had barely scraped by. We didn't feel strong. We felt broken. But here's what we've learned: Courage isn't always obvious in the moment. It doesn't roar like a lion. Sometimes, it's a whisper in the dark that says, "Rise up, you will be okay."

And sometimes, we only recognize it in hindsight, when we are standing in a more grounded place and realize: that breath, that pause, that decision to turn right instead of left, that moment to let someone go, was courage showing up from the depth of our being when we weren't sure it existed.

A Thousand Mile Heartache

MARIS SEGAL & KEN ASHBY

Maris Segal and Ken Ashby are transformational and quantum leaders who consult, coach, and collaborate with executives, entrepreneurs, and rising leaders to bring their professional, personal, and philanthropic vision to life.

Segal Leadership Global (SLG) was launched to meet the shifting needs of leadership with a focus on evolving and transforming human relations skills into powerful tools to drive a people-first culture with bottom-line impact. The SLG Relational Leadership experience is designed to empower leaders at every stage and age of their journey with the mindset, heart-set, and skillset needed to drive vision and positive change within themselves, their teams, and the broader organization.

Their book, *The RFactor*, an entertaining story of evolving relationships, sits at the core of their work. In addition, Ken and Maris have been TEDx speakers and featured co-authors in over twenty-five inspiring leadership-centered books.

They were individually recognized by the White House with the Presidential Lifetime Achievement Award for their philanthropic dedication and were awarded internationally with the Gentlemen and Women of Heart Awards. IG @_the_rfactor

Author's Website: *www.SegalLeadershipGlobal.com*

Charity Awareness: *www.UnsilencedVoices.org*

MICHELLE MARIE SHOCKLEY
COURAGE AT THE CROSSROADS

Have you ever felt like you were at a crossroads in your life? Sometimes, it seems as if we're at an intersection, waiting for a traffic light or, better yet, a heavenly sign to tell us which way to go. We feel stuck, waiting for something to happen, unsure if the light will ever turn green.

Staying on the same course, or doing nothing, is often the safest way. It's familiar, and the to-be-expected pain is predictable. However, having the courage to turn right or left at the crossroads is a step out of our comfort zone, and where life truly begins. In 1994, I made the decision to move out of the intersection and take a courageous turn: I decided to leave the United States to live in Europe.

I had been dating a German national for six years. We met early in my college career, and he made it clear from the beginning: "If we stay together, we're going to live in Germany." As a very naïve student, I said, "Sure." I even became somewhat arrogant about the move, as if a higher calling were waiting for me overseas. Of the six-year relationship, three years were long-distance, with Andreas living in Germany and me in Indiana.

Many who found out I was engaged to a German national and maintaining a long-distance relationship slightly discouraged me, if not outright mocked me: "He's just using you." Determined to prove the critics wrong, I dedicated myself even more to the relationship, fueled by both love and defiance.

Months of preparation preceded my move. About fifteen boxes were packed and sent to Germany via friends and his work. My college and consumer debts were paid off. I resigned from my job. Bridal showers were held. Friends were seen one last time, hugs exchanged, and tears shed over dinners and late-night conversations.

The big day finally came. On April 6, 1994, I left Standiford Field Airport in Louisville, Kentucky, to fly to Cincinnati and then on to Frankfurt, Germany. At the airport, one of my friends, two of my nieces, and my stepfather cried and said their farewells. The moment of courage had arrived.

On the plane, I began to cry. I cried the entire trip from Louisville to Cincinnati. Confusion, happiness, nervousness, doubt, regret, joy—everything came pouring out. The people around me were probably confused, perhaps wondering what life event had just unfolded. Once in Cincinnati, I regained my composure, and the international flight was less emotional, although my heart remained heavy.

On the morning of April 7, 1994, I landed in Frankfurt to begin my new life with Andreas. He picked me up, and we went to look for wedding rings. Four days later, we were married at the city building in a civil ceremony. The next few days revealed that the courage I'd needed to board the plane was nothing compared to the courage I would need to stay in Germany.

The first two years of our marriage were difficult. I felt like a mail-order bride. Although Andreas and I had spent time together in college, the three years of separation had taken a toll. We had to completely re-acquaint ourselves. He was frustrated, too used to being independent, insecure about money, and had developed a sort of disdain for America. It was not an ideal starting point for a God-led marriage.

My career prospects also seemed minimal. We had married for love, not money—but we all know that money helps in a young marriage. It didn't help that I was in a new culture, far away from my own network, with no clear path forward.

I began an internship with the city of Mainz, in cooperation with the Freundschaftskreis Mainz–Louisville (The Friendship Circle for Mainz and Louisville). It lasted two months and brought in a small amount of money. Although I had a bachelor's degree in German language and literature, I still didn't speak fluently. I had to demonstrate courage every day just to communicate. I would start a sentence in German, and the listener would often finish it— for me, or in English. How frustrating! Sometimes, just getting dressed in the morning and leaving for work was an act of courage.

After the internship ended, I had to look for a new job. In any market, this is challenging. But looking for a job where you lack fluent communication skills feels like a mammoth task. Each application felt like sending a piece of myself out to be judged in a language that didn't yet fully belong to me.

Registering with the employment office was an experience. After just two months of work in Germany, I was allowed to list only one type of job for consideration. That was it. Outside of fast food, my chances were slim. My husband grew antsy—he wanted me to contribute financially. I was nervous. I hadn't made friends yet. I felt alone, other than my husband and in-laws. Loneliness has a way of clouding even the brightest intentions.

Luckily, my in-laws saw an ad for an apprenticeship about thirty-five miles away. I applied and got the position—it was in accounting. Since I had a college degree, I was able to reduce the training time by a year. My next courage challenge began: attending vocational school in a foreign language.

Again, I couldn't speak as quickly as my native classmates, but the teachers were sympathetic because I tried. In the first course I attended, I knew the instructor was speaking German—but the rest was beyond comprehension. I often sat through lectures, grasping at context clues and visual aids to piece together understanding. With each passing month, my skills improved. My confidence grew. I made friends. Slowly, I no longer felt like a visitor, but like someone building a life.

As my German improved and I settled into the rhythm of daily life, something inside me began to shift. What had once felt like pure survival slowly became a foundation for growth. The apprenticeship that began with so much uncertainty eventually blossomed into a fulfilling career in accounting. Over time, I gained not only technical skills but also confidence in my ability to navigate both professional and cultural landscapes.

Years passed, and I found myself no longer asking, "Can I do this?" but rather, "What else is possible?" After two decades in my field, I took the leap to start my own business—something I never would have imagined during those tearful moments on the airplane or the frustrating early days of language barriers and loneliness. What once felt like an unfamiliar and sometimes hostile land became home, and the woman who once doubted whether she could stay became someone others turned to for strength and guidance.

Courage, I've learned, doesn't always roar. Sometimes it's a whisper: getting out of bed, showing up for a conversation, applying for that next opportunity. It's the quiet determination to believe in something better when nothing around you feels familiar. My story began at a crossroad, but it didn't end there. I turned, I stumbled, I grew, and ultimately—I thrived.

We all have a story that matters. Mine is just one among many, but if sharing it helps someone else find the courage to take her next step, then every hardship was worth it.

Let's make the world a better place, one story at a time.

MICHELLE MARIE SHOCKLEY

Born in rural Tennessee, Michelle lived in Mississippi and Michigan before her mother and stepfather settled down in Southern Indiana. She lived there until the age of twenty-four, when she moved to Germany in 1994 to marry her college sweetheart. From the marriage, Michelle has two children, Alexa, who lives in America, and Carsten, who lives in Germany.

After twenty-two years of marriage, Michelle separated from her German husband and decided to remain in Germany, where she today runs her own business as an interim manager, trainer, and public speaker. Michelle has been training sport clubs, companies, and executives in Martial Arts, Aerobics, English, and Human Resources topics since the year 2000. She enjoys traveling and reading.

Michelle has a Bachelor of Arts degree from Indiana University in German language and a vocational certification as *"Steuerfachgehilfin"* (tax accountant) in Germany.

Author's Website: *www.MichelleMarie.world*
Charity Awareness: *www.Wir-Fuer-Kinder.net*

DR. MICHELLE MRAS

HUMBLE BRAVERY

Courageous and brave are adjectives used to describe many of us who have battled some sort of hardship. I survived multiple trials throughout my life, but not once have I considered myself brave. Even though many of my huge trials are far in the past, I still look back and see a young woman who was determined to give everything she could to stay alive.

As a young college student, I was abducted and human trafficked for just under two years. Brave was not in my vocabulary. I simply did everything I could avoid causing my untimely death. When I share this part of my past, I hear, "You are so brave to have survived such an ordeal. How did you get away?"

When I hear that statement and question, I smile and respond with my honest opinion that I merely managed to get up every day with all my limbs intact, no big bruises, my mental state not completely shattered, and with an avid determination to not die today. Getting away was not like you see in the movies. No dashing hero came to my rescue. It took many small self-made plans over time that singularly seemed meaningless but added up to my survival and eventual escape.

How did I do it all? I really don't know. I think my guardian angel was guiding me while I moved through life in a zombie-like state for the year and a half I was captive. My mantra at the time was, "Don't die."

A year after escaping, I began to date a young man I met at my old roommate's wedding. He got me a bookkeeping job at his family's art gallery. He and I became very close. He helped me feel safe again. His strong moral code and tight family affiliation provided me the security I needed. I laughed and danced again. It felt good to regain the happy, joyful person I used to be.

He was more than a boyfriend; he and his sweet-hearted father were my reality check that not all men were monsters. I worked on addressing many of my immediate fears while with him: hair-trigger jumping at noises, crying if someone looked at me strangely, or having panic attacks from the sound of passing cars. He'd give me a big hug and say, "It's okay," and laugh. He had no idea what I was freaking out about. He never asked. He just reassured me about my safety. That's all I needed.

When I'm told that I am brave because I went through my fear of being near a man after all I endured, I explain that I wasn't brave; I was strategic. There is safety in numbers. When I was alone, I was a target.

Many years later, in October 2016, I began my official battle with breast cancer. I was told that I was brave for opting for an immediate Bilateral Mastectomy to head off this seemingly unending battle. The multiple surgeries and the series of complications resulting from the cancer battle never caused me to feel courageous.

Just as I felt with my human trafficking experience, I woke up each day thankful to still be breathing. There were days when I had difficulty getting up, many days where I missed having breasts, days where I cried that I was so broken and beaten that I wondered if I would ever feel normal again. Not once did I see my survival as being courageous. Once again, there was no knight in shining armor to be the hero to save me from all of my torment. My mantra remained, "Don't die."

The two experiences I shared above were definitely traumatic. Not once did I look into the mirror during these long-term traumas and think, "Wow, Michelle, you are so brave. Good job!"

Understand that when you find yourself in your version of hell, don't stop. Keep dragging, crawling, limping, walking, hopping, and running toward whatever exit you can imagine until you can see it. Don't wallow in despair. You'll get lost in your emotions and fall victim to the dark side of fear. It's okay to feel fear and succumb to emotions.

There were weeks when I was terrified and temporarily paralyzed by fear. To heal, I had to give myself permission to feel all the feelings I was denied when captive. The release of these emotions helped me free the scared young girl who was hiding in my psyche. The secret is to not allow yourself to remain in that space.

Now that I am far from the lessons, I have noted all I've learned about human nature, resilience, and the power of a positive attitude. My lessons from both my trafficking and cancer experiences were that it is *human nature* to want to hide from the truth. I lived in denial of what was happening to me even while actively experiencing horrible things. It was easier to restructure this horrid life in my mind and define it as a captive rape situation.

When fighting cancer, I noticed that it caused people close to me to distance themselves because they had no idea how to help. It's not bad or evil, it's just avoidance of what is too much for their psyche to handle—they choose not to see.

Resilience is developed through the tiny efforts of not giving in to whatever is attempting to knock you down. We are born with resilience, but we forget as we get older. As infants, we flex the resilience muscles immediately after we are born. We shift our lungs from a water environment to breathing air; from darkness and warmth to bright lights and cold; then we learn to communicate our nourishment and comfort needs by developing language skills.

When we begin to move, we learn to roll over, crawl, stand, and eventually walk. None of these efforts are for the weak at heart. We fall, scrape ourselves, bruise our legs, etc. Even learning how to use our mouths to eat is a repeated act of resilience. As humans, we are innately gifted with the quality of resilience, and, dare I say, courage. We are protected and directed away from harm as we grow up, and we forget to use the muscle as we age. We forget about resilience until we are given no other choice but to start using it. We would be a world of crawlers if we didn't have the instinct to get up after a fall.

Regardless of what you are experiencing, the power of a *positive attitude* will change how you perceive your circumstances and, therefore, help you see options. Neither human nature nor resilience work without a positive attitude. The ability to shift your mindset to see the positive side of whatever situation is the key to a successful outcome.

My mentor, Dr. Paul Scheele, introduced me to a mindset that I have embraced as a way of life. During a particularly rough patch of my healing, he asked me to "Embrace your toddler mindset."

At first, his suggestion confused me, but once I put it into practice and looked at each issue or circumstance through the inquisitive perception of a toddler, my issues became less troublesome. The pains I held for years lost their hold on me. Toddlers live in the present. The past is done and gone. The future is unknown and open to adventure. Toddlers are courageous!

Personally, courageous is not an adjective that I claim. I believe that courage is never realized in the moment. Those deemed as courageous through their circumstances are just doing their best to do what's right for them at the moment. Courage is realized on the other side of hardships. It's a reflection of how human nature, resilience, and a positive attitude played their part in getting survivors to thrive on the other side.

If you are seeking a hero to save you, look in the mirror and become the hero you need. No number of medical staff, therapies, or avoidance will save you. Make a mental note that whatever happens in your life, you will have the courage to advocate for yourself.

"Courage reveals itself on the other side of hardship."
~ Dr. Michelle Mras

DR. MICHELLE MRAS

Dr. Michelle Mras is an award-winning global and TEDx keynote speaker, executive speaking coach, international bestselling author, and co-author of thirty books, including twenty Amazon bestsellers. Michelle is the host of the MentalShift show on *The New Channel (TNC)* in the Philippines, and co-host of the Denim and Pearls podcast. She has speaking parts in several sci-fi movies; check *IMDB.com* for her. Her music EP album can be found on *MichelleMras.com*. Dr. Michelle was nominated for the Most Influential Filipina in the World and is a United Nations Ambassador for Peace.

Dr. Michelle Mras is a survivor of multiple life challenges, including a traumatic brain injury, breast cancer, and human trafficking. Dr. Michelle is a proud military daughter and spouse who has traveled and lived around the world. She uses her vast experience to guide her clients to recognize the innate gifts within them, to stop apologizing for what they are not and step into who they truly are. Dr. Michelle's driving thought is that every day is a gift. Tomorrow is never promised. Every moment is an opportunity to be the best version of you… Unapologetically!

Author's Website: *www.MichelleMras.com*

Charity Awareness: *www.Kenna-Foundation.org*

MR. WHISKEY
THE INTERSECTION OF MORALITY & COURAGE

When most people think of courage, they instantly imagine a heroic scene—a man fighting a bear or a woman rushing into a fire to save her children. These are definitely brave acts, but not all of us have experienced such events. Many of us live simple yet meaningful lives, not realizing that they're actually full of courage—specifically, moral, emotional, and spiritual courage.

I want to pivot from the mainstream ideas of "physical" bravery to focus on the emotional and morally straining acts of courage, starting with me stopping a possible homicide-suicide.

Wait a minute! Didn't I just say that I wanted to focus on common events that relate to everyone? While a homicide-suicide sounds drastic, the unfortunate truth is that almost everyone knows someone who is struggling with addiction, unresolved trauma, depression, or suicidal ideation.

In the military, this is especially true. During my time in the service, and even as a veteran, I've prevented several suicides. It's not a burden, and I'll never call it that, but doing so has definitely put me in morally conflicting positions that weighed heavily on me.

My first experience with such a situation required the most courage and was the most difficult one—not just because I had never been in that kind of situation before, but also because I was significantly less developed mentally and emotionally than I was later on when facing the others. It happened just a few weeks into boot camp.

There was a sailor who was a bit of an outcast in our division, and he had difficulty getting along with others and even got into trouble a few times with our leaders. I always tried to understand his perspective. From this, we formed a bond, where he shared with me about ongoing trauma with his mother and an abusive stepfather. It had followed him into boot camp, and in general, it didn't seem like the military was the right fit for him at that time.

The tension between this sailor and the others continued to worsen each day. His little remarks to me about wanting to hurt others in his anger and sorrow had drastically grown into a kill list. A suicide is one thing—a homicide followed by suicide is another thing. This was unexpected, and it was unlike anything I had come across prior in my life.

He told me that I was his best friend and that I'd be spared. The others, however, whom he did not like, had been written down on a kill list, in a specific order of priority targets to extra kills. According to the plan, it would end with his own death or possible escape. He did not care if he died in the process, though.

It may initially seem like an easy situation—report the sailor and go back to your day. Unfortunately, that's not the case—not for me, at least. Allow me to give some military context first.

In the military, your job is also your lifestyle. When your job in the military changes, it can mean everything else changes, both for you and your loved ones. Due to the nature of certain jobs in the military, medications or mental health difficulties can get you removed from your position and either changed to a new job or separated from the service entirely.

While a suicide report may affect a person's career in the civilian world, officially reporting a suicide to the military can drastically change a person's life—again, it's not just their job, it's *everything*.

So, while everyone in the military is supposed to be a mandatory reporter when it comes to a service member mentioning anything that seems suicidal, many of us find ourselves at a moral crossroads. We'll explore that now with my situation, but I am not encouraging disobedience to any military authority.

What happens if I report him? Where will they take him? Are they going to kick him out of boot camp? Will he be unable to join any military branch afterward? If I'm the only person he told, then he'll know I reported him, right? Will he resent me? Will he try to find me one day? What about the abusive stepfather? What of his income? What if he can't get another job? Is this just talk, or will he actually do this?

These questions are generally universal regarding a suicidal military member. That last question—the gauging of how real it is —can be the most difficult part. While we're always supposed to assume suicidal remarks are serious, drastically altering a person's life over what was just a joke or passing feeling can be a majorly regrettable decision.

This is the morally conflicted battle of which I spoke earlier: Do you or do you not report a suicidal individual?

I continuously contemplated the many questions in my head. It was tearing me apart. In a way, my division's lives were in my hands, and while that sounds dramatic, it was possible that he would kill some of us, and possibly, himself. After talking with a trusted shipmate about the situation, I knew that I had to report it.

However, I was still afraid to do so—I was afraid of making the wrong decision. I had a small fear of becoming his priority kill, but even worse, I had a fear of ruining his life by making a decision that I would extremely regret.

Yes, many would've considered my decision to report him the right one, but if there had been an alternative path where he overcame his feelings and became a successful military member, and I had chosen that route… What then is right and wrong?

Morality is complex, as we all know. Human emotions are amorphous and ever-changing feelings inside of us, tied to this world, religion, society, ourselves, and others in complicated ways.

In my case, I was afraid either way. Even if I wanted to report him, would his life get better? What if it got worse and pushed him to actually do what he had mentioned that he wasn't actually going to do? Then, that would mean that *I* caused it to become a reality when it had only been a passing thought.

Yet, there were lives potentially at risk. I was the involuntary maker of this decision, and I needed to act on it. So, I did.

The sailor was taken away. When he showed back up to get his belongings, my heart dropped. I swore that he was going to kill me, but it turns out that he didn't know I had reported him, nor had he realized that I was the only one who could've done so. Our division leader had ensured my anonymity and safety by generalizing the situation and incorporating his personal assessments.

When I packed the sailor's belongings, I was still very uneasy about the whole situation. A few days later, however, I saw him with the separation division, and he was smiling, excited to go home, and glad to be out of the military before he had gone too far in and been pushed beyond his breaking point.

Since seeing that, I've been able to sleep a bit easier, and I try my best to drown out the questions and alternate timelines. Since then, I've also dealt with several sailors who were suicidal and didn't report them, and with my help and others, we took care of them, and they are still in today, serving this country, successful and healthy.

So, I encourage you to have the courage to make bold and heavily weighted moral decisions, to trust yourself when doing so, and to continually serve others and do good.

MR. WHISKEY

Mr. Whiskey, formerly an Electrician's Mate Nuclear Operator, is a U.S. Navy veteran, podcaster, author, speaker, preacher, comedian, and entrepreneur. As the founder of Couple O' Nukes LLC, he is dedicated to helping individuals improve their lives through global networking, information sharing, and community building—both virtually and in person. Through the Couple O' Nukes podcast and his travels around the world, Mr. Whiskey focuses on mentoring young adults, connecting with outcasts, and empowering passionate dreamers. His mission spans suicide prevention, addiction recovery, fitness, health and wellness, military matters, relationships, parenting, career development, financial literacy, and faith.

When not actively working, Mr. Whiskey can often be found outside with his three-pound Chihuahua, running several miles at a time, writing fiction or poetry, designing women's Kaiju-based fashion, or spending quality time with his elderly neighbors. He also dedicates a significant amount of time to studying the Bible, as well as Hebrew and Greek.

Author's Website: *www.CoupleONukes.com*

Charity Awareness: *www.ProjectCallisto.org*

NANCY E. MOORE

THE STRENGTH TO BE SEEN

Courage is one of those words we often misunderstand, or we add to the definition and make it out of our reach. We tend to associate it with dramatic moments—soldiers in battle, first responders racing toward danger, superheroes with capes and supernatural strength. Those forms of courage are real, powerful, and deserving of admiration.

But there is another kind of courage—quiet, personal, and important moments in our own lives and in the lives of others. It lives in the everyday choices we make—the moments when we stand up for ourselves, speak out for others, or simply choose to show up when we'd rather hide.

Courage is the inner strength to take meaningful action in the face of fear, pain, uncertainty, or adversity. It is not the absence of fear —it is the decision to move forward despite it. True courage is not always bold or loud. It can be as simple as saying "no" when everyone is saying "yes." Courage is the openness to show vulnerability, have a difficult conversation with someone, or admit when we are wrong. At the very core of courage lies the belief that you, your truth, and your voice matter.

Growing up in a first responder family, courage was all around; I just didn't know it. I've learned that courage is not like having green or blue eyes—it's not something you're simply born with. Courage is like a muscle. In the beginning, it is not very strong, and as you step out and work on it, it becomes stronger and stronger.

As children, my siblings and I were taught the importance of community. Our parents told us it was our job to protect those who needed help, no matter our age. One day, when we were no older than six, five, and four, we saw a couple of third-grade boys picking on a girl with special needs. My siblings and I looked at each other, and we knew—we had to act.

So, we told the boys to stop. When they didn't, and we insisted, they turned on us. It was terrifying. However, my siblings were good fighters, and somehow, we managed to handle it. Later, the boys told their dad they had been beaten up by a group of older kids. Their father stormed over to our house, demanding to see the "older boys." My dad laughed. "Those were my kids."

Looking back, I'm not sure if we acted out of courage or because we feared our parents would find out we had done nothing. Maybe it was both. Either way, that moment taught me a lesson: sometimes we're more afraid of not living up to our values than we are of the consequences of standing up.

My journey of learning about courage led me to explore the concept of FEAR. One of the best things I ever learned was that fear is our feelings—and feelings can be fickle. What I learned was that FEAR stood for:

F – False

E – Evidence

A – Appearing

R – Real

Fear can lock us in a space that courage cannot reach. It can freeze us to where we cannot move; it convinces us that we are nothing, and not worthy of help. But courage reminds us otherwise. And one of the greatest things I learned is that I can be courageous and fearful at the same time. It is the choices and actions I take that are important.

I remember the first time I stood up to a bully. I was terrified. Not of being hit, exactly. As I thought more and more about it, I realized I was more afraid of surviving being hit—I was afraid of the hospital, of the unknown, of what came after. But when I choose courage over fear, nothing happened. The bullies backed down. I stood there stunned. Courage doesn't always look like victory—it often feels like trembling and standing your ground anyway.

Being small in stature, people often tried to use me as a sounding board for their power. They'd stand over me, yell, try to intimidate me. I trained myself not to blink. One person even said I looked like a devil because I wouldn't move or blink as they were yelling at me. I was learning to be courageous.

Over time, I've realized how essential my faith is in developing courage. I believe God is always with me, guiding, listening, encouraging me to take the right step, even if it's scary. I've learned to quiet myself and ask, "Is this where You want me?" That inner dialogue has helped me show up with integrity and courage.

Courage doesn't come all at once. It grows slowly. For me, it's made me more reflective. I see the big picture more. I ask better questions: *Is courage instinctual? Can it be taught? Why aren't we teaching it to children in schools, the way we teach reading or math?*

I believe soldiers and first responders don't just *have* courage—they've learned to make their sense of duty bigger than their fear. They build courage through repeated practice. So can we.

Sometimes just being fully yourself is an act of courage. This world wants to mold you, shrink you, or silence you. It's easy to dismiss yourself and you're feelings because someone else's struggles seem "bigger." But what's courageous to me might seem simple to you—and vice versa.

Courage is in the hands of the person using it at the time. Every act of courage—big or small—needs our recognition. We need to recognize people in their early steps of courage. One person's quiet step of courage becomes the light someone else needs to find their own.

I once believed courage belonged only to heroes. I thought it meant being stoic, shutting off emotions, pushing through without weakness. But I know now that courage and vulnerability go hand in hand. Courage is not about being unaffected. It's about being *authentic*.

There's a quote often misattributed to Edmund Burke:

> *"The only thing necessary for the triumph of evil is for good men to do nothing."*

When I looked it up, I learned it had been paraphrased. Whether he wrote it or not, the meaning is the same. We have choices. Choosing to do nothing is the most courageous act of all—when that silence means resisting provocation or not giving energy to hate. These days, courage calls us to speak. To act. To stand in the gap for someone who can't.

Courage doesn't always come naturally. It is a decision. A commitment. A belief that your actions matter.

It's not about being fearless—it's about honoring your values even when fear is present.

It's not about grandeur—it's about truth.

It's not about applause—it's about integrity.

And sometimes, it's just about feeling the fear and being courageous anyway.

NANCY E. MOORE

Nancy E. Moore is an Image Strategist and Digital Entrepreneur Coach with over fifteen years of experience transforming personal style into powerful branding across the beauty, television, film, and commercial industries. From working behind the scenes as a makeup artist, educator, and creative director to leading high-profile editorial shoots and ad campaigns, Nancy has mastered the art of visual storytelling and understands how personal image shapes confidence, influence, and opportunity.

Today, she merges her creative flair with digital strategy to guide entrepreneurs in building magnetic, authentic brands that stand out online. As the author of *Style Made Simple: Your Guide to Daily Looks* and the co-founder of a wealth-building company for women, Nancy is passionate about equipping others with the tools to thrive—both in business and in life.

Her signature offering, the Digital Entrepreneur Essentials Package, is a step-by-step framework that helps clients develop a clear and cohesive online presence through brand identity, color analysis, marketing visuals, and strategy—all with a personal touch.

Author's Website: *www.NancyEMoore.com*

Charity Awareness: *www.SurvivalToThrivalSeries.com*

NEETU N. PRABHU
THE FIRE WITHIN

THE QUIET BEGINNING

People talk about courage like it's a lightning bolt. A moment. A headline. A roar. But for me, courage came quietly. Not in a scream—but in a decision. Not in public—but on the way to the hospital in an ambulance, in the stillness of the hospital room, a courtroom hallway, my dark garage, my small, precious closet.

It didn't feel like power. It felt like survival. It felt like: "I'll take the next breath." "I'll open the next bill." "I'll say no this time." And that was enough.

THE BREAK & THE COMING

I didn't grow up imagining I'd ever end a marriage. Especially not one I gave my entire twenties and thirties to. But the truth was clear: What was once home had become a battlefield. And no matter how long I stayed, it would never become safe again.

So, I left. With nothing but my children, my breath, and my name.

Except... even my name didn't feel like mine. Not yet. I had even given up my maiden name when I got married. And now, I had to earn it back. Not from anyone else. From myself.

Leaving cost me everything the world calls stability:

- Financial security
- Physical health
- Professional momentum
- The illusion of "having it all together"

There were days I was curled up on the floor with medical records in one hand and legal bills in the other. There were nights I sang lullabies to my children while sobbing inside. There were weeks I couldn't eat. Couldn't speak. Could barely breathe. But I kept going.

Not because I wasn't afraid, but because I chose not to abandon myself again. I promised to take care of me. For the first time, I chose *me*.

I was done being "rescue 911" for everyone else—for my family, friends, clients, society. I realized, in the end, I was all alone. I was done. I was more than done.

THE VOICE THAT CARRIED ME

I didn't post on social media.

I didn't tell the world.

I didn't write a memoir.

And I didn't ask for permission this time. I gave myself permission instead. I made a promise to myself this time. I got up. I showed up. I chose again.

I had even completely lost all faith in what the world calls "God." I had even destroyed my temple with my own bare hands. I didn't believe there was anyone watching over me or protecting me—it was all a big cosmic joke.

Until I discovered—it really *is*. I prayed more in that season than I had in a lifetime. And the voice I kept hearing—the only one that didn't judge me—was this presence: "I am okay." "I am here." "I am alive." "You are not what happened to you."

You are who you choose to become—*starting now*. I leaned in. I listened to this voice inside of me—this knowing I had that belonged to something greater than this woman others called "Neetu." This power carried her.

This awareness breathed her. She was born again. I was born again.

THE RISE

And I rebuilt. Not from the floor up, but from the fire within. Not with vision boards or timelines. With boundaries. With breath. With brutal honesty.

I said no to things that looked good, but cost me my peace.

I said yes to rest, to nourishment, to nature, to things that felt good.

I cut ties with people who loved the old version of me, but couldn't handle the truth of who I was becoming.

I created a sacred space in my calendar. I let my body heal on its own time. I learned to trust my nervous system again. And slowly... I became the woman I used to pray for.

And today? My girls see me—from afar. And up close. They don't just feel safe—they see what strength looks like in a woman. In their mother. Because this isn't just my story—it's theirs, too.

I stepped into this new version of me. I had watched her fall. Fail. Fumble. Tremble. Crumble. And I watched her wake up. I watched her rise again. Build her heart again. Bring her babies back to a safe place they called home again. And build a whole business from scratch again.

I was with her the entire time. I saw her rise. I saw her shine. It was her time. It was her time to shine.

Keep reading, because this is all unfolding on a quiet timeline.

In 2022, I founded Unity Wealth Strategies. No ads. No pitch decks. No chasing. And yet—the right people came. They came because they could feel something. Not a brand, but a presence. They trusted me, and not just as a wealth strategist, but as a woman who had walked through fire... *and* was still warm, not hardened.

I didn't get bitter. I just got better. I didn't need to prove I had courage—I had already lived it.

Courage, I've learned, is not about loud declarations. It's about quiet decisions. It's the decision to walk away. To shut the door. To whisper, "Enough." To rest when your body says rest. To rise even when no one is clapping.

Courage is choosing yourself—without needing permission. And the day I chose myself?

That was the day I finally came home. It was finally quiet. All the drama, trauma, chaos—done.

The police, courts, lawyers, bills—done. The gossip, the stories, the chatter, the noise—done.

It just got really quiet inside of me. There was craziness around me, yet calm inside of me. Panic amidst me, yet a deep, peaceful presence inside of me.

It looked like a chaotic zoo on the outside, yet I was more than courageous on the inside. I didn't know *how*, but I had a knowing. And I followed that voice.

I tuned everything and everyone out. I tuned in. I turned it on. I let that voice inside speak to me. Guide me. And for the first time, I listened. It turned out, I left God... but He never left me.

Today, He walks with me. He flows to me and through me. And I'm so, so thankful for this moment. Every time I breathe, I realize this is a gift.

I am still here. I am meant to be. And I even got my maiden name back.

MY MESSAGE TO YOU

If you're still walking through your own fire—*I see you.* You don't need to know the whole path. Just the next step. You don't need a perfect plan. You just need one honest moment with yourself.

Courage isn't the absence of fear. It's the presence of truth. It's the presence of YOU.

And the truth is? You're still here. Get to know the *real* YOU. **You are enough.** And that is enough to begin again.

With all my love,
Neetu N. Prabhu

NEETU N. PRABHU

Neetu Prabhu, Founder and CEO of Unity Wealth Strategies, is a distinguished wealth strategist serving ultra-high net worth clients and business owners. She specializes in wealth building, legacy planning, and multigenerational wealth transfers, utilizing tax-free income strategies to revolutionize her clients' financial futures. Neetu is recognized for her fiduciary excellence and ethical service, earning accolades such as the prestigious Million Dollar Round Table Court of the Table award and multiple honors for her impactful decade-long tenure in financial services.

Beyond her professional endeavors, Neetu is passionately committed to empowering single moms and survivors of domestic violence. A philanthropist at heart, she champions financial literacy for women, acting as a guiding force to foster independence and resilience. She is also a multi-time #1 Amazon Bestselling Author and a featured speaker alongside notable figures like Brian Tracy and Erik Swanson.

Author's Website: *www.LinkedIn.com/in/NeetuPrabhu*

Charity Awareness: *www.SurvivalToThrivalSeries.com*

DR. ONIKA SHIRLEY

THE COURAGE TO CREATE YOUR OWN PATH

EMBRACING RESPONSIBILITY AS A YOUNG ADULT

At just sixteen, I found myself standing at a crossroads, the weight of responsibility settling heavily on my young shoulders. While my peers fretted over homework and social gatherings, I was navigating the uncharted waters of adulthood—balancing high school and the daunting quest for independence.

Securing my own place wasn't just about physical space; it was a bold declaration of my desire to take control of my life and shape my future. In a world that often questions the capabilities of youth, I discovered that true courage lies not in the absence of fear, but in the willingness to embrace it.

This journey became my catalyst for growth, teaching me the invaluable lesson that taking responsibility can be the first step towards creating a life filled with purpose and empowerment.

"Courage is not the absence of fear, but the triumph over it. It is in the moment we choose to take responsibility for our lives that we unlock the power to create our own future."
~ Dr. O

Standing on the edge of adulthood, the reality of my circumstances began to sink in: I was not just preparing to navigate this turbulent transition alone, but I was also carrying the life of a little person within me. The absence of the father loomed over me like a shadow, amplifying my fears about the future. The prospect of single motherhood was daunting, filled with uncertainties about finances, stability, and the immense responsibility of nurturing another life.

Yet, amid that fear, I discovered a reservoir of courage deep within me—a fierce determination that ignited my resolve to forge ahead. I understood that while the road ahead was fraught with challenges, the love and commitment I felt towards my unborn child became my guiding light.

I was ready to embrace this new chapter, not just for myself, but for the little soul who would rely on me entirely; it was this powerful mix of fear and courage that propelled me forward, reminding me that I had the strength to rise above my circumstances.

I refused to become just another statistic, a teen mom who dropped out of school and relinquished her dreams. The thought of relying on my mother or anyone else to raise my child was never an option; I was determined to take full responsibility for my daughter's life. With unwavering resolve, I balanced the demands of motherhood with my education, pushing through the challenges of high school while holding down a job.

Each day was a testament to my dedication—I graduated with my class, driven by a relentless determination to defy expectations and chart my own course. Even when I faced the adversity of two car wrecks that could have derailed my progress, I kept moving forward.

Walking by faith, I embraced each obstacle as an opportunity to grow stronger, proving to myself and to the world that I could overcome any challenge life threw my way. My commitment became my compass, guiding me toward a future that was wholly my own.

Graduating high school was merely the beginning of my journey, a steppingstone toward a much greater aspiration. After a grueling four-year recovery from my car accident, I found the courage to return to school, reinvigorated and more determined than ever.

Over the next decade, I committed myself to my education, acquiring not only my associate and bachelor's degrees but also my master's and, eventually, my doctorate. Each milestone was a testament to my resilience—a transformation from mere survival to a vibrant thrival.

Alongside my academic pursuits, I embarked on a fulfilling career in manufacturing that lasted eighteen years, where I learned the value of hard work, teamwork, and innovation. It wasn't just about achieving degrees or titles; it was about pure determination, walking by faith, and placing my trust in God while believing wholeheartedly in myself.

Through every challenge and triumph, I learned that true growth comes from embracing life's obstacles and using them as fuel to propel one's journey forward. My story became a testament to the power of perseverance, transforming fear into faith and adversity into opportunity, all while nurturing a vision for a future that was rich with possibilities.

As I reflect on my journey, I recognize that the path from survival to thrival is not limited to my experiences alone; it's a universal journey that anyone can embark upon, regardless of their circumstances. Each of us faces challenges—be it the end of a marriage, the loss of a loved one, or unfulfilled dreams—but we all have the power to rise and create a life of purpose. Here are five actionable tips to help you reclaim your narrative and inspire your transformation:

1. Embrace Your Story:

Acknowledge where you've been and how it's shaped you. Your past is not a determinant of your future; it's a foundation upon which you can build. Reflect on your experiences and allow them to empower rather than define you.

2. Set Clear Goals:

Identify what you truly want out of life. Whether it's furthering your education, starting a new career, or nurturing personal relationships, setting clear and achievable goals provides direction and purpose, guiding your journey from survival to thrival.

3. Cultivate a Strong Support Network:

Surround yourself with individuals who uplift and inspire you. Whether it's friends, family, mentors, or support groups, engaging with others who share your vision can provide strength, encouragement, and invaluable perspectives as you navigate your path.

4. Practice Resilience:

Challenges are a natural part of life. Instead of allowing setbacks to pull you down, view them as opportunities for growth. Cultivate a mindset that embraces resilience, knowing that every obstacle can lead to new strengths and insights.

5. Walk in Faith & Trust Yourself:

Allow your beliefs—whether spiritual or personal—to guide you in uncertain times. Trusting yourself and having faith in your ability to overcome challenges can be a powerful motivator. Remember, you have the strength within you to transform your story.

By implementing these strategies, you can take deliberate steps towards creating a fulfilling life that thrives beyond mere survival. No matter the trials you face, know that with courage, perseverance, and a sense of purpose, you have the ability to write your own narrative and lead a life rich with joy and meaning.

In closing, remember that the journey from survival to thrival is not a linear path, but rather a series of rich, intricate steps that reflect the essence of who you are. Each challenge you face holds the potential for growth, and every setback can serve as a springboard to new heights. Like a seed that must break through the soil to ultimately bloom, your struggles can cultivate resilience and strength within you.

By embracing your story, setting purposeful goals, building a strong support network, and trusting yourself, you can not only overcome obstacles but flourish in ways you never thought possible. The power to shape your destiny lies within you. Step boldly into your future, equipped with faith and the unwavering belief that you can thrive, no matter the circumstances.

"The only limit to our realization of tomorrow will be our doubts of today."
~ Franklin D. Roosevelt

DR. ONIKA L. SHIRLEY

Dr. Onika L. Shirley is the Founder and CEO of Action Speaks Volume, Inc. She is a Procrastination Strategist and Behavior Change Expert renowned for helping individuals build unshakable confidence, overcome procrastination, and transform dreams into reality. A Master Storyteller and International Speaker, Dr. O serves in Global Ministry and is an international bestselling author, multiple award recipient, serial entrepreneur, and global philanthropist who has impacted lives in the USA, Africa, India, and Pakistan.

As a Motivational Speaker and Christian Counselor, Dr. Onika is dedicated to making a positive difference. Her accolades include being recognized as an Exemplary Global Leader and a Woman of Excellence by I Change Nations, receiving the Passion Purpose Peace Award, and the Presidential Lifetime Achievement Award.

With a heart full of purpose, Dr. O continues to walk in service, striving to make a lasting impact on the lives of others.

Author's Website: *www.ActionSpeaksVolumes.com*

Charity Awareness: *www.FeedingAmerica.org*

PAM KURT

THE COURAGE TO UNLEASH FROM WITHIN TO GET TO FREEDOM

"Freedom is about what you can unleash."
~ Harriett Rubin

As I sit here to write my chapter, I have seen my last few years change dramatically, and they continue to change.

I am a very faith-based person and I know God will only give me as much as I can handle, but... oh my! Freedom means different things to different people. For me, and in this story, freedom means being the person I want to be, utilizing my God-given talents and strengths to be the best version of myself, and feeling the freedom that comes with being the authentic me—the best me. It means being unleashed to simply be myself. But doing this takes courage.

It was very important to be a part of this book. I have had to find the courage to "unleash" several times to get where I am today. What I have learned is that it is a constant action. I have to remember it is part of the journey to continue to unleash.

I have been praying for guidance and direction to be "free" for several years. There is a burning desire. I just want to be free! I am a mother, grandmother, wife, daughter, sister, aunt, business owner, coach, and many other titles that most women hold in their busy lives.

Like most of you, we do it all. I even coach ladies about having it all. But we need to take care of ourselves and unleash the restraints to truly be able to reach that level and achieve our goals. But what does "having it all" look like?

How can I help you unleash yourself to freedom? Do you choose for yourself, your own desires, or what you think everyone else wants from you? From society, family, friends, and employers? Whose life are you choosing? Most of us allow labels and expectations of others to guide us in our lives. It puts you in a box, and then one day, we realize that these boxes are restraining you.

Do you think having it all means meeting everyone's expectations, doing all of the errands, family chores, handling a career, and still finding time for self-care? I beg to differ—it's about your God-given purpose.

It's about you. We need to follow that purpose to our freedom and to be unleashed. But do you have the courage to be the best you?

Life's purpose is to be free and free to do your purpose, not that of others. Can we unleash the restraints that prevent our purpose? Trying to continue pleasing others and doing things only for others is a common lifestyle and daily struggle for many women. Society has recognized it by saying you are co-dependent or too motherly (if there's such a thing), or you pick your career over your family, or you're too masculine. These sayings keep many women in a mental, physical, and emotional bondage of restraints. They restrain you from being who you were really meant to be.

There is also poverty, gender discrimination, racial discrimination, stereotypes, and simply unkind and mean people that restrain you. But you can decide how to unleash yourself from even that type of restraint. Unleash!

What if you have a choice to be free?

What if you were able to be unleashed from all restraints? You can be!

Freedom is a state of mind and a means to unleash! You can unleash yourself with your choices and mindset. If you choose to please, blame, or feel shame for your choices, it will limit your life. You will be restrained. Freedom can unleash you! Freedom also requires constant and repeated acts of courage to be you. To unleash yourself, we need some daily reinforcement. A simple morning routine is a great tool for continuing to work towards being the best you can be. A morning routine helps many successful ladies.

To start the morning with a great mindset to be your best, you may happen to start with some of these small steps:

1. **Wake Up Early & Be Grateful:**

   There is so much peace in the stillness of the mornings—be grateful that you woke up! You can always add to that list.

2. **Stretch & Exercise:**

   Spend at least a few minutes letting your body wake up—we don't all have time for an hour of exercise every day. Spend at least a few minutes stretching, letting your body know that you respect it and are taking care of it, and be strong for *you*.

3. **Nutrition:**

   Try to eat something other than simply drinking coffee—you

haven't eaten in probably eight to ten hours, so treat your body well!

4. **Set Your Daily Goals, Intentions, & Make a Plan For the Day:**

   Knowing what to expect and having a plan helps you get through the day.

5. **Make Your Bed:**

   This is one I learned a long time ago—it helps set your mindset for the day!

In these still, quiet, peaceful moments, what do you desire? I want freedom. Freedom to choose what I can do and can't do; freedom to simply be; freedom to say "no;" freedom to change my mind; freedom to just let it out; and freedom to decide my next steps in life or for the day. Do you? If you are *not* totally free, why not?

You can decide to be free and follow your dreams. But know that your desire for freedom and what that means will change with the seasons in your life. My life has had ups and downs. I can tell you I have been through a lot of tragedy, drama, and trauma in my lifetime.

I lost my father as a child. I grew up with a very simple childhood, knowing my family lived paycheck to paycheck. I was in an abusive marriage; I got divorced and was a single mother by age twenty-five. I watched both my aunt and my grandmother die of cancer; my mother is currently fighting Ovarian cancer. My husband is an alcoholic; I have had financial problems; my car has been repossessed before, and utilities have been shut off. I worked multiple jobs, trying to get through college with my son. I have had business partners cheat me out of money. I don't tell you this for sympathy or empathy, I tell you because you can get through tough times, too.

You can unleash and become who you are meant to be. Unleashing to get to freedom means releasing restraints and becoming free to become the best YOU! I have tried it all—a new car, a new house, a new job, and professional recognition. I still wasn't happy. I still felt the emptiness and no peace. I needed to unleash myself. Find myself. Find my true purpose and direction.

During COVID, I started a coaching business, *Best Version of You, LLC*. It began as an attempt to find an alternative income source due to the pandemic. This company is everything I was meant to be. I started coaching. It became a passion, and *Best Version of You* has become a national movement to empower women. I always used this question for my legal clients: "If money and time were no obstacle, what would you do?" I realized this was it—*this was the key for my journey*. I want to empower women to unleash their full potential and be their best selves!

I developed a coaching program: "Dream.Believe.Achieve. DBA: You!"

I was able to break down all of the steps in the process to help ladies unleash their best selves. Through this journey, I have learned that all the experiences that led me there will give you the freedom you desire and help you be the best you can be.

What is the powerful force that allows me to be unleashed and free from restraints? For me and my clients, it's our faith. The only way I can get there is to pray for guidance and direction. I ask daily for guidance. This guidance provided me with a way to start the *Best Version of You.*

Working through issues in the coaching program allowed me to be free. I came to realize that I don't always have to be in charge. I just need to be me. It's not irresponsible to prioritize my own care over others. I developed the support through the coaching program. There really are many women with this mindset. Build that tribe and fellowship. It only builds and empowers more women.

One of my dear friends stated she made three goals for the year. To help her stay on task, she evaluates anything she does or is asked to do by asking herself this question: Does doing that help me reach my goal? If it doesn't, she doesn't do it! Sounds simple, but it works.

For example, what if one of your goals is to lose twenty pounds this year? You are at a party and are offered an extra piece of cake. Remind yourself: Does eating that cake help me reach my goal? If not, don't eat it.

If you honestly want the best for others and follow your purpose, you will find the way. Just dream. Believe. Achieve… You have the right to unleash your true self and be happy.

My wish for you is that you find your own path to freedom by unleashing your own restraints. You have made it through many heartaches, trials, and tribulations. There may be more to come. Keep moving; life is a journey, and you can make it your best. God believes in you. I believe in you. You deserve freedom, you deserve to dream, you deserve to believe, you deserve to achieve.

I wish you the courage to take the next steps on your journey to freedom. You deserve to be the Best Version of You!

PAM KURT

Pamela D. Kurt is an attorney, Bestselling Author, speaker, and certified 10X Business Coach dedicated to empowering women to unlock their fullest potential. With a thriving family law practice and a history of leadership roles and board positions, Pam has always been driven by a passion for helping others. Today, she channels that passion into her business, *Best Version of You, LLC*, where she guides women through personal development, spiritual growth, and business success.

A prolific author, Pam has co-authored twelve books and contributed to multiple bestselling series, including *The Everyday Women's Guide* and *Becoming an Unstoppable Woman*. Her works, such as *The Successful Woman's Mindset* and *The Path to the Best You*, have topped charts in categories like Women in Business, Self-Help, and Personal Transformation. Her writing journey, which began as an attorney drafting legal documents, has evolved into a powerful platform for sharing stories of resilience, success, and empowerment. Pam has also been featured in prestigious publications like *Enterprise World*, *Tycoon Magazine*, and *Brainz Magazine*, solidifying her voice as a thought leader in women's empowerment. Connect with her at *pam@bestversionyou.com*.

Author's Website: *www.PamKurt.com*

Charity Awareness: *www.ForbesHouse.org*

PATTY SHIH-MEI LEE CAMPBELL

COURAGE VS. FEAR

. . . .

I lived in fear most of my life. As a child, I was taught to fear authority. I was not allowed to have a voice. I was taught to be seen and not heard because I was a girl born in a Chinese culture in the 1960s. My job was to obey without question. Boys were considered more important than girls. Boys were groomed by their dads to do business and master their craft, but girls were raised to be married off.

We played outdoors a lot, and swam almost every day in the tropical island nation of Singapore. Children were pretty much left to play alone and fend for themselves, except during school and meal times. Once, my friend and I were playing house by the pool, and we were washing toy dishes in the pool. I turned around to put something away, and when I turned back to the pool, my friend was drowning in the pool with her face under the water. I quickly pulled her out, and she was coughing and crying, spewing out water. There was no adult supervision, and we just continued playing after she recovered.

I remember so many head injuries: from flipping around on the concrete, my uncle (who was only two years older than me) hit me with a hoe, and a car accident where I flew to the front of the car and hit my nose on the car knobs, leaving a moon-shaped scar on my nose. I remember the bright lights above the surgery table while they stitched me up.

My mom, who was bipolar, was negligent in leaving her pills on the table once. She was so busy complaining to the servant that she never saw me taking her pills and falling asleep on the couch. When she finally realized I was passed out on the couch, she rushed to the hospital to get my stomach pumped.

The adults in my life, especially my dad and grandpa, were very stern and strict. We were afraid to cross them or misbehave. My grandpa even yelled at me when I played the wrong note on the piano. And then there were the spankings. Once, my dad chased me around the dining table with his slipper because I did something he didn't approve of. Then there was the time I hung halfway out a five-story window, and my dad came in, pulled me back into the apartment, and spanked me. You bet I never hung outside the window again!

My fear of authority affected my relationship with not just my parents but all authority figures—teachers, bosses, pastors, and especially men in general. Because I went to an all-girls school, I couldn't talk to boys for a long time. When we moved to New York City and went to a co-ed middle school, I remembered looking at the boys and was afraid to talk to them.

I would have to muster a lot of courage and practice what I was going to say before speaking to anyone. People used to tell me to look them in the eye instead of looking down when I spoke, and to speak up because they couldn't hear my soft voice.

Perfectionism and people-pleasing ruled my life as I feared confrontation and making mistakes. I avoided confrontation at all costs and allowed people to treat me poorly and take advantage of me because they saw my weakness. I allowed people to "shush" me and speak over me because I didn't have the courage to stand up for myself.

I had to hit bottom before realizing that it was costing me my health and mental wellness. I suffered depression for years because I suffered a devastating loss, and I didn't feel in control of my own life. I lost my way, my identity, and my purpose.

My life changed when I had to face my worst fears and go through them to the other side. When the 2009-2010 economy crashed, I lost everything because I owned real estate. I had to sell one house and lost $70,000. I short-sold another property in Chico. I defaulted on my house and had to fight against foreclosure. I filed for bankruptcy and had only $300 to my name in February of 2010. To add insult to injury, I lost my baby girl at five months of pregnancy and fell into a deep depression. I had never been that stressed since my ex-husband left me in 2002, and I had the financial responsibility to take care of our son.

Sometimes, life takes us through all kinds of hardships, heartbreaks, and trials. How we handled these trials determines the difference between surviving and thriving. It took tremendous courage for me to face bankruptcy because that was one of my greatest fears.

In fact, I wasn't able to completely go through it the first time. It took extreme courage to face the attorney at a deposition during my fight against the bank foreclosing on my house. It took unfathomable courage to face abandonment and depression and to keep going after my ex-husband left without good reason. It took insurmountable courage, while depressed, to get up every day and work 80-hour weeks to provide for my son as a single mother. Life dealt me some harsh lessons and difficult times, but I not only survived—I thrived.

In 2004, on paper, I was wealthier as a single mom than at any other time in my life. I owned real estate, and I was a landlord. When the economy crashed in 2009, I crashed with it like millions of Americans across the United States. It took years, but my husband and I built our own businesses, and we are back to thriving in 2025. We own real estate again, and I have written and published two books since then. Having overcome numerous trials and lessons, we now have the ability to help those going through difficulties and provide them with solutions.

My questions to you are: What trials have you been through? What were your worst fears? How did you deal with these trials and situations to overcome them? How have these difficulties shaped you into the person you are today? What were some of your regrets? Were you proud of how you handled life? What was your attitude in life? Did you see your cup as half empty or half full? Was it okay to make mistakes?

Part of living life to the fullest and thriving is facing your fears head-on. I've heard FEAR defined as "False Evidence Appearing Real." When you are willing to face your fears head-on, you can dispel fear and turn your fear into courage. Courage is your inner lion coming forth, roaring loudly against anything that contradicts it. Courage is setting boundaries and saying "no" sometimes. Courage is standing in the full authentic you and showing up every day, no matter what happens.

Courage is not the absence of fear, but the facing of your fears even while you're still afraid. Courage can be lonely because many aren't willing to walk that narrow path. For those who do, they find strength within that they never knew they had. They realize they are much stronger than they thought, much braver than they imagined.

What have you overcome in your past that took courage? What are you proud of that you have accomplished? When was the last time you thought you weren't going to make it, but you did? That your heart was too broken, but you were able to go on? You are much more resilient than you think. You can turn survival into thrival. You do not need to succumb to the status quo or struggle your whole life.

Each day is a new beginning with a fresh start. You can choose a different path at any time. You can make new decisions today that will change your future. What will you do today that will impact your future in a courageous way? What visions and dreams do you have that you still want to attain? What steps and actions can you take today, this week, this month, this year to actualize those dreams? Do you have to go back to school? Do you have to quit your job? Do you have to step outside your comfort zone? Greatness happens outside the comfort zone. Courage happens when you defy and resist fear.

I hope you are encouraged to hope again, to dream again, to fight again for your deep beliefs and convictions. I hope to hear your story someday—hear about your failures and triumphs. I hope to see you on the other side of fear because you are willing to go through it.

PATTY CAMPBELL

Patty Shih-Mei Lee Campbell was born and raised in three different countries with three different cultural experiences. She has learned that there are more ways to be right than just one way. There is so much beauty in each culture, even when they are very different from each other.

She is married to a wonderful and supportive husband and has two sons, nineteen years apart. One just turned twelve and the other is thirty-one (and got married this year, May 25, 2025).

Patty loves to connect with people at a deeper level and tackles life with a positive outlook. Although her upbringing and experiences weren't the easiest, she has chosen to stay positive and overcome obstacles with grace and perseverance. Love is her chosen language.

Author's Website: *www.AbundanceGroup.us*

Charity Awareness: *www.TurnTable.com*

RITU CHOPRA

MY JOURNEY THROUGH RUGGED PATHS & WINDING ROADS

Little did I know that at the tender age of twelve years, life had begun to prepare me for the future.

Now, as I look back, I notice that sometimes, I followed the paths that opened up to me, and other times, I paved my own path. These paths were where the stories of my life were etched so deeply, the paths that opened themselves to guide me to the stories that were to be written on the jagged cobblestones. I grew up in a loving, protected middle-class home, where the highest education possible was our parents' goal for their children.

On one summer morning, when schools were out, I was, as usual, spending the morning by the fragrant *Champa* bush, its tiny flower petals loaded with fragrance, perfuming the summer air and humming of little bees nearby. It was a usual morning. My father, a civil law practicing attorney, called me when he was at home. His clerk had taken a day off. He asked me to fill out some important forms that he needed to take with him that day. It was simple to follow his instructions and to write in the blank areas of the form. He was very pleased, looking at my beautiful handwriting, and he complimented me.

The story just starts here.

What began as a small task, helping my dad with dictations, quietly sparked a journey neither of us foresaw. During summer breaks, I learned the language of legal papers, and soon I was taking notes for his typist. My teenage curiosity led to questions about law, which my dad answered with warmth and wonder, amused by his inquisitive thirteen-year-old.

Once, he asked me to go through the court documents written in a blend of two major local languages. In my fascination, I would read and re-read and ask Dad more questions. During this time, Dad gave me a diary that I used to write *"Golden Pearls of Wisdom"* every Sunday, which was published in a major local Newspaper's children's section.

He noticed my potential and would call me to join him in his home office when a client came for consultation, often for civil matters. I would make notes if he asked me to. I was learning so many new things. Looking back, these experiences have taught me confidence, the ability to communicate with experienced and accomplished people, belief in myself, ambition, problem-solving, and thinking like a grown-up in my mid-teens.

Slowly, assisting my dad became a routine. This unintentional learning process actually laid the foundation for my journey as a young bride when I moved to the United States with my husband at the age of twenty-one. The same opportunities were not available to me, as I had no access to pretty much anything.

Life changed drastically. My higher education was interrupted.

As a young, vibrant, aspiring woman, in just opposite circumstances, I had to find meaning and strength inside.

With many years of unhealthy and toxic relationships, facing threats to myself and my family, cultural stigma, shame, fear, uncertainties, and loss of dreams that I began with, my journey was very rough. I was fortunate to have had the education and burning desire to change my life's conditions. I was able to stop the physical abuse that often injured my spirit and my sincerity towards my loved ones.

I questioned myself but protected everyone else from the "shame and stigma" that comes with breaking away. I was preparing myself to embrace the roughest path and break the cycle of ongoing emotional and verbal abuse. Every now and then, I found myself picking up the fallen pieces scattered around in the shadows of life, spirits bruised, and confidence lost.

With nowhere to turn to for help, where would you go? Those who are supposed to protect you now are ready to harm you. How can someone reconcile this?

I was trying to find my place in my little universe. How did these challenges fit into my "ambitious world" that I had imagined growing up?

I sought answers and relied upon the strong values that were embedded in me, and sometimes I felt spellbound, as if I were in a crazy "scene" in a drama of life. I didn't find the answers I was looking for, only more disappointments. It was easy to let go of the glorious ambitions and fall prey to the vicious claws of "destiny."

Everywhere I turned, disappointments, hurt, sadness, and then an auto accident left me physically and emotionally in pain.

I remember reading, *"When life hits you hard and knocks you down, roll over and look at the stars."* These words of wisdom were just the medicine I needed. The faint voices of hope infused with faith suddenly emerged into the dark valleys and lifted my spirits. The rays of hope as the headlights on the road broke into the darkness, enough for me to see a small patch of the lit path ahead.

So, I looked up and had no choice except to create something out of this experience that was presented to me. *"Ask and you shall receive.*" My self-inspired moments gave me the courage to write a book. Oh! *"Into the memory lane again to relive the moment of the past,"* I thought to myself.

My inner voice responded, "No."

Seeking answers within, I remembered another pearl of wisdom written in my childhood diary: "A teacher shall appear when the student is ready."

Life amazed me, teachers appeared just when I needed them, often as fleeting strangers who answered my questions and vanished. Each encounter felt like magic, leaving me floating in a cloud of inspiration.

A WOMAN'S JOURNEY ALONE CONTINUES INTO UNKNOWN TERRITORIES

Life comes without instructions; we write our own manuals, shaped by our world. From dark valleys to inspired skies, I felt something greater emerging. I wanted to give hope, inspire strength, and rise after every fall, unknowingly writing a new chapter of faith, where faint voices of hope began to echo through the darkness.

Now, it wasn't just hope; faith walked beside it. Together, they pulled me from darkness toward a deeper purpose. It was time to rise. I found guidance in Dad's diary and, through writing my first book *Art of Life*, I discovered inner strength, courage, and a new outlook, one where true happiness is possible, no matter what the circumstances.

Aha, I thought. I had learned hard lessons and managed to swim across and stay afloat. Finally, it was a smooth ride. I gathered all my strength and was ready to aim higher.

"Not so fast, dear," Life whispered to me. "You're special. I have another test for you."

The economic meltdown of 2007-2008, "The Great Recession," arrived in our lives. Financial means were snatched away instantly, leaving me to grapple with a new reality. With many uncertainties around, I couldn't give up.

But wait, I am too tired, I need a few resting moments.

Time doesn't wait. Rushing to keep up, I searched for answers until my inner voice reminded me, *You've grown through challenges, mastered your skills; don't stop now.*

I turned to my diary for wisdom. My second book, *Mastering Life*, became my new expression, lifting me from the ordinary to a deeper purpose. Along the way, new teachers appeared, bringing clarity to my questions.

As I assembled the broken, scattered pieces one more time, I gathered my strength, reignited my dreams, and took a bold leap of faith into a new arena, armed with courage, clarity, and all the tools, skills, and strategy needed to succeed. Drenched with enthusiasm, courage, and audacity, I knew deep down: *I can make this work.*

"Not so fast, you brave ignorant," said Life. "It's a man's world, and you're a lone woman trying to compete in a world of the 'privileged' members of our societies. Can you prove your worth to compete with them?"
What I set out to accomplish, far away from my comfort zone, with the hope of causing change, was yet another stumbling block. Well, yes, it was a huge stumbling block indeed.

Suddenly, the inner voice went silent, very silent, almost feeling numb. Then it whispered again, "Hey, you, this is not a stumbling block, this is your launch-pad."

I remembered that faith had joined hands with hope, and both of them had just arrived on time once again to lift my spirits. With my spirits glowing, I found yet another way to inspire others. *Despite the Challenges* ®, my TV show, was born.

Of all the battles I have faced, I don't know how many I've won and how many I've lost. What I remember is that I fought all of them with all my strength. *How did life just slip away?* I've often wondered. Remembering my journey through the jagged paths, how can one get this far walking alone?

Today, I stand tall, grateful for every bitter-sweet experience that shaped me. Each challenge brought a lesson, each crossroads a teacher, and life kept whispering, *"Where there's a will, there's a way."*

RITU CHOPRA

Ritu Chopra inspires people with her sincerity in coaching and professional leadership experience, which includes managing business and IT operations.

Ritu has solved complex technical challenges in her work with Fortune 500 companies over the past twenty-plus years. Using proven methods and tools, she leverages her management and coaching expertise to bridge IT-business gaps, boost engagement, and empower teams.

As president of Chopra Management Services, Ritu is a creative force, motivational speaker, and certified leadership coach. She is the author of *Art of Life*, *Mastering Life*, *Women Leadership in 21st Century*, and her upcoming title, *Magic in Mindfulness*. As an executive coach, Ritu leads seminars and coaching programs tailored to niche areas, including personal mastery, women in leadership, and mindfulness in daily life.

Ritu brings her passion, humility, and dedication to inspire her clients to engage their heads and hearts in clarity and creation.

Author's Website: *www.RituChopra.com*

Charity Awareness: *www.SurvivalToThrivalSeries.com*

DR. SABRINA PATEL

COURAGE: LEAVING THE KNOWN FOR THE UNKNOWN

Courage isn't always loud. Sometimes it's the quiet decisions, the trembling yes to something uncertain, the brave goodbye to everything familiar. At seventeen years old, I left my home in Kingston, Jamaica, and stepped onto a plane that would take me away from my family, my culture, my comforts, and into the vast unknown of the United States. I didn't know it then, but that moment would shape the rest of my life. It would teach me what courage truly is—not the absence of fear, but the ability to act despite it.

I grew up in a world full of vibrancy and connection, where neighbors felt like extended family, Sunday dinners were sacred, and the sound of laughter mingled with the scent of island spices drifting from the kitchen. Jamaica gave me color, culture, and comfort. But alongside that comfort came a quiet knowing: that the future I envisioned for myself required something more. I wasn't running away from home, I was running toward possibility. I craved exposure, opportunity, and a broader stage to express the fullness of who I was becoming. Deep down, I knew that if I wanted to grow beyond the boundaries of my upbringing, I had to be willing to leave the familiar behind.

The decision to leave wasn't made lightly. I recall the months leading up to my departure, and the conflicting emotions that swirled inside me: excitement, fear, anticipation, guilt. I was young and determined, but I was also terrified. There's a certain pain in knowing that in choosing your path, you must also let go of a piece of your past. At seventeen, you're still figuring out who you are. And yet, there I was, preparing to say goodbye to my family, my childhood friends, and the country that made me.

I still remember the exact moment I hugged my mother goodbye at the airport. Her embrace was steady, but her eyes betrayed the worry and pride she was holding back. I had never seen her look so torn. "Be strong," she whispered, as tears welled up in both our eyes. "Go and become everything you're meant to be." That blessing carried me through the turbulence, both literal and emotional, of the journey ahead.

Landing in the United States was like stepping into another world. I arrived in a place that was colder in temperature and in spirit. The pace was faster, the people more reserved, and the systems unfamiliar. I was suddenly responsible for everything: rent, bills, transportation, meals, and my studies. I went from being a teenager in a household to being a young adult navigating life alone. There were days I questioned my decision. Days I cried silently in my dorm room, longing for the laughter of my sisters, the aroma of my mother's cooking, the familiarity of my old life.

But courage isn't the loud victories. It's the quiet persistence. The small choices to show up again and again—to class, to work, to yourself. I had to dig deep to find that inner strength. I found myself in libraries late at night, sometimes on an empty stomach, determined to keep up. I had to overcome moments of doubt, language barriers, cultural differences, and a lingering feeling of being "other." And yet, I knew I didn't come this far to only come this far.

As time went on, I began to rebuild. I created a new support system of friends who became my family. I learned to cook my favorite meals from back home, sometimes just to feel close to my roots. I studied harder than I thought I could, driven by the dream of becoming a physician. I learned not just how to survive, but how to thrive—and that transformation, that journey from fear to freedom, was powered by courage.

Courage also came in realizing that it's okay to be vulnerable. It's okay to say, "I'm struggling," and to ask for help. In my early days, I wore strength like armor, believing that I had to be tough all the time. However, over the years, I have discovered that true strength allows for softness. There is nothing weak about leaning on others, expressing fear, or resting. That realization changed how I approached my personal life, my education, and, eventually, how I care for my patients.

Looking back, I see now that leaving Jamaica was not just a physical journey. It was an emotional and spiritual evolution. I had to shed the safety of my childhood and step into a world that tested every part of me. But with every challenge, I discovered something new about myself. I learned resilience. I found my voice. I uncovered a sense of identity that was no longer tied to a place, but to a purpose.

My story is not unique. There are countless others who leave home in search of something more, something better. But I share mine as a testament to what is possible when we dare to follow the whisper inside us that says, "There is more." When we act not because we're fearless, but because we believe in the vision of who we can become.

Now, as a physician and mother, I often reflect on the courage it took to take that first flight. I remind myself of that young woman who stood at the airport, both terrified and hopeful, and I honor her every time I step into a new challenge. Whether I'm speaking at a conference, launching a wellness program, or guiding a patient through their healing, I carry that legacy of courage with me.

Courage is what moves us from comfort to calling. It's what

allows us to say yes to growth, even when it means saying goodbye to ease. It's what lets us hold space for fear while still choosing faith. And it's what transforms lives—not just our own, but of everyone we touch.

So, to anyone standing at the edge of a decision, staring into the unknown, wondering if they're strong enough, I say this: You are. You were not given your dream by accident. The path will be hard. You may cry. You may fall. But if you choose courage, you will rise stronger than you ever imagined.

And one day, you will look back, as I do now, and smile at the brave soul who chose the harder road. Because that road leads to everything that is beautiful, meaningful, and true.

DR. SABRINA PATEL

Dr. Sabrina Patel is a board-certified family medicine physician and the founder of Zia Health, a concierge functional medicine and wellness clinic based in Ormond Beach, Florida. With advanced training in hormone optimization, root-cause medicine, and functional wellness, Dr. Patel helps patients restore balance, reclaim energy, and align with their healthiest selves.

After facing personal health struggles postpartum and being diagnosed with an autoimmune condition, she pivoted from conventional protocols to integrative approaches that transformed her life—and now her patients' lives too. Born and raised in Kingston, Jamaica, Dr. Patel brings a unique cultural lens to healing, blending evidence-based science with compassion and intuition. She is a devoted wife and mother of two young boys, with a love for baking, the arts, and travel. Through her work, she empowers others to reconnect with their bodies, rediscover their vitality, and live in alignment with their purpose.

Author's Website: *www.SabrinaPatel.com*

Charity Awareness: *www.SurvivalToThrivalSeries.com*

SAMARA BETH

DISCOVERING COURAGE THROUGH EVERY STORM

. . . .

THE BAMBOO WITHIN

"Everything can be taken from a man but one thing: the last of the human freedoms—to choose one's attitude in any given set of circumstances, to choose one's own way."
~ Viktor Frankl

I didn't set out to be courageous. I set out to survive. Somewhere between survival and thrival, I became "Badass Bamboo."

My journey wasn't paved with ease; it was paved with pivots, heartbreaks, and hard choices. I've lived in thirteen big cities, across thirty homes, reinventing my life every few years. Each move, each heartbreak, each challenge demanded courage I didn't always feel I had. I discovered that true strength wasn't about standing tall without ever wavering. It was about bending without breaking, about being willing to root, grow, and reach again, no matter how many times the winds of life tried to knock me down. Rinse and repeat.

Before the nickname was given to me, I became "Lil' Bamboo" during the darkest chapter of my life. At fourteen weeks pregnant, I learned that my son, Cameron, had Giant Omphalocele, a severe condition that made survival nearly impossible. His tiny heart had a hole. His lungs were too small to sustain life without breathing tubes. His liver, intestines, and stomach grew outside his body in a fragile membrane.

After months of experimental genetic testing, three-dimensional ultrasounds, and consultations with five world-renowned specialists in Houston, I was told that no one would blame me if I let him go. I clung to hope, desperate for a miracle. There was no way I was going to give up on my son.

But reality painted a different picture. Caring for my beautiful five-year-old son Gavin, who had been diagnosed with autism at just thirteen months old, forced me to face an impossible situation. My heart broke, but I caved to the bravest decision I could as a mother. I let Cameron go, releasing him back to God, and releasing myself from a burden no mother should ever have to carry.

Or so people thought. That moment cracked me wide open. Grief flooded in, and yet, in some mysterious, sacred way, so did strength. I didn't break. I bent. I grieved deeply. I mothered Gavin with everything I had left. I moved forward, one unsteady step at a time. Courage, I learned, is not the absence of fear—it's standing up when you want to collapse, loving when your heart is shattered, believing in tomorrow when today feels unbearable.

Life didn't give me much time to recover. While raising Gavin and navigating depression, I juggled my husband's intense weekend MBA program, his constant oil industry work travel, and the endless logistics of our lives. At the same time, I was still working at a corporate event planning and destination management firm in Houston, producing marketing events, all while carrying Cameron and battling heartache.

After a beautiful funeral for our son, attended by twenty-five friends and family from all corners of my life, surviving Hurricane Ike in a closet, and enduring the economic crash of

2008, I was laid off from my part-time corporate job. After a good, cleansing cry, I did something most people thought was insane during a recession: I opened my own event planning company, Celebrations by Samara.

Just when I thought I couldn't possibly carry more, life handed me another surprise: I was pregnant again. Exhausted beyond belief, falling asleep on the HOV lane while driving Gavin forty-five minutes to his new school, I had no choice but to dig even deeper. I kept bending. I kept growing. I rooted myself wherever life planted me.

Military life had conditioned us to move every few years, and staying in one place for too long felt unnatural. We staged the house, sold it within a week, and searched for a new home closer to Gavin's school.

During this season of chaos and transition, I continued growing our family. I was pregnant with our daughter while rebuilding our lives again. We found a beautiful house just six minutes from Gavin's school, where I finally started to breathe. We made new friends. I dove back into volunteering as a room mom and fundraising co-chair. I was high-risk, attending endless doctor appointments requiring more courage, but I had hope.

One night after indulging at a moms' club cheesecake event, I woke up in a pool of blood. Panicked, we rushed to the emergency room, and the same team of nurses who had cared for me during Cameron's loss was there. They remembered us well. No one at that hospital had ever seen a case of Giant Omphalocele before; it had been heartbreaking for them, too. Having them by my side again, prepping the newer staff, was an unexpected comfort. And I seemed to have discovered a way to induce labor —candybar cheesecake.

My daughter wasn't waiting for anyone. Her lungs were underdeveloped, my OBGYN was at a conference in Florida, and my husband was in the middle of MBA midterms. As if orchestrated by fate, we scheduled a cesarean around his exams. He even called the hospital and casually asked, "How's 2 PM for delivery?" A stranger delivered my daughter, but she arrived strong, feisty, and full of life.

Armed with nothing but my dream home office, a passion, and an undefeated heart, I built a successful business in a city where I knew very few people. Through sheer willpower, innovation, volunteering, and networking, I became one of Houston's most sought-after social event planners, crafting spectacular celebrations and winning awards, not because I had a magic formula, but because I had the courage to keep showing up, committing first and figuring out the rest later, even when doubt whispered otherwise.

When life moved me again, first to Vancouver, British Columbia, then to Scottsdale, I celebrated what was possible. I planted new roots. I built new villages. Even when COVID-19 forced me to shut down my business, refund clients, and start from scratch, I chose courage again. I chose to believe that endings are often disguised beginnings.

I leaned fully into who I had become: the woman who W.I.N.s— Willpower, Innovation, Networking. From the ashes of disappointment, I birthed Samara Beth & Co., a coaching, *experiential events, branding, and marketing company* dedicated to helping others bend without breaking and thrive through every storm.

Transitioning from thirty years of consulting to becoming a business coach presents its share of challenges, but I welcome and enjoy the process of helping others share their messages and positively impact millions of people.

"Courage doesn't always roar. Sometimes courage is the quiet voice at the end of the day saying, 'I will try again tomorrow.'"
~ Mary Anne Radmacher

If I could whisper to the woman standing where I once stood, exhausted, heartbroken, unsure if she could take another hit, I would tell her this:

- Courage is a daily choice, not a one-time act. You don't wake up fearless; you wake up willing—willing to get dressed and put on your shoes; willing to show up scared but determined. Commit to one act of bravery each day, even if that act is simply getting out of bed and trying again.

- You may not control the storm, but you can control how you view yourself and your environment. Anchor yourself in something deeper than circumstances, whether it's faith in yourself and your higher power, community, journaling, or creativity. My daughter and I love diamond painting and finger-knitting blankets as a way to focus on art. Water your own spirit daily (no green thumb required) with activities such as stating a positive message or intention while tapping, practicing relaxing meditation, walking alone in silence to think, or allowing fresh ideas to surface.

- Allow yourself to bend. Bending is not weakness; it's wisdom. Let yourself grieve. Let yourself sway. Resilience isn't about being unaffected—it's about refusing to be undone.

- Turn your pain into purpose. Your hardest seasons will become your most powerful testimony if you let them. Your scars are not signs of failure; they are signposts for others searching for the way through.

- Finally, surround yourself with bamboo believers. You become like the people you spend the most time with. Find those who see the courageous warrior in you, even when you feel broken. Find coaches, mentors, and friends who pour belief back into your dry places. And if you haven't found them yet, come find me, where we help you WIN your brand and WIN your story.

Today, I no longer call myself "Lil' Bamboo." I stand courageously as "Badass Bamboo:" rooted, radiant, flexible, fierce. I am the storm and the shelter. I am the woman who didn't break. I am the woman who bent and rose stronger and grew taller (five feet no more).

And so are you.

If you are reading this, let it be a reminder: you are braver than you believe, stronger than you feel, and more capable than you even know. The world needs your light. It needs your legacy. It requires the courage to grow quietly, powerfully, within you.

Let's grow your bamboo forest together.

Connect with me. Let's WIN your brand. Let's WIN your story. Let's WIN your life.

SAMARA BETH

Samara Beth is a keynote speaker, 10X Certified Business Coach, national award-winning event producer, and best-selling author with a career spanning over thirty years across North America. As the founder and CEO of Samara Beth & Co., she empowers entrepreneurs to W.I.N. their brand by creating powerful and memorable events, experiences, retreats, and stages. By increasing their revenue, visibility, and brand impact, Samara Beth & Co's W.I.N. Pillars—Willpower to overcome challenges, Innovation to think creatively, and Networking to build powerful communities —have helped countless businesses grow successfully.

Having lived in thirteen cities and thirty homes, mostly as a military and expat spouse, Samara's journey is one of resilience, adaptability, and transformation, leading to her nickname "Lil' Bamboo." She has built multiple businesses, cultivated thriving communities, and navigated personal and professional challenges with unwavering determination. Known for her contagious energy and light, Samara has inspired thousands through her speaking engagements, courses, retreats, and books, helping individuals turn obstacles into opportunities. Recognized as a "Volunteer of the Year" and a recipient of the "Humanitarian Award," she continues to uplift others, leaving a lasting impact wherever she goes.

Author's Website: *www.SamaraBeth.com*

Charity Awareness: *www.AFMDA.org*

STEPH SHINABERY
BRAVE ENOUGH TO BEGIN

. . . .

Courage isn't the absence of fear; it's the ability to face it. It's standing toe-to-toe with your fear, looking it in the eye, and moving forward anyway.

There are moments in life that feel like a crossroads—where one road is comfort, and the other is courage. And the truth is, courage rarely feels safe. It usually appears wrapped in uncertainty, laced with fear, and demands action before you're ready.

I've lived that moment.

I've been planning a live event—something I've dreamed of for years. It was supposed to be co-led with someone I deeply respect and felt brought the exact masculine energy the event needed. But life happened, and my partner didn't show up. No call. No explanation. I could feel myself spiraling.

I started doubting myself. Could I do this on my own? Was this event even going to work? My brain went into protective mode: "Don't do it. You're not ready. You might fail. Everyone will see that you weren't enough."

The voice of fear was loud, but then something shifted. I paused. I breathed. And I chose love. I sent my partner silent gratitude, trusting he was walking his own journey. Then I asked myself: "Steph, how can you move forward anyway?"

So, I booked the Airbnb. I started ordering materials. I reached out to others who could support the vision. I decided I would show up. I will offer this event. Whether it succeeds or flops, I will walk through the door.

And honestly, I felt exposed. The people in my circle and my community expected him to be there. We've always done things together. I worried they'd ask, "Where's your partner?" And part of me feared that I'd be perceived as less than without him. But I had to ask myself, "Am I willing to let fear write this story—or am I willing to trust that I can stand on my own two feet and lead something meaningful?"

That's courage.

It's not about having all the answers. It's about being willing to step into the unknown because something inside of you is calling you forward, even if it's shaky or not perfect.

I've faced this before—big time. At age forty-two, I was stuck in a job I didn't love. I had been a nurse for twenty years, and although I had returned to art school for a time (which I absolutely loved), something was still missing. I craved fulfillment. I wanted more.

So, I made the terrifying decision to leave it all behind and go to anesthesia school. I walked away from my job. I ended a relationship. I took out over $120,000 in student loans. I could've stayed at my job and coasted into retirement. It had great benefits. It was stable. It was safe.

But I didn't want safety—I wanted a life that lit me up.

People around me thought I was crazy. Who goes back to school at forty-two? Who gives up a retirement plan for more debt and uncertainty?

But I did it anyway.

And that choice gave me a new life—a life where I actually love what I do. I joke with patients, calling myself their sedation bartender. I enjoy my work. It provides me the flexibility to grow in new directions, to invest in myself, and to pursue my true purpose.

Courage cracked open a door I didn't even know was waiting for me.

I often hear from people in their thirties who are hesitant to make a significant life change, such as returning to school, switching careers, or pursuing a long-held dream. And I always tell them, "You've got decades left. Why stay stuck in something that dims your light?" It's never too late. Courage is deciding you're worth the risk.

But this isn't just about jobs and education. For me, courage has also meant redefining identity.

As a girl, I was labeled. I wanted to compete. I wanted to play with the boys. I didn't want to be confined to roles that didn't align with who I was. And I recall how challenging it was to constantly defy what people expected of me. But I kept going. I loved the game. I loved the growth. I loved proving to myself that I was capable, no matter what others thought.

That spirit lives in me still.

Even now, as I prepare to pivot again in my life—to leave anesthesia someday and build something new, my next passion—I remind myself that every step forward has been built on the foundation of courage. Not perfect nor certain. Just a willingness to begin.

I've learned that staying in dissatisfaction, just because it's familiar, is its own kind of suffering. There was a time when I focused too much on what I didn't have. I think, "I'm not where I want to be. I'm not doing what I love yet." That mindset drained me until I returned to a mindset of gratitude.

I began to realize how my current work provided me with freedom, connection, and opportunity. That shift in perspective changed everything. It allowed me to show up differently. It reminded me that the courage to change isn't always in walking away—it's in choosing how you see what's already in front of you.

Even now, I still get scared. I still worry. However, I continue to choose to move forward. Because if I don't, I'm not just holding myself back—I'm withholding something from the people I'm meant to serve. My community misses out. I miss out. And I know I'd be kicking myself for not trying.

I think of the people who changed the world by being courageous. And then I think, "Can't I, at least, do this one brave thing today?" The answer is yes.

Write This Down:

"Courage doesn't wait for clarity. It moves with purpose even in the fog."

So, here I am. Still figuring it out. Still scared. Still showing up.

Because sometimes courage is just being brave enough to begin— and brave enough to keep going.

STEPH SHINABERY

Steph Shinabery is The World's Best Possibility Coach, a Nurse Anesthesiologist, Artist, Speaker, and the Founder of Genius Code Academy.

After spending much of her life in a career that lacked the inspiration and fulfillment she knew was available to her, she began a journey to answer the question: "What is it I truly desire?"

Her journey led to the creation of the Genius Identity Code™, a process for unlocking your gift, purpose, and path, and helping people see, believe, and execute their unique genius to achieve miraculous outcomes.

Steph works with creative experts, entrepreneurs, and coaches to help them embrace their authenticity and create a life that gets them excited to jump out of bed every day!

You can find her talk, "Wake Up Your Genius Machine," on Amazon Prime Video's *Speak Up: Empower Your Ideas, Season 4.*

Author's Website: *www.StephShinabery.com*

Charity Awareness: *www.SurvivalToThrivalSeries.com*

TYLER WATSON

FROM STRIVING TO THRIVING: HOW DESPERATION BIRTHED CREATION

Most people never realize they are living in survival mode. They call it "working hard." They call it "being responsible." But underneath the surface? They are striving. Gripping. Desperate.

I know this because I lived it. Years ago, I worked as a massage therapist, earning less than $13,000 a year. I had dreams of being something more—maybe a coach, maybe a doctor of natural medicine—but I was stuck between survival and destiny. I was good at coping. I wasn't great at creating.

I remember the moment the universe forced my hand. I was standing at an event, overwhelmed, watching a speaker pitch a program that cost half my entire yearly income. Half. It felt impossible. I barely had enough for groceries, let alone some big "coaching program."

My first thought? I'll do it once I have the money. But then something deeper whispered to me: "Tyler, if you wait, you'll never have it." I froze. Then another thought, even stronger, hit me: "Who are you going to serve—money or me?"

It wasn't a random thought. It felt divine. In that moment, I realized something painful and freeing: For my entire life, I had been serving money. Not God. Not my purpose. Not my higher self.

I was serving lack. I was enslaved to fear.

And right there, in that sweaty conference room, I made the decision that would define the rest of my life: I would never again make decisions based on money. I would only make decisions based on inspiration and truth.

I didn't have the money. I didn't have credit. But I had a decision. I started calling people. Borrowing. Asking for help. And against every ounce of logic... I chose to say yes to my destiny.

THE HIDDEN GIFT OF DESPERATION

Looking back now, I realize that desperation was a gift. Not because I enjoyed it—but because it demanded that I choose.

When you're desperate, you'll do things you wouldn't do when you're comfortable. You'll call strangers. You'll swallow your pride. You'll push past rejection. You'll humble yourself. And, at first, that desperation fueled my creation.

I hustled. I studied everything I could get my hands on. I failed and got back up again.

I applied every broken, messy step with complete fire because I was done tolerating a mediocre life.

I didn't just want to survive anymore. I wanted to thrive. And over time, that fire became focus. The desperation that once drove me to fight started making me build.

In seven months, I made my first six figures. The next year, I had weekends where I made six figures in just a few days. But the real breakthrough wasn't the money. It was that I was no longer a slave. I was no longer owned by fear, by doubt, or by lack.

FROM DESPERATION TO INSPIRATION

There comes a point where desperation must evolve. It's a powerful engine—but it's not meant to drive you forever.

Once I proved to myself that I could create, a deeper question arose: What if I could create—not because I needed to, but because I chose to? What if business, money, relationships, and even personal growth didn't have to be fueled by fear of "not enough" but by a desire to serve more powerfully, love more deeply, and create more joyfully?

That question changed everything. I recall a specific moment when I was relaxing in my bathtub, letting my mind wander, when an unexpected thought suddenly occurred to me: "Create an offer worth $65,000 and sell it at your next event." I laughed at first. It felt outrageous. Impossible. Unrealistic. But this time, I knew better.

It wasn't about logic; it was about alignment. So, I listened. I designed a new program, built around solving bigger problems for people who were ready to transform their lives at a higher level.

I pitched it to a room of fewer than thirty-five people, and within three days, I sold four packages—bringing in over $260,000. No desperation. No striving. Just creation.

That day, I realized a truth that few ever discover: True thriving isn't about escaping desperation. True thriving is about choosing from inspiration.

THE REAL SHIFT: FROM VICTIM TO CREATOR

For most of my life, I made decisions based on what I could afford, not what I was called to.

I settled for what felt safe, instead of choosing what felt true. And because of that, I lived in constant striving—working harder but never feeling fulfilled.

What shifted wasn't just my income—it was my identity. I stopped seeing myself as a victim of circumstances. I stopped making choices because of fear. I stopped waiting for money to give me permission.

And I started creating. Choosing. Owning.

It wasn't easy at first; it took practice to trust that inner voice. It took persistence to move even when fear whispered in my ear. But once I tasted creation without desperation, there was no going back.

THE SECRET TO THRIVING: FULL CHOICE

Here's the truth no one talks about: Freedom isn't about how much money you have. Freedom is about how you choose.

If your choices are still being dictated by fear, lack, guilt, shame, or obligation—you're still enslaved. Even if you're "successful."

But when you choose based on inspiration, when you decide based on alignment rather than fear, you step into your full power. You become the Creator you were always meant to be.

True choice is not logical; it's not based on what your bank account says. It's based on what your soul knows. When you choose from that place, you stop striving. You stop surviving. You start thriving. And it gets to be powerful.

It gets to be easy. It gets to be fun. Because creation, in its purest form, is joy.

YOUR TIME TO CHOOSE

Maybe today, you're standing where I once stood. Maybe you feel the tension—the pull between fear and future. Between settling and soaring. Between survival and soul.

If that's you, let me say this as clearly as I can: You were not born to be a slave to money, fear, or lack. You were born to create. To choose. To thrive.

So, the next time life asks you, "Who will you serve—fear or truth?" you'll know your answer.

And when you choose truth—fully, completely, cellularly—the entire universe will rise to meet you.

TYLER WATSON

Tyler Watson is a coach, speaker, and mentor specializing in turning survival-mode strivers into powerful creators. After escaping the cycle of depression, financial struggle, and striving for worthiness, Tyler dedicated his life to helping others break free.

Through his Cellular Alignment Technique and personal mentoring, Tyler has helped thousands accelerate their breakthroughs, generate quantum leaps in income, relationships, and confidence—and most importantly, choose from truth instead of fear. Tyler's mission is simple: to help you remember your divine ability to create without limits and thrive with full choice.

Start your journey from striving to thriving with Tyler's free gift here: *https://www.AlignmentEffect.com/More*

Author's Website: *www.AlignmentEffect.com*

Charity Awareness: *www.SurvivalToThrivalSeries.com*

VICKI PARKER

FROM HOPEFUL ESCAPE TO INTENTIONAL LEADERSHIP

THE REAL COURAGE

They called it courageous, that decision to leave behind a lifestyle that many found glamorous, boarding flights, facilitating retreats, coaching from lounges in places like Delhi, Paris, and Key West, and carrying the energy of twelve-week training programs around the globe. But when I chose to move into a 177-year-old farmhouse tucked inside a national park in Ohio, I didn't experience it as bravery.

I experienced it as faithfulness, obedience.

The truth is, my "yes" to this new life wasn't a departure from the extraordinary; it was a response to the sacred.

Faithfulness brought me here. This opportunity placed itself gently on my path like a divine nudge, and I answered without fully knowing what I was stepping into. I said yes to Him, yes to what I believed was being orchestrated, not by chance, but by God. And I was promised I could still travel when needed, as long as we had staff. That was all I needed to begin.

And yet... no amount of divine prompting shields you from the learning curve when building something human.

Today, I live in two small rooms above the dining room and library. My once high-ceiling condo has given way to pitched wooden beams that creak in the morning. It's a life that's quieter, but not simpler. My schedule now flexes to the rhythm of seasons, turnover days, and 5 AM descents to the kitchen before the first coffee is brewed.

There are days I miss the energy of twelve-week training programs. I miss the pace, the maker energy, and the glossy confidence that came with being in demand.

But slowly, by holy design, I am learning to experience power differently: not in performance, but in presence.

I came to the Inn to apprentice myself to a new kind of leadership, the kind that takes root behind the scenes. I manage promises and personalities, navigate expectations, and build teams that not only function but also flourish. It is nothing short of spiritual training: experimental, high-stakes, and deeply humbling.

There have been days I haven't lived up to my own standard. Times I let communication slide. Moments I slipped into gossip rather than guidance. There have been stretches where I quietly deferred to my co-Innkeeper and then resented her control, when, in truth, I wasn't standing in my own leadership or honoring the gifts I bring.

All of this, I now realize, is part of the work.

God didn't call me here to replicate my old life in a pastoral setting. He invited me to practice what I've learned over a lifetime and discover where I still shrink from leading in love. And that means doing the real work of alignment. Of honoring my word. Of managing promises with the same care I manage bedsheets and breakfast trays.

The hardest pill to swallow? I've given people reason to doubt me. That isn't about shame, that's about accountability. Seeds of mistrust are easy to plant in soil that isn't consistently tended. And if courage looks like anything these days, it looks like me standing toe-to-toe with my reflection and choosing again.

I am not a victim of this small-town chapter. I am an author in it.

Managing a historic home with uneven floors and guests from around the globe is not everyone's idea of a thriving career. For me, it's a living classroom. Every moment presents an invitation, a chance to deepen trust, cultivate grace, and practice presence.

I no longer confuse frantic movement with progress. I know now that true growth is rooted, not rushed. This looks like taking five extra minutes to create a welcoming breakfast table. This looks like asking forgiveness faster than I used to. This looks like holding myself with the same grace I give to guests. And that looks like choosing, over and over again, not to coast.

I'm not waiting for someone else to organize my joy.

Sure, I still desire jet-set experiences. I want to speak to global audiences, hang out of train windows in Zurich, and sip matcha lattes overlooking unfamiliar street corners. I believe all of that is still part of the harmonic lifestyle God and I are co-creating.

But harmony, unlike balance, is not staged or symmetrical. It doesn't mean sacrificing one life for another. It means acknowledging that everything meaningful gets to live in the same score.

And faithfulness, that quiet, consistent returning to your yes, is how I'm learning to play the middle notes.

That's how I begin my days now, not with roaring ambition, but with resolve.

Some mornings, as I'm wiping down the countertop before our guests wake, I hear an inner whisper: "Lead." Not loudly. Not like on a stage. But gently. Like a seed sprouting in warm soil.

And I know in that moment the question isn't: Will you lead others today?

The question is: Will you lead yourself?
There is a courage that comes with being seen. But there's another courage, the kind that increases when no one is watching. My co-Innkeeper, the guests we host, the fog slipping through the meadows at dawn, it all teaches me: I've been entrusted with a sacred stewardship. The Inn is the outer lens, but the real stage is within.

A SPIRITUAL REFLECTION

Take a moment and consider the areas of your life that may be inviting you into deeper faithfulness:

• Where are you being asked to rise, not for applause, but for alignment?

• Where do you feel a whisper inviting you to return to what you once committed to?

• What is one promise you can make to yourself that would bring harmony into your day-to-day?

Don't worry about being perfect. If anything, courage is about hearing the invitation... and once again choosing to answer "yes."

A PRAYER TO BEGIN

Dear God,

Thank you for the quiet voices that lead me when the world is loud. Thank you for the sacred assignments that don't come with applause but call for presence. Give me companioned strength to be faithful to what You've placed before me. Help me lead myself in the small things so I can trust myself in the great things. May my courage be rooted in obedience, and my joy found in harmony.

Amen.

VICKI PARKER

Vicki Parker is a women's empowerment and wellness coach, innkeeper, entrepreneur, and connector of souls. With deep reverence for family and conscious living, she supports women in remembering who they are, reclaiming confidence, and cultivating authentic relationships.

Vicki is a certified NLP practitioner, licensed BANK Trainer and Coach, creator of the Unstoppable Confidence 5-Day Challenge, and an experienced speaker on emotional intelligence, feminine leadership, and frequency-based living. Known by her family as the "spark plug," she travels with intention, presence, and gratitude. She currently resides in the Cuyahoga Valley National Park, where she tends to both souls and spaces with care at The Inn at Brandywine Falls.

Author's Website: *www.VickiParkerUnlimited.com*

Charity Awareness: *www.MDA.org*

YURI CHOI

FROM SURVIVAL TO THRIVAL: THE COURAGE TO CROSS THE BRIDGE

I could hear the waves crashing, and I could feel the salty breeze against my face. It was a bit soothing, honestly, but it still could not stop the tears from rolling down my cheeks. I sat there on the beach in Southern California a moment longer after my dad's memorial ceremony was over, just quietly looking at the sunset.

After his memorial in October of 2017, I wasn't sure what was ahead of me. At the time, I was at a job that I felt imprisoned by, a job where I had already tapped out my growth potential. But while Dad was sick, I had no space to really think about making a change, or what I wanted to do instead. I felt empty. I felt stuck. I felt directionless. I didn't know a life without my dad—or my now-widowed mom—and I knew everything was about to change, though I didn't know how or in what ways yet.

I was scared.

The previous two and a half years leading up to that moment had been nothing but slow-burning grief and constant fear, as I watched my dad slowly die from cancer. It broke my heart. It left me feeling shattered. I wouldn't wish that type of pain on any human being—to watch one of your beloved parents wither away for years, and to feel helpless through it all.

After his passing, I started to realize that everything I once thought was important in my twenties and early thirties didn't seem relevant anymore. His passing left me with some big questions instead: *When I die one day, what do I want to not regret? What would make my dad proud of his daughter? What kind of life do I want to consciously and fearlessly create from here, knowing that everything eventually ends? What is my purpose?*

When my dad was battling cancer, with constant doctor visits, emergency room stays, and surgeries, I didn't realize it then, but my dominant energetic state had become survival mode.

And even after my dad went to heaven, I couldn't just snap out of survival mode, because I had been "practicing" living in that state for over two years.

Any emotional state we stay in long enough becomes habitual. It becomes part of who we believe ourselves to be. Survival mode is present when we are operating from any variation of fear—guilt, shame, apathy, anger, stress, or anxiety. As a Performance Coach for high-achieving entrepreneurs and professionals, I often share this: survival mode isn't bad. It's functional. It protected us in our earliest days as humans—it kept us alive when we needed to escape threats.

Today, most of our threats are no longer physical. They are emotional, mental, or internal.

This means, if survival is happening primarily in our mind, we can also shift it. It's not really who we are naturally.

The realization came through that after my dad's passing—I realized that if I didn't consciously choose to move out of survival mode, it would unconsciously continue to choose for me.

And survival—while necessary at times—was not the place from which I wanted to create the rest of my life. We aren't supposed to be creatures that barely survive this planet. We are creatures who get to create, play, and enjoy, most of the time, while our survival mechanisms are supposed to be activated only occasionally, when absolutely necessary, for short and intense bursts of focus that can be beneficial to our physical safety.

And I can tell you, it certainly wasn't an instant shift. It was terrifying to even imagine living differently when all I had known for years was grief, stress, and fear. What if I dreamed and failed? What if I hoped and got disappointed again? It's in these moments —standing on the edge between what was and what could be— that we meet the true nature of courage. Courage is not the absence of fear. Courage is moving anyway, with fear tucked under one arm and hope tucked under the other.

During this season, I stumbled across a documentary called *The Secret*. At the time, it wasn't so much the concept of manifestation that moved me—it was the idea that I could take back the authorship of my own mind and that I could choose to imagine a future that wasn't dictated by fear, but by possibility. So, I began my practice.

Every single day for a year, I reconditioned my thinking. I watched *The Secret*. I journaled.

I ritualistically envisioned what it would be like to live from a creative, thriving state—not because it felt easy or natural yet, but because I made the courageous decision to imagine something different. At first, it felt awkward. Survival mode thoughts still ran through my mind on autopilot. And with time—and with a thousand tiny moments of courage—I began to carve new mental and emotional neural pathways.

I visualized myself meeting mentors and teachers I once thought were unreachable: John Assaraf, Jack Canfield, Michael Beckwith, Marie Diamond, and Loral Langemeier, among others.

I visualized myself writing and publishing books, speaking on stages, and sharing the message and stories of creating my own life on my own terms, one that I would be proud of.

I visualized myself helping others find their own version of aliveness, of expansion, of thriving.

And one by one, those visions became my reality.

I ended up meeting some of those very mentors. I co-authored books with transformational leaders such as John Assaraf, Loral Langemeier, and Marie Diamond from *The Secret*.

I published my own book, *Creating Your Own Happiness*. I even became the designated Executive Coach for a client who was the CEO of *Psych2Go*—the largest YouTube channel in the world for mental health, with over 12 million subscribers.

None of this was born out of a life without fear. It was born out of learning how to walk—daily—with fear in one hand and vision in the other and consciously giving increasingly more energy and attention to the one with vision over time.

Courage is the bridge between survival and thriving. It is the willingness to feel uncomfortable, to take action while your voice shakes, and to dream even when the past has taught you to expect disappointment.

Courage is the energy that says, "I don't know how this will turn out—but I am moving forward anyway because it aligns with who I envision becoming." It's not a clean, clear path at times. Courage will often feel messy, clumsy, and emotional. And yet, each time we choose courage over comfort, we expand the edges of who we believe ourselves to be.

Today, when I coach high-achieving clients, I often tell them: Courage is a frequency that exists between fear and excitement.

It's the threshold emotion. It's the portal between who you were in survival—and who you can become when you dare to thrive.

The reason many people feel stuck is not because they aren't talented enough, smart enough, or capable enough. It's because they've been taught that fear is a stop sign, when really, it's an invitation.

Fear is not the end of the story. It's the beginning of your transformation—if you choose courage. Reaching a state of thrival isn't a reward reserved for the few. It's a way of living that becomes available to anyone who chooses to meet life's unknowns with brave, open hands. You don't have to wait until you feel "ready." You don't have to wait until the fear disappears. You only need to be willing to walk forward, just as you are, holding both your fear and your vision. One trembling—yet life-changing—courageous step at a time.

And most importantly, through thousands of big and small acts of courage over the last eight years, I believe my dad would be proud of me now.

I think back to that girl sitting alone on the beach in Southern California, her heart cracked open, staring into the sunset with no map for what came next.

She didn't know then what I know now:

That grief would forge resilience.

That fear would become a bridge, not a prison.

That courage, one trembling step at a time, would lead her here—to a life not merely survived, but fully, magnificently lived.

And that sunset, once marking an ending, had really been the beginning all along.

REFLECTIVE JOURNALING QUESTIONS

1. Where in my life right now am I being invited to choose courage over comfort?

2. What would it look like to move forward while holding both fear and excitement?

3. If I fully trusted my capacity to thrive, what courageous decision would I make today?

YURI CHOI

Yuri is the Founder and creator of Yuri Choi Coaching. Choi is a performance coach for entrepreneurs and high achievers. She helps them create and stay in a powerful, abundant, unstoppable mindset to achieve their goals by helping them gain clarity and understanding, leverage their emotional states, and create empowering habits and language patterns.

She is a speaker, writer, creator, connector, YouTuber, and the author of *Creating Your Own Happiness*. Choi is passionate about spreading the messages about meditation, the power of intention, and creating a powerful mindset to live a fulfilling life. She is also a Habitude Warrior Conference Speaker and emcee, and she is a designated guest coach for Psych2Go, the largest online mental health magazine and YouTube Channel.

Her mission in the world is to inspire people to live leading with L.O.V.E. (which stands for: laughter, oneness, vulnerability, and ease) and to ignite people's souls to live in a world of infinite creative possibilities and abundance.

Author's Website: *www.YuriChoiCoaching.com*

Charity Awareness: *www.SurvivalToThrivalSeries.com*

~ COURAGE ~

Habitude Warrior Mastermind

Join a team of
AWESOME
Entrepreneurs, Coaches, Business Owners, and Leaders to support you in your journey of success!

Be one of my personal guests for a session!
www.MastermindGuestPass.com

HABITUDE WARRIOR & INTEGRITY PUBLISHING EDITORIAL TEAM

Habitude Warrior International and Integrity Publishing International take great pride in our editorial team, who put their heart, sweat, and tears into each and every project and national bestseller! Thank you, team!

JON KOVACH JR.
Team Manager

Jon Kovach Jr. strives to assist every author and every team member in the process of self-development for ultimate success.

PAT MINTON
VP of Operations

Pat Minton has been with the Habitude Warrior International team for over 20 years getting her start with Brian Tracy & Erik Swanson.

JILLIAN KOVACH
Editorial Manager

Jillian is a vital team member of Habitude Warrior & Integrity Publishing, bringing her expertise in managing our Editorial Department.

To inquire about joining our team please send us an email to *team@HabitudeWarrior.com!*

~ COURAGE ~

Team@IntegrityPub.com
www.IntegrityPublishingInternational.com